Understanding and Teaching
Primary
Mathematics

Companion Website

For open-access **student resources** specifically written
to complement this textbook and support your learning,
please visit **www.routledge.com/9781447929994**

ON THE WEBSITE

Lecturer Resources

For password-protected online resources tailored to support
the use of this textbook in teaching, please visit
www.routledge.com/9781447929994

Understanding and Teaching

Primary Mathematics

Tony Cotton

Routledge
Taylor & Francis Group

LONDON AND NEW YORK

First published 2010 by Pearson Education Limited
This edition published 2013

Published 2013 by Routledge
2 Park Square, Milton Park, Abingdon, Oxon OX14 4RN
711 Third Avenue, New York, NY 10017, USA

Routledge is an imprint of the Taylor & Francis Group, an informa business

ISBN 13: 978-1-4479-2999-4 (pbk)

British Library Cataloguing-in-Publication Data
A catalogue record for the print edition is available from the British Library

Library of Congress Cataloging-in-Publication Data
A catalog record for the print edition is available from the Library of Congress

Printed and bound by CPI Group (UK) Ltd, Croydon, CR0 4YY

BRIEF CONTENTS

FULL CONTENTS

Chapter 12 ICT and teaching and learning mathematics

PREFACE

Introduction

I hope that this book will engage all trainee teachers in developing their subject knowledge in mathematics to support them in becoming skilled and confident teachers who enjoy teaching mathematics to learners in primary classrooms. Many beginning teachers I have worked with have told me that when they are confident in their own understandings of a subject they feel much more able to teach that subject creatively and with a passion. This confidence stems from what has been called 'deep' mathematical subject knowledge and a clear understanding of the different teaching approaches that can be taken to teach the subject.

The particular approach of this book is to develop your mathematical subject knowledge through exploring the learning and teaching of mathematics. The book will support you in developing your own understanding of mathematics by examining the misconceptions of the learners you will work with and by developing your own repertoire of teaching strategies so you can immediately see the impact of your own learning on your teaching practice.

This approach is supported by Ofsted. In their review of teaching mathematics published at the end of 2011 (available at http://www.ofsted.gov.uk/resources/good-practice-primary-mathematics-evidence-20-successful-schools) they emphasise the importance of good subject knowledge and subject-specific teaching skills. They suggest that the most effective schools recognise the importance of good subject knowledge and subject-specific teaching skills and seek to enhance these aspects of subject expertise. They also support the focus of this book on misconceptions, saying '(Effective) schools are quick to recognise and intervene in a focused way when pupils encounter difficulties. This ensures misconceptions do not impede the next steps in learning.'

The aim of the book

The book aims to support you in developing the three key areas of mathematical subject knowledge. These are:

- **Mathematical knowledge:** The book will support you in developing your own understanding of mathematics through engaging you in activities and investigations.
- **Curriculum knowledge:** Through reading the book you will come to learn exactly which areas of mathematics should be taught to each group of children you may be working with and understand the progression within learning and teaching mathematics. So you will know which areas of mathematics your learners should have encountered and where they will go next.
- **Pedagogical knowledge:** The book draws on examples from the classroom so that you can see the best ways to introduce your learners to particular mathematical ideas.

The book is practical and models good primary practice in the way it supports you in developing your own knowledge and understanding. In this way you will develop both your own understanding and your teaching repertoire.

Who should use this book?

This book is aimed at all those who wish to develop their own mathematical knowledge in order to improve their confidence in teaching mathematics.

Trainee teachers

Trainee teachers will find this book can be used throughout their course to develop a personal portfolio and to support them on their school experiences. They will find it useful for assignments which look at particular areas of mathematics and when on your school experience to give you ideas on how to teach particular topics.

Newly qualified teachers

Newly qualified teachers will be able to draw on the book to support them in areas they have not previously taught or which were not covered specifically during their training.

Experienced teachers

Experienced teachers will find this book useful when visiting areas of mathematics new to them or when working in new year groups. They may also find the book useful to refresh their understanding of areas they have not taught for some time.

Distinctive features

Big ideas

Each section starts with the big ideas which underpin the particular strand of mathematics covered. This allows you to see the big picture immediately and understand how the mathematics you are teaching falls within the overall landscape of the curriculum.

Progression

Each chapter gives you an overview of progression across the primary years so that you understand which mathematical ideas are appropriate to the children you are teaching. It also helps you understand what knowledge your pupils will bring with them and which mathematical ideas they should progress on to next. This is structured so that you are introduced to the foundations for learning in each area of mathematics, and then the ideas which support learners in beginning to understand this area of mathematics are described. The skills and understandings which learners should be taught to become confident mathematicians are outlined, and finally suggestions for extending those learners in your classroom who are skilled mathematicians are described.

Links to the classroom and research

Each chapter makes links to key pieces of research and curriculum development. This will support you in writing assignments and in seeing direct links to the classroom. There are also activities that you can try out in your classroom and ideas to support you in developing your own resources.

Audit and portfolio tasks

These tasks allow you to build a portfolio of evidence to show that you have acquired the subject knowledge you need to gain qualified teacher status. There are additional activities for you to consolidate your knowledge available on the companion website.

Teaching points

These draw on common misconceptions in learners and support you in knowing how you can deal with these misconceptions in the classroom. As I mentioned earlier in this preface, it is important that you see your learners' misconceptions as teaching points. By understanding what the most common misconceptions are likely to be, you can prepare to overcome learners' common difficulties.

Assessment

Assessing is a key part of learning. It helps you know what your pupils currently understand so that you can plan for the next piece of learning. It also helps you understand how effective your teaching has been and to uncover any areas of difficulty that you need to revisit. Each chapter offers you an assessment activity to use with the pupils you are teaching.

Case studies

Each chapter contains a case study which gives you a lesson plan and an evaluation for each strand of mathematics. This makes a direct link between your own subject knowledge and your teaching. You will also be directed to a lesson which is available on the companion website. This allows you to carry out an observation of a piece of mathematics teaching which links directly to the mathematical area you are exploring.

Using ICT

As well as a chapter focusing specifically on using ICT in your teaching, there is a range of software on the companion website which you can use both to develop your own mathematical understanding and in your own teaching

Drawing on my own teaching of mathematics education in three teacher education institutions over 15 years, as well as 10 years' experience teaching mathematics in secondary and primary schools, I hope I have written a book which will support you in developing your subject knowledge through encouraging you to reflect on your own mathematical understandings and by exploring your teaching of mathematics. My aim would be that through using this book you will develop your subject knowledge and your teaching so that you can confidently and skilfully teach any area of mathematics to any year group.

ACKNOWLEDGEMENTS

The publisher gratefully thanks the following reviewers for their valuable comments on the book:

Sal Jarvis, University of Hertfordshire

Ko Poon, University of East London

Jacqueline Launders, Sheffield Hallam University

Helen Martin, Aberdeen University

Jill Turner, University of Worcester

Nigel Hutchinson, Bishop Grosseteste University College Lincoln.

Publisher acknowledgements

Figures

Figure on page 130 reprinted with permission from http://illuminations.nctm.org, copyright 2009 by the National Council of Teachers of Mathematics. All rights reserved.

Tables

Table on page 19-20 adapted from paper by Askew, M., Brown, M., Rhodes, V., Wiliam D. and Johnson, D. (1997) 'Effective Teachers of Numeracy in Primary Schools: Teachers' Beliefs, Practices and Pupils' Learning', London: King's College, University of London.

Text

Extracts on pages 24-5, 48-9, 83-5, 107-8, 132-4, 158-60, 177-8 and 222-5 adapted from National Strategies, http://nationalstrategies.standards.dcsf.gov.uk/, The Department for Children, Schools and Families, Crown copyright, Crown Copyright material is reproduced with permission under the terms of the Click-Use Licence; Activity on page 154-5 reprinted with permission from http://illuminations.nctm.org, copyright 2009 by the National Council of Teachers of Mathematics. All rights reserved; Extract on page 212 from National Autistic Society website, www.nas.org.uk/autism, © National Autistic Society, Visit www.autism.org.uk for further information; Box on page 215 reproduced with kind permission of the NRICH website (http://nrich.maths.org) University of Cambridge.

Photos

Alamy Images: TP 140; Corbis: Michael Boys 152.

In some instances we have been unable to trace the owners of copyright material, and we would appreciate any information that would enable us to do so.

Author acknowledgements

The most important groups of people to thank are all the young learners I have worked with and all the beginning teachers I have worked with. They have taught me more than I could ever teach them about learning mathematics. It has been an honour to share what they have taught me with a wider audience. My wife, Helen, has proofread everything in this book too – her willingness to have a go at the mathematics, despite her own admitted lack of confidence in the area, has supported me in writing a book that might do some good! Thanks also to the team of reviewers who commented on early drafts of the materials. Your comments were valuable and insightful. I hope I have addressed the issues you raised in the final drafts. Finally, thanks to Jennifer Seth, my development editor at Pearson, for her incredible hard work in making sure that the book is the best it can be.

GUIDED TOUR

CHAPTER 3
PROBLEM SOLVING USING MATHEMATICS

Introduction

Whenever I share the story that follows with students they tell me that they don't believe it really happened. However, when I suggest that I also used to sit reading a book to myself in the reading corner and that very quickly my class would start to gather round to share the book they can see that this would happen. Honestly, children can find mathematics as fascinating as reading. It is important that we show the learners we work with that we enjoy doing mathematics for its own sake. This is one way of doing this.

I had been experiencing difficulty in engaging a group of 9- and 10-year-olds in a problem-solving activity. They seemed happy simply completing exercises that I gave them but would not investigate mathematics in a more open way. So I decided on a new tactic. While the group were out at playtime I surrounded myself with

Chapter introductions and Starting points include a mathematical problem or piece of research to illustrate a concept or theme that is built upon within the chapter.

---

teaching measurement we should spend time finding out how and when our learners measure outside the classroom and use this learning as our starting point. We should also draw on as many real life, practical contexts as possible when teaching the skills of measurement.

Progression in 'Measuring'

Foundations for 'Measuring'

Initially children will begin to understand the language of measurement and comparison using vocabulary such as 'greater', 'smaller', 'heavier', 'lighter' to compare quantities. To introduce children to ideas of time you should also use vocabulary such as 'before' and 'after'. So, at this stage children should be engaging in a wide variety of practical activities which allow you to develop this vocabulary with them.

Beginning to understand 'Measuring'

At first children should carry out activities which involve measuring and weighing in order to compare objects. They will use suitable **uniform non-standard units** and then **standard units** for this comparison. (In non-standard units, uniform means that we use something that has a uniform measurement, so we can measure length using multilink cubes, or use a fixed number of wooden blocks to compare weights. Standard units are those in common usage, such as metres, litres and kilograms and all the related units.) Once children have an understanding of using non-standard units to compare they can start to use a range of measuring instruments such as metre sticks and measuring jugs. Pupils will continue to estimate, compare and measure, by now relying on standard units. They will be able to choose suitable measuring instruments to help them. At this stage you should introduce them to scales and teach them how to read the numbered divisions on a scale, such as a

158

---

it is 4 or less it remains the same. For instance, if I were to round 4.72 to one decimal place I would write 4.7. If I were to round it to the nearest whole number I would write 5.

Towards the end of their time in primary school most learners should be able to express one quantity as a percentage of another (for example, express £400 as a percentage of £1000). You should also be working with them to see the connections between equivalent percentages, decimals and fractions.

Extending learning in 'Counting and understanding number'

The transition to secondary education will focus on developing children's use of **ratio notation**. Percentage notation is 30%, ratio notation is 30:100, and decimal notation is 0.3. Here the pupils you wish to extend can learn to reduce a ratio to its simplest form and divide a quantity into two parts in a given ratio. They will be able to use this understanding to solve simple problems involving ratio and direct proportion (for example, to identify the quantities needed to make a fruit drink by mixing water and juice in a given ratio).

The next section of the chapter focuses on the big ideas of 'counting', 'place value', 'fractions, decimals and percentages' and 'proportionality' which are at the heart of 'Counting and understanding number'. If you are confident with these ideas you will be able to teach children successfully throughout the primary school years and will have a clear understanding of the development of these ideas across the 3-11 age range.

Big ideas: counting

Many children will start school already able to count - but it is important to be aware of the principles of counting, both to support the children who cannot yet count and to recognise the processes that young children who have already learnt to count have mastered. The key research which supports us in understanding the process of learning to count was described by Rochel Gelman and Randy Gallistel in their book *The Child's Understanding of Number* published in 1986 by Harvard University Press. Gelman and Gallistel are both psychologists. They are married and work at Rutgers University in New Jersey, USA. Their

49

Each chapter provides an overview of **Progression** across the primary years to aid understanding of which mathematical ideas are appropriate to the children you are teaching.

Big ideas deal with the fundamental ideas which underpin each particular strand of mathematics covered. This allows you to see the big picture immediately and understand how the different strands knit together.

Teaching point 6: Misreading clocks

The best way to support children in learning to tell the time is to have both analogue and digital clocks in the classroom, and to refer to them as often as possible. Children rarely see analogue clocks – they will have a digital reading on their mobile phone, or on a TV at home, so you may need to model using an analogue clock frequently.

Taking it further

In *Mathematics Teaching* 209, July 2008, Rona Catterall describes the way she introduced 'telling time' to her class of 6–7-year-olds. This is a detailed article about the methods Rona used after she became frustrated with her children struggling with the skills of telling the time and is available online at http://www.atm.org.uk/ mt/archive/mt209.html.

One example she uses is how you can use a child's understanding of their age to help with telling the time. She reminds us that a child sees their age to be of great importance. So she asks one of her class how old they are. 'I'm 6,' they reply. The teacher asks if they can say they are 7? 'No,' says the pupil, 'I'm not 7 until my next birthday.' 'It's just the same with this clock,' says the teacher, with the time set at half-past six, 'we can't say it's seven o'clock until the hand has gone all the way round.'

I introduced a class of mine to an analogue clock a few years ago and they laughed almost as if I had brought in an ancient timepiece. I set the clock at half-past twelve (12:30) as this was lunchtime and asked the group what time was shown by the clock. The range of answers included:

- 6 past 12
- 6 to 12
- 12 and a half.

Portfolio task 8.1

Write a list of the units of measurement you have a sense of as I did above. Try to complete the list below – what do you think weighs about 1 kg, has a capacity of about a litre or measures about 1 cm?

1 mm	1 g	1 ml
1 cm	1 kg	10 ml
1 m	100 kg	500 ml
1 km		1 litre
10 km		100 litres

Which measurements did you find easy and which did you find hard? Talk to your friends about it and think about how your prior experiences have informed your knowledge of measurements.

Measuring is not just about units of measurement; other key skills are reading scales and measuring instruments, including clocks, and understanding concepts such as area and perimeter. We will explore all of these areas in detail throughout the chapter. Firstly, let us see how children's understanding of measuring is developed during their time in primary school.

Taking it further

In their book *Children Doing Mathematics* published by Blackwell in 1996, Terizinha Nunes and Peter Bryant show how children can be very successful in mathematical activities outside the classroom as they bring their intuitive understandings to bear on everyday problems. However, when they are faced with the same problems in school they often struggle as they try to apply 'school learning' to the problem rather than following their own strategies. Chapter 4 in the above book describes how children's

157

Taking it further boxes make links to key pieces of research and curriculum development, to support you in writing assignments and in seeing direct links to the classroom.

Data handling can be an exciting and motivating area to explore with the children you teach. It is also, arguably, one of the most important areas of mathematics in which to develop skills in order to be able to make sense of and understand the world around us as presented through the media. I would hope that by gaining confidence in seeing data handling as a process of posing questions, gathering data which is then interpreted to answer those questions, and finally using this process to ask new questions, you will have become excited at the prospect of working through this cycle with your learners.

It is possibly the only area of mathematics that can be taught through a totally cross-curricular approach; indeed it can possibly only be taught in this way. Similarly it is an area of mathematics that can be taught by drawing on the children's interests as a starting point. Several years ago I was having a drink with a cousin of mine whom I don't see very often. Out of the blue she asked me if she should stop taking the contraceptive pill. I was taken aback and asked why she wanted to know. She told me that she had read in the paper that being on the pill doubled her chance of getting thrombosis in her legs. I asked her to show me the article and was able to explain to her that even doubling the risk still meant that the risk of thrombosis was very small. I realised she had asked me because I was 'good at maths', in her words. She didn't feel confident in making important decisions based on her data-handling skills. So, I would argue that teaching data handling is very important – enjoy it!

Self-audit

Gather some achievement data that you have on a class that you are teaching. This may be previous achievement on optional SATs, it may be results on reading ages – it can be any quantitative data. Decide what you want to find out from the data, such as comparing boys' and girls' achievements, or a particular subject area you have been focusing on, and write a list of questions. Use the data-handling techniques you have met in this chapter to analyse the data. Make sure you use range, mean, median and mode, and comment on which of these measures is the most useful. Also use a range of ways of representing the data. Use your analysis to write a short report on the achievements of your class. Include this report in your portfolio.

Big ideas

Children are also expected to be able to interpret pie charts. Pie charts show the proportions of data. Work on this in the task box below and add it to your portfolio.

Portfolio task 9.2

Examine this pie chart. Write down three different sets of data that it could represent. Choose one of your sets of data and write a short paragraph analysing the data. This question is deliberately open as it exemplifies how data can be interpreted in many different ways.

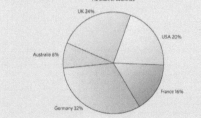

Pie chart of countries

UK 24%
USA 20%
Australia 8%
France 16%
Germany 32%

Venn and Carroll diagrams

Venn diagrams and Carroll diagrams are used to sort objects. Carroll diagrams are actually named after the author Lewis Carroll, who wrote *Alice in Wonderland* and was fascinated by mathematics. People have explored *Alice in Wonderland* for the mathematics it contains,

Audit and portfolio tasks allow you to build a portfolio of evidence to show that you have acquired the subject knowledge you need to gain qualified teacher status.

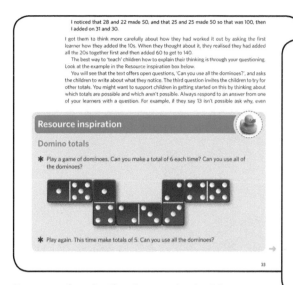

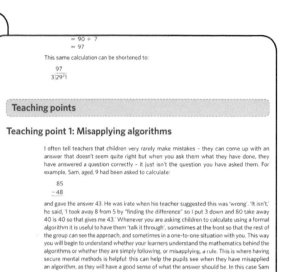

Resource inspiration boxes give inviting examples of different activities to explore with your class and provide inspiration for your own teaching.

Teaching points highlight common mathematical misconceptions made by children.

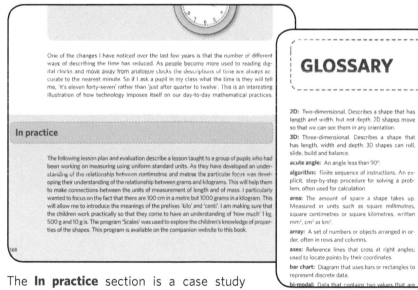

The **In practice** section is a case study which gives you a lesson plan and an evaluation for each strand of mathematics. This makes a direct link between your own subject knowledge and your teaching.

Key terms are highlighted in the text when they first appear. These terms are also included in the Glossary at the end of the book.

As well as a chapter focusing specifically on using ICT in your teaching, the accompanying **companion website** gives you six interactive programs which you can use both to develop your own mathematical understanding and in your own teaching, videos to accompany the Observing section of each chapter, an audit for you to monitor your progress and develop your teaching, glossary flashcards and web links.

CHAPTER 1
TEACHING AND LEARNING PRIMARY MATHEMATICS

Introduction

Learning maths was like a dagger going through my skull – no matter how hard I tried it wasn't good enough. This was really frustrating because I knew there were really important things to discover and when I'm teaching and the kids really get it it's like they've found diamonds. I don't know whether it was my fault or the teachers.

This is the way a student of mine described the experience of being both a learner and a teacher of mathematics. I had asked my students to describe to me their memories of learning mathematics at primary school. It vividly describes the concerns that some of you may have that you don't have sufficient mathematical understanding to be as effective a teacher as you want to be. It also describes the joys that come with seeing that you have been able to describe a complex mathematical concept well. During the same activity another student described how a feeling of panic can set in if you feel as though you have not got a good grasp of the area that you are teaching.

My problem is being put on the spot – I can't think then, lots of little warnings run through my head the moment I'm asked a question. I was literally running for my life during that activity.

Some of you will have had very positive experiences of learning mathematics and some of you may have felt as though you couldn't understand what was being asked of you. Whichever is true for you, working at your own subject knowledge will support you in feeling much more able too find those diamonds that are lurking, and to feel confident that you will be able to answer whatever question a pupil will throw at you. All of my students have worked through the kind of exercises you will find in this book.

Through working on research projects such as the one I have described above I have become convinced that the best way to develop mathematical subject knowledge is by engaging teachers in actively questioning and reflecting on their learning. Some beginning teachers do not see themselves as 'good' at mathematics because of the way in which they have experienced mathematics as a learner. Through exploring mathematics in a new way they gradually change their view of what being 'good at mathematics' is and can begin to see themselves as mathematicians. Introducing their pupils to a form of mathematics that they have recently experienced themselves allows them to be both tentative in terms of the possible outcomes while being secure in the process. They know, or they trust, that interesting things will happen in terms of children learning mathematics. And they notice that through exploring mathematics in an open and investigatory way their learners are themselves developing as young mathematicians. These beginning teachers are moving towards a belief that mathematics is about questioning, exploring and justification.

The beginning of this process is to understand what we might mean by subject knowledge. This chapter offers a definition of subject knowledge for teaching mathematics, as well as setting the scene for the rest of the book. It describes how working with the book will support you in developing your own mathematical subject knowledge. Armed with this understanding you can plan how best you might use the book.

Starting point

Whenever I am asked to describe a teacher with good mathematical subject knowledge I use the following example from my observation of a trainee teacher. The trainee had placed a multiplication grid (you fill in the blanks by multiplying together the numbers at the end of the row and column) on the whiteboard for the pupils in the class to complete as the mental/oral starter to a mathematics lesson:

×	8	2	1/2	5	1/4	10	4
6							
3							
7							
9							
4							
5							
12							

As the multiplication grid was revealed there were sounds of complaint from the pupils. One of the pupils said to the trainee, 'You don't put fractions in a number grid and we only go up to 10!' The trainee, patiently, persuaded the pupils to accept this 'new' version of what had become an everyday activity for the pupils and then asked them to complete the grid.

Portfolio task 1.1

As a starting point for working on this book get a notebook or file. This will act as a record of all the activities you engage in whilst you use the book. The companion website to this book links these activities to the NQT standards for those of you that need to evidence your learning. Now try the activity before reading on. It may take you a few minutes.

After 10 minutes the trainee stopped the class and asked, 'Which column did you fill in first?' One of the pupils put their hand up and said '48'. The trainee paused and said, 'I don't want you to tell me any answers – I want you to tell me which column you filled in first.' At first the pupils did not understand why the answer for the 'first' square wasn't seen as important. Then realisation struck – one pupil said, 'You could do the 2s first – that would be really easy.' Another suggested starting with the 10s for the same reason. By the end of the discussion the class had come to understand that mathematical thinking was about looking carefully at a problem and finding the most effective, or efficient, way of solving it rather than simply following a process which had 'worked' previously. So for this grid, if you complete the 2 column you can then complete the 4 and 8 columns by doubling. Similarly, filling in the 10 column allows you to complete the 5 column by halving. The same process will sort out the 1/2 and 1/4 columns.

Reflect on the process you went through if you tried the activity. Most trainees I work with start at the top-left corner and work systematically through the grid. This shows how deeply engrained the feeling is that there is a 'right' way to carry out the mathematics. When I suggest the alternative, several trainees have suggested that this is 'cheating'. It is hard to break away from the image of the mathematical subject that we carry with us from our own experiences at school. However, if you do not feel confident in your own mathematical subject knowledge this is, in part, due to your experiences as a learner of mathematics. I hope this book will allow you to make such a break.

Why is mathematical subject knowledge important?

You may be training to become a teacher or you may be an experienced teacher who wants to improve their mathematical subject knowledge. I believe that someone with good mathematical subject knowledge is able to be confident in what they are teaching and, more importantly, will be seen as confident by their pupils. We all learn better from someone who we believe is both confident in their own knowledge and is passionate about sharing that knowledge with us.

That is why this book focuses on developing your mathematical subject knowledge by concentrating on the types of activities you can use in the classroom. I hope that by engaging you in mathematics that you see as relevant to your teaching you can become as passionate as me about mathematics itself. This will ensure that the pupils you teach will learn well. I will have been successful as a writer if you, as a teacher, and your pupils as learners, enjoy your mathematics and become more confident learners of mathematics together.

It is often argued that there is a direct link between good mathematical subject knowledge and effective teaching and learning of mathematics. I would also argue that there is a direct connection between having good subject knowledge and being able to make appropriate choices about the way in which to teach particular mathematical ideas. But before we move on we must define exactly what we mean by 'good mathematical subject knowledge'.

What is mathematical subject knowledge?

Research on teaching suggests that teachers draw on three forms of knowledge in order to teach effectively. The first is knowledge of the subject itself – you need to feel confident in your own mathematical subject knowledge in order to be able to teach effectively. Teachers also need an understanding of the curriculum they are expected to teach, so you need to be clear which mathematical ideas and concepts are appropriate to the age range of the pupils you are teaching. Finally you need to understand which are the most appropriate strategies and activities to engage your pupils in learning a particular mathematical idea. In order to develop your skills in teaching and learning primary mathematics this book must focus on these three areas. The book aims to do this in the following ways.

Mathematical subject matter knowledge

The activities within this book ask you to explore mathematical ideas through engaging in investigations and practical activities. My aim here is that you develop what is called a relational understanding of mathematics rather than an instrumental understanding. In an article first published in *Mathematics Teaching* in 1976 Richard Skemp introduced this idea, and it has been drawn on ever since. Relational understanding means that you move beyond a mechanical or rote view of mathematical processes in order to see and understand the links and connections between the different areas of mathematics. You will not be forced to try and 'remember' mathematical rules and processes that you were taught at school; instead you will come to an understanding of how these processes actually work.

Mathematics curricular knowledge

The book supports you in developing an understanding of the progressive nature of coming to understand mathematics. Each chapter opens with an outline of the key concepts which pupils will be taught. These are divided into four groups:

1 Foundations for learning

2 Beginning to understand

3 Becoming confident in

4 Extending learning in

Having this understanding of the progression of mathematical skills and concepts within an area allows you to make decisions about what is appropriate for your pupils at their stage of learning. Through careful assessment you can understand the stage that your pupils have reached. Your curricular knowledge then allows you to carefully plan for the next stage of learning. You will also become aware of the ideas that your pupils will meet when they move on from your classroom. It is important for us to be clear about the next stages of learning, not only so that we can extend individuals' learning, if appropriate, but also so that we can feel comfortable that our pupils are ready for the next stage.

Pedagogical content knowledge

When you teach any area of mathematics you make choices: you choose examples to introduce a particular concept; you choose a particular teaching approach; you choose a way to group your learners; and you choose particular teaching strategies. A teacher with good pedagogical content knowledge has an awareness of the choices that they made and why they made those particular choices. This area of subject knowledge develops as you become more experienced – as you become more experienced you are able to draw on an ever-growing bank of activities and strategies. This book allows you to share other teachers' experiences through drawing on a wide range of activities and strategies and offering you a reflective commentary as to the rationale for choosing these particular approaches.

To summarise, a teacher with good subject knowledge has the following understandings:

- Mathematical subject matter knowledge (they understand the mathematics).
- Curriculum subject knowledge (they know the requirements of the curriculum).
- Pedagogical subject knowledge (they can make good choices to help them teach the mathematics).

What makes a 'good' teacher of mathematics?

You probably have in mind a mathematics teacher that you learnt from at school whom you see as a 'good' teacher. The fact that you remember them as a good teacher of mathematics probably means that they had good subject knowledge drawing on the three areas described above. I would suggest that this meant they had some or all of the following skills.

They could anticipate possible misconceptions or misunderstandings, and knew how best to support learners at coming to new, more effective conceptions. (Some examples are given below.) This knowledge does not just come through experience – one of the aims of this book is to share common misconceptions with you so that you can plan ahead to support your learners. Knowledge of common misconceptions allows you to respond flexibly and appropriately to the difficulties that children experience.

Examples of such misconceptions might be:

- You can't divide smaller numbers by larger ones.
- Division always makes numbers smaller.
- The more digits a number has, the larger its value.
- Shapes with bigger areas have bigger perimeters.

You may want to take a moment to think of counter-examples to these statements. (For example, $5 \div 10 = 0.5$; $15 \div 0.5 = 30$; 0.000526 is smaller than 2; for the shape example try exploring different rectangles with a perimeter of 12 cm.)

Teachers with good subject knowledge can also generate probing questions that allow children to articulate their current understandings and through this articulation come to better-developed understandings. Often a probing question simply asks how a pupil has worked something out rather than asking for the result of their thinking. So faced with a pupil who has written $28 + 53$ a probing question would be 'How will you work out the answer?' as opposed to 'What is the answer?'. Or, similarly, if a pupil has written $56 - 19 = 43$, a probing question would be 'Tell me what you did first to work this out' rather than asking the pupil to 'Check this one again', which signals an error. By asking probing questions you come to understand the pupil's thinking processes rather than simply knowing whether they got an answer 'right' or 'wrong'.

When observing teachers at work, one way in which good subject knowledge is apparent is in the way that they deal with children's unexpected questions. Teachers with good subject knowledge are never thrown by these questions. They deal with them with confidence.

Finally a teacher with good subject knowledge can support pupils in making the connections between different areas of mathematics so that the pupils see mathematics as a whole rather than a series of separate and often disparate ideas. They can do this because they themselves see mathematics as a whole. This is another example of Richard Skemp's idea of relational understanding.

How will this book develop my subject knowledge?

The three facets of subject knowledge are developed throughout the book. First your knowledge of the curriculum and guidance is developed by directly linking every chapter to a clear progression in terms of the mathematical concepts covered.

Each chapter also develops your knowledge of the learners and learning processes so that lessons and activities can be structured effectively to meet the needs of all pupils. This is done through the use of case studies and direct reference to how children learn mathematics. A focus on common misconceptions within each chapter also allows you to develop your understanding of how individual learners come to understand mathematics.

The book also focuses directly on developing your knowledge of teaching and learning resources and how they can be effectively used to support learning. There are many ideas for activities that you can use in the classroom. These both allow you to see how mathematics can be taught and give you resources to try out for yourself in your own teaching. They also mirror the process you will often go through to plan a session. You may be given a resource with which to teach a particular concept. As a teacher, your role is to plan the most appropriate way to use this resource to develop the children's mathematical understanding. My aim is that this process will support you in becoming skilled designers of your own resources which you can tailor for the children that you teach.

No book on subject knowledge could teach you everything you need to know across the whole of the curriculum. However, this book will ensure that you feel confident in all the key areas of mathematics. Perhaps more importantly it will give you the confidence to develop further your own subject knowledge in a range of curriculum areas through extending and generalising the ideas in the book with a focus on applying them in classroom situations. It will also allow and encourage you to reflect on your own thinking processes in order to develop your own subject knowledge.

A framework for teaching mathematics

You will see that within this book specific attention is paid to progression within specific areas of mathematics. This is to allow you to plan over the longer term as you gain an understanding of what children's previous experiences will have been and how they will draw on your teaching to support them in the future.

I have split the mathematics curriculum into seven broad areas. These are:

1 **Using and applying mathematics** This comes first, as I think the most important facet of your subject knowledge is your ability to solve problems applying the mathematical understandings that you have.

2 **Counting and understanding number** This includes place value, fractions, decimals, percentages and ration and proportion.

3 **Knowing and using number facts** This chapter will help you understand the underlying rules behind number patterns and number facts including your times-tables.

4 **Calculating** This includes number operations, mental methods for calculation and solving number problems.

5 **Understanding shape** This chapter covers the properties of shapes and areas such as symmetry and the language of position, including using coordinates.

6 **Measuring** This chapter covers areas such as conservation and comparison of measures, units of measurement, area and perimeter, and volume and capacity.

7 **Handling data** This chapter covers the data–handling cycle including collecting data, analysing data and presenting data. It also explores chance and probability

All the mathematical ideas that you are likely to meet when teaching the 3–11 age range appear within these chapters. The next chapter offers you a range of audit tools which allow you to assess your current subject knowledge against these broad areas. You can then prioritise your own learning and decide which chapters of the book to focus on first. At the beginning of each chapter the 'big ideas' underpinning the mathematics within the chapter are detailed. This allows you to understand what the most important ideas are within a concept. It is amazing how often teachers have not been given an understanding of the 'big picture' and, as a result, their own subject knowledge consists of a rather disjointed series of tricks and rules. Having an understanding of the 'big picture' allows you to understand the connections between areas of mathematics and develop your relational understanding.

Foundations for learning mathematics

Although the focus for this book is primary mathematics it is important that all teachers of learners in the early years feel secure in their knowledge of mathematics. The areas below offer all early years practitioners broad areas on which to focus to ensure that young learners begin to enjoy and become confident in their mathematics. Chapter 10 explores teaching in the early years in more detail – in particular I emphasise that mathematics learning should take place through child-initiated activity and discussion.

The task of a good teacher of mathematics in the early years is to plan a wide range of activities which offer young learners opportunities across the breadth of the mathematics curriculum. As an early years practitioner your assessments will allow you to track children's learning in the different areas of mathematics. Then your mathematical subject knowledge will allow you to make useful and pertinent interventions to support your learners' mathematical development.

Areas which will allow your learners to develop a broad understanding of mathematics could include:

- Saying and using number names in order in familiar contexts.
- Counting up to 10 everyday objects.
- Recognising the numerals 1 to 9 in a range of everyday contexts.
- Using the vocabulary involved in adding and subtracting.
- Using language such as 'more' or 'less' to compare two numbers.
- Finding one more or one less than a number from 1 to 10.
- Beginning to relate addition to combining two groups of objects, and subtraction to 'taking away'.
- Using language such as 'greater', 'smaller', 'heavier' or 'lighter' to compare quantities.
- Talking about, recognising and re-creating simple patterns.
- Using language such as 'circle' or 'bigger' to describe the shape and size of solids and flat shapes.
- Using everyday words to describe position.
- Using the developing mathematical ideas described above to solve practical problems.

Practical activities to develop these ideas are described in more detail in Chapter 10.

Using this book will ensure that all early years practitioners have the knowledge and understanding to teach these concepts well. It is not the case that early years practitioners need a less well developed mathematical subject knowledge than their colleagues who teach older children. On the contrary it is vital that early years practitioners have solid subject knowledge across the mathematics curriculum so that they can see how these early mathematical concepts develop. In order to plan for mathematics to be developed in a broad range of contexts, and to plan for children to gain confidence and competence across the very broad range of standards, teachers need to have a secure subject knowledge themselves.

Organisation of the book

The second chapter of the book allows you to audit your subject knowledge in three ways. You can use these initial audits to create an action plan that will personalise your study to develop your subject knowledge in a way that suits your own individual needs.

Chapters 3–9 are structured in the same way so that you can easily manoeuvre your way around the book and so that you can see your subject knowledge develop across the whole mathematics curriculum. Each chapter is introduced using a **Starting point**. Here you will be asked to engage in an activity which illustrates the main mathematical ideas underpinning the theme of the chapter. This is followed by a detailed breakdown of the **Progression** within the mathematical ideas which are covered in the chapter. This supports the development of your curricular subject knowledge and allows you to plan appropriately for all of your learners, whatever age or stage they have reached.

The subject knowledge which underpins the strand is then discussed in more detail, explaining the **Big ideas**, with particular care taken to emphasise key terms, which are highlighted in the text when they first appear. These key terms are gathered together and defined in a Glossary at the end of the book. Careful explanations of the key areas of mathematics are also given so that you are able to understand how to explain important areas of mathematics to pupils. The main bulk of each chapter is constructed around key **Teaching points**. These teaching points often use a common misconception as a starting point for the discussion of a key mathematical idea together with suggestions of how best you may introduce this idea to your pupils. The chapters also offer examples of activities which you can use in your classroom. The text offers a rationale and a critique of the examples to help you develop your own skills in developing effective activities to support you teaching. This allows you to develop your own bank of teaching activities while developing an understanding of how best to use these examples.

Each chapter also includes an **In practice** section. Here you are given an exemplar lesson plan focusing on a key concept from the mathematics covered in the chapter. This lesson plan also draws on an interactive teaching program which can be used to support your teaching and to develop your learners' mathematical skills. There is one interactive program within each chapter. These programs are available on the companion website for personal study and for you to use in the classroom. The 'In practice' section also includes a commentary by the teacher on the effectiveness of the lesson when they taught it. The final part of this section refers you to video of a mathematics lesson which you can watch on the companion website. This supports you in developing your mathematical subject knowledge by watching skilled teachers at work.

Each chapter also contains **Portfolio tasks** which can be used to help you reflect on your learning and can be included in your portfolio. In addition each chapter contains sections which direct you to the most important research exploring the learning and teaching of this particular area of mathematics. These **Taking it further** sections are contained in boxes labelled **From the research** for articles which take a research focus and **From the classroom** for articles written with a classroom focus. These features will be of specific interest to those of you who are studying at Masters level.

At the end of each chapter you are also offered ideas for **Assessing mathematics** in the particular area you have been studying. This section consists of a range of tasks and activities you can use in your classroom to assess your learners' understanding of the areas you have been teaching. There are also ideas for **Cross-curricular projects** which will allow you to explore the ideas introduced in the chapter in an extended project which draws on other areas of the curriculum.

Finally there is a **Self-audit** at the end of each chapter, and you are also invited to construct a lesson plan focusing on one facet of the subject knowledge covered in the chapter. Your response to these two activities will form part of your portfolio. There are additional activities available on the companion website to give you more practice.

Chapters 10–12 further develop your expertise in teaching mathematics – your pedagogical subject knowledge – through exploring subject knowledge in terms of early years practice, inclusive teaching and learning, the use of calculators and using ICT to support the learning and teaching of mathematics.

The companion website

The **companion website** (www.routledge.com/9781447929994) which accompanies the book contains the initial audit activities and the proforma for your personal action plan. The proformas for the lesson plans are also included here, as well as supporting software. Everyone who purchases the book is given access to the companion website.

Summary

This chapter has two aims: to describe to you what is meant by subject knowledge and to outline to you how the book will support you in developing your mathematical subject knowledge in order to become a confident teacher of mathematics. You have seen how subject knowledge can be described as having knowledge in three areas:

- Mathematical subject matter knowledge (you understand the maths).
- Curriculum subject knowledge (you know the requirements of the curriculum).
- Pedagogical subject knowledge (you can make good choices to help you teach the maths).

And you have been introduced to the key features in the book which will allow you to develop across these areas. Your next task is to complete the audit in Chapter 2 – and then enjoy yourself as you draw on the appropriate chapters to complete your personal portfolio.

Going further

'Diamonds in a skull: unpicking pedagogy with beginning teachers' by Tony Cotton
This is the research paper which I based the opening of the chapter on. This article describes a piece of research which involved 20 trainee teachers in describing and exploring how they developed their subject knowledge in mathematics. These trainees had described themselves as lacking confidence in teaching mathematics, and the research tracks their development into becoming skilled teachers of mathematics.

Cotton, T. (2010) 'Diamonds in a skull: unpacking pedagogy with beginning teachers' in Walshaw, M. (ed.) *Unpacking Pedagogy: New Perspectives for Mathematics Classrooms pp. 43–63.* Charlotte, NC: Information Age Publishing.

'Relational understanding and instrumental understanding' by Richard Skemp
This is seen as one of the most important pieces of writing about mathematics teaching and learning of the last 50 years. Skemp uses a metaphor which describes mathematics as a landscape to be explored rather than seeing mathematics as a ladder to be climbed. Through gaining an understanding of how different points in a landscape are connected, and the different paths we may take to navigate this landscape, we come to a much better understanding than if we have to blindly follow paths without any sense of where they might lead. The full text of the article is available at http://math.coe.uga.edu/olive/EMAT3500f08/instrumental-relational.pdf and is well worth reading.

Skemp, R. (1976) 'Relational understanding and instrumental understanding'. *Mathematics Teaching*, 77(3), 20–26.

CHAPTER 2
WHAT SHOULD I KNOW? WHAT DO I KNOW?

Introduction

Very often, at the end of an explanation which in my mind was very clear, one of the children I am teaching will put their hand up. When I ask them what they want they will tell me 'I'm stuck.' Sometimes I reply, 'What are you stuck on?' 'Just every-thing' they say! Developing your subject knowledge in mathematics can feel a bit like this – it is hard to focus on the particulars when at first you are not sure what you understand and what you need to work on. Similarly, I have often told people that my dad was my best teacher. I remembered him being able to explain things to me really clearly, especially mathematics that I was 'stuck' on. It was only recently that he told me he did not always understand the ideas himself but that he just encouraged me to explain things to him until I was able to discover myself what it was that I was 'stuck' on. If you find yourself struggling on any of the questions here try to see this as a positive. You have found an area that you need to work on. Then carefully reflect on what you do understand, and ask yourself exactly what questions you have. If you can identify your questions carefully you may well be able to move forwards yourself.

Chapter 1 described what I mean by subject knowledge. This chapter expands on this by offering you audit tasks so that by the end of the chapter you have a clearer understanding of what knowledge you already have and the steps you might take to build on your previous experiences.

Starting point

Two groups of trainee teachers I was working with were discussing the ways that their courses assessed their subject knowledge to ensure that they could teach mathematics effectively. Neither group were happy. One institution asked its trainees to take examinations at the end of each year. This group asked me, 'How does an exam show that we can teach mathematics well – if we've got GCSE mathematics why should we have to do more exams?' The other group were equally unhappy. They had to complete subject knowledge files and felt that gathering 'evidence' showing that they had 'revised' all the mathematics necessary didn't support them in their teaching either. They felt that although this file contained evidence that they had covered all the areas of mathematics it didn't necessarily show that they could use this knowledge to teach others.

It is clearly important that trainee teachers are confident in their mathematical subject knowledge before embarking on teaching particular mathematical ideas. However, what the stories above show is that it is also important that you can see, and make explicit, the connections between your own subject knowledge and your teaching.

During an inspection an inspector asked these questions of the students I was teaching:

- How do you know what mathematics you should know?
- How do you know if you know it?

I thought at the time that these were very helpful questions in terms of assessing our own subject knowledge. So answering these questions and making connections between your answers and your teaching is the aim for this chapter.

Auditing your current knowledge

This chapter will ask you to consider your subject knowledge in three ways. Firstly, you will reflect on your previous experiences of learning mathematics and think about your current levels of confidence in teaching mathematics. It is important to explore this area in an initial audit as confidence is a key facet of good subject knowledge. The audit will allow you to recognise your developing confidence as one measure of your improving subject knowledge.

The second part of the audit explores your personal beliefs about what makes up effective mathematics teaching. Your own beliefs play a central role in the way in which you teach mathematics, and this again links back to how confident you feel when teaching mathematics. As I have already suggested, feeling confident in the classroom is a large part of demonstrating good subject knowledge. This section of the audit allows you to illustrate how you will develop in order to plan appropriate activities in order to ensure effective learning of mathematics.

Finally you will audit your current understandings of mathematics in the areas of:

- Using and applying mathematics
- Counting and understanding number
- Knowing and using number facts
- Calculating
- Understanding shape
- Measuring
- Handling data

These areas correspond to the chapters which follow in the book. This section of the audit takes the form of presenting you with common misconceptions for you to analyse in the areas listed above. Using the proformas available on the companion website you will be able to complete these audits online and they will form the introductory section of your personal e-portfolio of mathematical subject knowledge.

Exemplars of completed audits are given in the following sections. Before you start the audit online have a look at these exemplars to support you in working through them for yourself.

Audit: Section 1 – Previous experience in learning mathematics and confidence in teaching mathematics

This section of the audit documents your previous experience in learning mathematics and allows you to document your developing confidence both in teaching mathematics and in planning for teaching and researching your own subject knowledge.

Visit the companion website to complete the audit online. You will see that the audit is in two columns. Complete the first column before using the book to develop your subject knowledge and then return to this section and complete the second column after using the book. This allows you to document any changes in the way you view your previous experience of learning mathematics as well as any changes in your confidence levels as a result of your studies.

The comments do not have to be detailed – you may not have many memories of your primary school in order to make comments, for example. The aim of this section is to allow you to take some time to think through your prior experiences and achievements and to reflect on how this makes you feel at the moment as a learner and teacher of mathematics. The second part of this opening section allows you to record statements about how you feel about teaching, planning and working on mathematics. The aim here is that you can 'take note' of how your feelings develop as a result of your studies.

The final part of this section explores your initial confidence levels across the mathematics curriculum and then allows you to reflect back to these initial thoughts after you have worked through the activities in the book. If you are uncertain as to the content of any of these areas of mathematics turn to the appropriate chapter and skim through the 'progression' section. This will remind you of the mathematical content contained within each of these areas.

Mathematics subject knowledge – Personal profile

Name	Tony Cotton	
Previous experience and qualifications Comment on your learning and achievement at the following points.	Before using *Understanding and Teaching Primary Mathematics*	After using *Understanding and Teaching Primary Mathematics*
Age 11:	Felt very confident in learning maths – was always placed in the high achieving table	I realise that I was often not challenged in my primary classroom. I simply spent a lot of time completing exercises that I could already do. I did not really develop my mathematical thinking skills
Age 14:	Achieved an 'average' level in my SATs. I was not really enjoying maths and it seemed like we were repeating a lot of the work that we had already covered	
GCSE or equivalent:	I got my grade 'C' – I was still not enjoying maths as a subject	I realise that I feel a bit frustrated that my secondary teachers did not make the subject enjoyable or interesting. I'm determined to make sure my pupils enjoy maths
Post-16 experience and qualifications:	I have avoided maths ever since I got my GCSE!	
My confidence in teaching mathematics	Complete the sentences below Before using *Understanding and Teaching Primary Mathematics*	After using *Understanding and Teaching Primary Mathematics*
When teaching mathematics in school I feel . . .	OK. I do seem to just follow the school's plans or use ideas from the Web rather than thinking up ideas for myself	That it is important for me to have a really good grasp of the maths rather than simply read through the maths at the same level as the children – it helps me see where the maths is leading in the future
When planning for teaching mathematics I feel . . .	See above	That I need to ensure the activities are challenging and interesting – not simply find something that will cover the curriculum
When researching mathematics in order to develop my own subject knowledge I feel . . .	That I can find activities that will help the pupils. I find it hard to find exciting activities, though	See above

Initial audit of confidence

Please complete this audit using the following key:

1 I feel very comfortable with this area of mathematics and could answer questions from children with confidence.

2 I feel fairly comfortable with this area of mathematics and would be happy to teach it with some preparation.

3 I am a little uncertain with this area of mathematics and would need to spend a lot of time preparing before I could teach it.

4 I do not understand this area of mathematics at all.

| | Before reading book | | After reading book | |
Area of mathematics	Confidence level	Comment or evidence	Confidence level	Comment or evidence
Using and applying mathematics	3	I'm not really sure what is meant by 'using and applying' as it is an area I feel I did not learn in school	2	I feel much more confident that I understand what I need to teach – I still find it a challenge to find appropriate activities, though. I have included my response to the initial audit task here as well as my notes from reading the chapter to show how my understanding has developed
Counting and understanding number	2	This is an area I feel OK about – it has been an area I have previously focused on. My successful response to the initial audit tasks supports me in this comment	2	I did not focus on this area
Knowing and using number facts	2	As above	1	I read the chapter and found the ICT task interesting. I have included a lesson plan which uses this piece of software which I use in school. I am now very confident in teaching this area of mathematics
Calculating	2	As above	1	I also completed the tasks at the end of the chapter and was very pleased with the results. I have included these as evidence of my growing confidence in this area

	Before reading book		After reading book	
Area of mathematics	Confidence level	Comment or evidence	Confidence level	Comment or evidence
Understanding shape	2	This is another area I feel comfortable with. I have a good memory for the names and properties of shapes. I have included my successful initial audit as evidence of this	1	After working on the chapter I realise that there is a lot more to 'shape' than simply remembering the names. I really enjoyed working through this chapter and have included all my notes in my portfolio
Measuring	3	I am uncertain about areas and volumes and need to study this in some detail	2	I feel much more confident with my knowledge in this area. I have included my response to the tasks in the chapter and an exemplar lesson plan in my portfolio
Handling data	3	This is not an area that I feel confident in at all as it is something that I avoided at school and have not had to teach at all	2	After working on the chapter I realise that this area is not as complex as I thought. I have included my notes from working through the chapter as evidence of my improvement

Audit: Section 2 – Beliefs about learning and teaching mathematics

For this section of the audit you are asked to reflect on your beliefs about learning and teaching mathematics and comment on any changes to your thinking after working through the book. You do this through completing a questionnaire based on important research into effective teaching of mathematics carried out by Mike Askew and others at King's College in London. They carried out a wide range of observations across many primary schools exploring the impact of teachers' beliefs on learning mathematics and divided these beliefs into three categories: 'connectionist', 'transmission' and 'discovery'.

To summarise these beliefs, connectionist teachers think it is important to make connections between all the different areas of mathematics. They are likely to draw on a wide range of mathematical ideas to solve problems themselves and will make these links for their learners. These teachers will favour open-ended, investigative approaches to learning and teaching mathematics. Teachers who feel comfortable with a transmission model take the view that mathematics is a fixed body of knowledge that their learners should be introduced to by a teacher who can 'transmit' this knowledge effectively. A model here would be that the teacher works through examples with their learners who then practise similar examples on their own. Finally a teacher who believes in a discovery approach will plan activities that allow their learners to explore mathematics at their own level, coming to their own understanding of how mathematics operates.

Your own beliefs are likely to have been influenced to a large extent by your prior experiences of learning mathematics and how this makes you feel as a learner of mathematics. They will also have been influenced by your experiences in the classroom as a trainee teacher and the beliefs of teachers you have worked with in schools.

Once you have completed the initial questionnaire you may like to explore the differences between your own beliefs and those that you would ascribe to your own teachers and to teachers that you have worked with in schools. Differences in beliefs may account for personal feelings of inadequacy as both a teacher and a learner. Visit the companion website to this book containing the questionnaire and highlight the statements that most closely mirror your current beliefs using the highlighter tool. You can select statements from different columns – in fact it is very likely that you will want to select statements from across the spectrum of beliefs. You may even want to choose more than one statement per row. The idea is to engage you in thinking about your beliefs before you embark on working with the ideas in this book. When you feel as though you have completed working through the book revisit the questionnaire and underline those statements you now agree with. Of course, many of these may be the same. Then complete the comment box to reflect on the impact of your working at your mathematical subject knowledge on your beliefs about learning and teaching mathematics.

Look at the completed table below as an example before completing the online questionnaire.

	Connectionist	Transmission	Discovery
	Being numerate involves:	Being numerate involves:	Being numerate involves:
Beliefs about what it is to be a numerate pupil	The use of methods of calculation which are both efficient and effective	Primarily the ability to perform standard procedures or routines	Finding the answer to a calculation by any method
	Confidence and ability in mental methods	A heavy reliance on paper and pencil methods	A heavy reliance on practical methods
	Selecting a method of calculation on the basis of both the operation and the numbers involved	Selecting a method of calculation primarily on the basis of the operation involved	Selecting a method of calculation primarily on the basis of the operation involved
	Awareness of the links between different aspects of the mathematics curriculum	Confidence in separate aspects of the mathematics curriculum	Confidence in separate aspects of the mathematics curriculum

	Connectionist	Transmission	Discovery
	Being numerate involves:	**Being numerate involves:**	**Being numerate involves:**
	Reasoning, justifying and eventually proving results about number	An ability to 'decode' contextual problems to identify the particular routine or technique required	Being able to use and apply mathematics using practical apparatus
Beliefs about pupils and how they learn to become numerate	Pupils become numerate through purposeful interpersonal activity based on interactions with others	Pupils become numerate through individual activity based on following instructions	Pupils become numerate through individual activity based on actions on objects
	Pupils learn through being challenged and struggling to overcome difficulties	Pupils learn through being introduced to one mathematical routine at a time and remembering it	Pupils need to be ready before they can learn certain mathematical ideas
	Most pupils are able to become numerate	Pupils vary in their ability to become numerate	Pupils vary in the rate at which their numeracy develops
	Pupils have strategies for calculating but the teacher has responsibility for helping them to refine their methods	Pupils' strategies for calculating are of little importance – they need to be taught standard procedures	Pupils' own strategies are the most important: understanding is based on working things out yourself
	Pupil misunderstandings need to be recognised, made explicit and worked on	Pupils' misunderstandings are the result of a failure to 'grasp' what was being taught and need to be remedied by further reinforcement of the 'correct' method	Pupils' misunderstandings are the results of their not being ready to learn the ideas
Beliefs about how best to teach pupils to become numerate	Teaching and learning are complementary	Teaching is separate from and has priority over learning	Learning is separate from and has priority over teaching
	Numeracy teaching is based on dialogue between teacher and pupils to explore understandings	Numeracy teaching is based on verbal explanations so that pupils understand teachers' methods	Numeracy teaching is based on practical activities so that pupils discover methods for themselves
	Mathematical concepts and the ability to apply these concepts are learned alongside each other	Learning about mathematical concepts precedes the ability to apply these concepts	Learning about mathematical concepts precedes the ability to apply these concepts

	Connectionist	Transmission	Discovery
	Being numerate involves:	**Being numerate involves:**	**Being numerate involves:**
	The connections between mathematical ideas need to be acknowledged in teaching	Mathematical ideas need to be introduced in discrete packages	Mathematical ideas need to be introduced in discrete packages
	Application is best approached through challenges that need to be reasoned about	Application is best approached through word problems which offer contexts for calculating routines	Application is best approached through using practical equipment
Comment on impact of self-study on personal beliefs	*I think I have moved more towards the 'connectionist' viewpoint. This was quite a difficult move for me as I have never been taught by a 'connectionist' teacher and most of the teachers I have observed have focused on 'transmission'. However, I am now much more able to see the links between different areas of mathematics and think it is important for pupils to be able to make this link too*		
	I have also realised that using children's misconceptions as a starting point for teaching is really useful. I think my own growing understanding of where misconceptions come from has helped me		

Audit: Section 3 – Exploring subject knowledge

The final section of the audit asks you to work with a range of questions across the strands of mathematical subject knowledge covered in the book. This allows you to decide which areas of mathematics you already feel comfortable with and those areas you need to concentrate on for further study. Please visit the companion website to carry out this section of the audit. The questions and worked answers are available on the companion website (www.routledge.com/9781447929994).

Don't worry at all if you find yourself thinking 'I don't know what to do in this question' or if you become 'stuck'. This is a signal for you that it will be worth working through the appropriate chapter in the book. This is an initial audit of your subject knowledge so that you can focus on the areas you most need to develop. Once you have worked through all the questions you can complete a personal action plan on the companion website which will help you to prioritise your use of the book. You should make your first priority those areas that you have assessed as 3 or 4.

Summary

This chapter has asked you to reflect on your own starting point in terms of your subject knowledge of mathematics. I hope that you are now able to answer these questions for yourselves:

- What do I need to know?
- What do I already know?
- Which areas should I focus on to develop my own knowledge?

The audits have provided you with the opening sections for your personal portfolio. You will develop this portfolio as you complete the portfolio tasks throughout the following chapters and the audit sections at the end of these chapters.

Going further

'Effective teachers of numeracy in primary schools: teachers' beliefs, practices and pupils' learning' by Mike Askew and his colleagues
This paper describes the research, discussed in the chapter, that explored effective teaching of numeracy, and introduced the idea of connectionist teaching.

Askew, M., Brown, M., Rhodes, V., Wiliam, D. and Johnson, D. (1997) 'Effective teachers of numeracy in primary schools: teachers' beliefs, practices and pupils' learning' (paper presented at the British Educational Research Association annual conference in 1997). London: King's College, University of London.

CHAPTER 3
PROBLEM SOLVING USING MATHEMATICS

Introduction

Whenever I share the story that follows with students they tell me that they don't believe it really happened. However, when I suggest that I also used to sit reading a book to myself in the reading corner and that very quickly my class would start to gather round to share the book they can see that this would happen. Honestly, children can find mathematics as fascinating as reading. It is important that we show the learners we work with that we enjoy doing mathematics for its own sake. This is one way of doing this.

I had been experiencing difficulty in engaging a group of 9- and 10-year-olds in a problem-solving activity. They seemed happy simply completing exercises that I gave them but would not investigate mathematics in a more open way. So I decided on a new tactic. While the group were out at playtime I surrounded myself with large sheets of flip chart paper and began to explore a particular number chain. (The rule was that if the number is divisible by 5 I divided by 5, otherwise I added 4 – the aim was to see how long the chains were, depending on which number I started with.) As the group came back into the classroom they started to gather round and asked me what I was doing. They then started to ask me other questions – How long do you think this chain will be? What happens if you start with a number bigger than 10? They then made suggestions about how they could help me in finding the answers. Before I knew it the whole class was engaged in exploring number chains.

Sometimes exploring mathematics alongside our pupils engages more effectively than always working at something which we already know the answer to.

The aim of this chapter is to support you in becoming confident in teaching how to use and apply mathematics. To do this you need to explore your own learning of mathematics, so I would like to ask you to work on a piece of mathematics as an initial step. This will give you some insight into how your learners may feel when you ask them to carry out a mathematical activity they have not met before. By reflecting on your learning process you will be better able to see the support you might offer to your learners.

Starting point

Portfolio task 3.1

Look at this number square. Imagine you can extend it as far as you like both horizontally and vertically. You may want to sketch your own enlarged version in a notebook. What patterns do you see in the number square? Jot down anything you notice.

1	3	5	7	. . .
2	6	10	14	. . .
4	12	20	28	. . .
8	24	40	56	. . .
. . .	. . .	. . .	. . .	. . .

Now let us focus your thinking a little. Do you think every number will appear if you extend the square far enough? If you think every number will appear, write down why you think this is the case. Will every number appear once, or more than once? Again try to make notes describing your reasoning.

Now, to focus even more, will 1000 appear in an extended version of the square? If you think it will, describe its position. If you think it won't, explain why this is the case.

I often use this activity with my students and many tell me that they find the first question too open. They say, 'I don't notice anything!' or even 'What am I supposed to notice?' Hopefully one group of students will make a suggestion like:

1	3
2	6

'If you look at a block of four numbers from the grid, by adding the two numbers in the first column you get the number at the top of the next column.' Once someone has noticed a pattern, any pattern, this seems to give others permission to look for other patterns. I think perhaps at this stage my students realise that I am not asking them to find a particular pattern that will give the 'right' answer, but genuinely asking for any patterns.

Unlike the other chapters in this book, the ideas which underpin 'Problem solving using mathematics' cannot be summarised as a set of content to be taught; rather it is a structure which you can use to solve and investigate problems across all areas of mathematics. Later in the chapter you will see that ideas of communication, reasoning, and enquiry are at the heart of this mathematical problem solving. It is for this reason that I have chosen to open the main body of the book with this chapter. I think that these ideas are at the heart of all mathematical activity. If you become confident and skilled in the areas of mathematical communication, if you are able to use your mathematical knowledge to investigate and solve problems through applying mathematical reasoning, you will have become a mathematician.

If you tried to share your insights into the previous number square task with friends or children you would start to see the centrality of communication. Sometimes our own thoughts and ideas become much clearer when we try to share them with others – or we gain new insights through asking questions as other people try to explain their thinking. You may have realised that the prompt questions asked you why you thought your solutions were correct – this is to enable you to begin to articulate your 'reasoning'. It is only when we ask 'why' that we begin to explore mathematical reasoning. Finally, the process of enquiry and problem solving encourages learners to engage with open questions. I asked, 'What patterns can you see?' This may have felt too open for you at first. How would you know when you had finished? Were there particular patterns I wanted you to spot? This unease perhaps comes from your prior experience of mathematics, which may have been presented through a series of closed questions and answers supplied by the teacher, followed up by a series of exercises to practise a particular skill. When developing problem-solving skills we often start with a fairly open question so that we can investigate the mathematics in a number of different ways.

Before moving on to explore problem solving in more detail I want to outline how the ideas above can be developed across a learner's time in primary school. This allows you to see how the activities you design for the children you are working with build on ideas which they will have met already.

Progression in 'Problem solving using mathematics'

Foundations for 'Problem solving using mathematics'

Initially young learners should be asked to recognise and re-create simple patterns and talk about what they see. Early skills include matching similar objects and sorting objects into categories they can describe. Children will also start to talk about the decisions they are making: for example, they may arrange blocks in colours and tell you that the blocks 'go red, blue, red, blue'.

Beginning in 'Problem solving using mathematics'

At this stage children will use diagrams and numbers to represent problems and to organise their thinking. For example, they may choose to use cubes if you ask them to carry out calculations they cannot work out mentally. They will be able to describe more complex patterns to you and complete patterns that you start from. They will identify, describe and explain simple patterns involving numbers and shapes. They might notice that answers all end in 2, or that answers are all odd or all even. Children will also start to use ICT both to explore problems and to present their solutions using simple word processing programs and software which allows them to sort and categorise.

Becoming confident in 'Problem solving using mathematics'

By this stage children are coming to an understanding of the way in which mathematics can be used to communicate and explain ideas from a range of curriculum areas. For example, a geography unit that the children will study explores 'Our school and local area'. The children will draw on their mathematical skills to undertake this learning. When you offer them an open-ended investigation they will also be able to follow a specific line of enquiry, explaining the choices they are making. For example, in the number square at the beginning of this chapter they may choose to look at patterns in specific rows or columns. If appropriate they will relate their solutions back to a real-life context to check the reasonableness of their solution. So if they are working on a series of word problems based around shopping they will be checking to see that the prices are reasonable. They will be making well informed decisions about the most appropriate way to represent and report their thinking. They will suggest a range of possible lines of enquiry given a starting point, and discuss a range of approaches to the problem, offering a clear rationale for the approach they take. By the end of their time in primary school children will enjoy using mathematics as a problem-solving tool across the curriculum and will be able to explain their thinking clearly.

Extending learning in 'Problem solving using mathematics'

Children operating at this level will be able to break down two- and three-step problems into simple steps and prioritise the information they are offered in order to make sense of a problem. They will continue to describe and explain their methods using a wide range of appropriate pictures and diagrams and an increasingly sophisticated mathematical vocabulary.

The next section of the chapter focuses on the 'big ideas' of communication, reasoning, and enquiry and problem solving. These 'big ideas' are the starting point for all the mathematical problem solving we will carry out with our learners. You will explore ways in which you can become a confident mathematical thinker and in this way you will be able to model mathematical thinking successfully with the learners with whom you work.

Big ideas

One of the most influential texts exploring this aspect of our subject is *Thinking Mathematically* by John Mason with Leone Burton and Kaye Stacey, published in 1985 by Pearson Education. (John Mason is the Professor of Mathematics Education at the Open University (OU).) He has written for 25 years about the processes of mathematical thinking and was the director of the influential Centre for Mathematics Education at the OU for 15 years. He has a particular interest in the ways in which we search for generality as a way of thinking and making sense of the world.

In *Thinking Mathematically* we are offered five key assumptions to support our teaching of mathematical thinking:

1 Everyone can think mathematically.

2 Mathematical thinking can be improved by 'practising reflection'.

3 Mathematical thinking is provoked by contradiction, tension and surprise.

4 Mathematical thinking is supported by an atmosphere of questioning, challenging and reflecting.

5 Mathematical thinking helps in understanding oneself and the world.

You may realise that these assumptions underpin the approach I have taken to developing your subject knowledge in this book – and that they offer a classroom ethos rather than a series of skills to be taught. However, there are 'skills' which underpin the process of problem solving using mathematics which will be outlined in this chapter.

Two other ideas which are important when working with children on their mathematical thinking are **specialising** and **generalising**. Specialising is the process you use when you look at specific examples in order to get started on a problem. So, for example, if you suggested that the 'numbers doubled as they move down the rows' you will have started by noticing that 2 is double 1 and that 4 is double 2. You may even have checked that this was always the case by extending the number square to look at further examples. You will have used this to come to a generalisation – this is when you make a statement about all numbers in the square. So generalising is making a statement that is true about a wide range of cases. An example might be 'if you add two odd numbers together you get an even number'.

The ideas of specialising and generalising appear throughout mathematics. A common confusion you will see with children is that they will take a 'special' case as true for all cases. If you were to ask your learners to draw you 'a triangle' it is most likely that they would draw an equilateral triangle. We see the special case – a triangle with all sides and angles the same size – rather than the bigger picture. In general, any three-sided shape is a triangle.

Taking it further

In *Mathematics Teaching* 182 (available at **http://www.atm.org.uk/mt/archive/ mt182.html**) Laurinda Brown, a mathematics education lecturer and researcher, reports on a research project where she worked with four teachers on problem-solving activities in the classroom. She suggests that the approaches they took which we discuss in this chapter will encourage children to become mathematicians rather than simply 'learn' mathematics. Her criteria for mathematical thinking will be very useful if you are devising activities or trying to analyse the mathematical thinking that is taking place in your classroom.

She suggests that thinking mathematically involves:

- Being systematic and organised.
- Being able to analyse situations and make generalisations.
- Predicting and testing predictions.
- Being precise in our definitions.
- Developing precise mathematical vocabulary to describe situations.
- Being aware of the big picture while working in a particular direction.
- Being able to pose our own questions.
- Being able to share ideas and being able to work independently.
- Challenging other peoples ideas by asking 'what if?' questions.

Next time you engage in some investigational work, ask yourself which of these criteria you have met. Similarly, the next time you work with children on developing their mathematical thinking skills, use the list to evaluate your own practice.

Enquiry and problem solving

I think it may be useful at this point to explore a mathematical problem to exemplify what I mean by 'Enquiry and problem solving'.

Portfolio task 3.2

Look at the number line below:

1	2	3	4	5	6	7	8	9	10	11	12	13	14	15

Look at chunks of the number line which consist of two consecutive numbers, such as 1,2 or 6,7 or 13,14. Add these pairs of numbers together. What do you notice? Do you think this result is true for any two consecutive numbers? Why do you think this happens?

Now try adding together three consecutive numbers, or four. What are you noticing? What do you think is the reason for these results?

You may feel a little insecure with the openness of this task. You may not be sure if you have 'answered the question'. This isn't unusual. There is in fact no 'question to answer' – the point is to 'plan and follow lines of enquiry', which is one of Laurinda Brown's themes. Hopefully, by trying to answer the 'why' questions you are beginning to 'communicate your mathematical thinking'.

Reflect on how you approached this problem. One definition of numeracy offered by the 1999 English framework for teaching mathematics suggested that learners should 'have an inclination' to solve problems. This suggests that it is not sufficient to teach children how to solve problems but that we should teach them to *want* to solve problems. Is this how you felt when faced with the problem above – did you want to extend the problem and find out why certain results were happening, or did you feel rather confused by the apparent openness of the problem? Many of my students when faced with this problem will ask me how they will know when they have 'done enough' or 'finished'. I would suggest that this attitude to problem solving is learnt – many of you will remember having to submit coursework as a part of your GCSE examination. And many of you will have been given very clear guidelines as to the approach you should take and the way you should present the problem in order to maximise your mark. However, this places a reliance on the teacher to give you answers and to keep you on the right track, rather than an inclination to solve problems through following your own lines of enquiry. An important way to develop your own subject knowledge is to explore mathematical problems for yourself, if possible with the children you teach, and model how problem solving can be open ended. If you show your learners that you have an 'inclination' for problem solving they will follow your model. I offered a view of how this can be effective as a teaching approach at the beginning of the chapter.

Similarly, the investigation modelled a line of enquiry in the following way:

1   Start with a question – what do we notice about consecutive numbers?

2   Find a starting point to examine this question – in this case look at pairs of numbers.

3   Specialise – that is, look at specific pairs of numbers to see what you notice. You may have noticed that adding together pairs of numbers gave you an odd number as an answer.

4   Try a range of similar cases to see if the result can be generalised – does the result always happen whichever pairs you choose?

5   Try to 'prove' the result – why does this happen? Proving is being able to convince someone that your explanation is correct.

Portfolio task 3.3

I have used this problem with young children and they proved the result for me by building towers from cubes. Try to prove the statement 'The sum of two consecutive numbers is always an odd number' through a drawing.

Here is a drawing that may get you started:

Representing

In the book *Assessing Children's Mathematical Knowledge: Social Class, Sex and Problem Solving*, published by the Open University Press in 2002, Barry Cooper and Mairead Dunne showed that many children fail to demonstrate their skills in problem solving as they find it difficult to decode representations of mathematical problems. For example, if children are asked the question 'If there are 77 children in a year group and the coaches to take them swimming hold 35 children, how many coaches are needed?', some children responded 'Two'. When asked for the reason for their answer they said it would be silly and too expensive to hire three, and that seven children could have lifts in parents' cars. They did not realise that the answer expected was three, as in a sense the 'real' context was a mathematical context and not a genuine problem to solve. The children who are most successful in solving problems which appear on high-stakes tests are those who can make the link between a realistic mathematical problem and the mathematical processes they will need to carry out to solve the problem. In the example above these children would realise that the question was asking for a repeated addition to be carried out until an answer greater than 77 was reached. The best way to support children in developing their skills in decoding different representations of problems – in words, in tables, in graphs, in pictures – is to allow them to explore a range of problems which are represented in a variety of ways. This range of representations can then be shared with the class so that your learners begin to understand the range of representations that are possible. While children are exploring the range of ways in which they may represent problems, they also need to be developing their skills in communicating their mathematical thinking, which is discussed below.

Reasoning and communication

Reasoning is the process of being able to plan an enquiry: that is, deciding how you will tackle a problem, and then being able to draw on the range of mathematical skills that you have available to work at the enquiry. You can teach reasoning by asking children questions that allow them to draw on the knowledge they already have to solve a problem, and most importantly by encouraging them to articulate their thinking processes. Think back to the portfolio task that opened this section – could you explain the thought processes you went through? In his book *Thinking Mathematically*, John Mason describes a process of rubric writing to help develop mathematical reasoning and communication. Rubric writing is following a routine every time you notice you are 'stuck'. The key processes in rubric writing are noticing when you are 'stuck' and writing down how you know you are stuck – what is it that you don't know? When you have a new idea, described as an 'aha' moment, you write down 'aha' and describe the discovery you have made. Finally, at regular intervals you pause to 'check' your calculation or reasoning and make note of this. Then, at the end of a process of problem solving, you take time to 'reflect' and notice what you have discovered and what you have learnt.

Portfolio task 3.4

Take a sheet of A3 paper and fold it in half – use a 'portrait' orientation. On the left-hand side of the paper revisit the consecutive numbers problem above. Try to re-create in as much detail as you can the thinking process you went through when you explored the problem. Now on the right-hand side of the paper use the method of rubric writing to annotate your thinking. When were you stuck? Why were you stuck? Jot down your 'aha' moments. What did you do immediately following these thoughts? At what stages did you check back over your calculations? What did you discover? Finally, take time to reflect. What did you learn from working at the problem? How might you approach a similar problem in the future? How might you explore this problem further?

If you can try this problem with a class you are teaching, encourage them to tell you when they are stuck, or have 'aha' moments. Support them in checking back over their solutions and most importantly give them time to reflect on the process.

Teaching points

When you introduce your class to mathematical problem-solving activities you will notice misconceptions and misunderstandings. It is important that you don't treat these as mistakes or errors but that you use them as prompts to intervene and to support the pupils in coming to a better understanding of the mathematics they are working on. The following teaching points are based on my own experience of teaching problem solving. You may recognise some of the areas as ones which you have difficulty with yourself. You will also see how they link to the big ideas described above.

Teaching point 1: Not carrying out appropriate steps in multi-step word problems

This can take two forms. Some children will scan a problem to see if they can quickly spot the **operation** that is being asked for – these children might put their hands up and ask a question such as 'Miss, is this one a divide?' Other children may carry out the first operation within a problem and then stop. They have become used to problems having a single answer each.

I was working with a group of Year 6 children on solving word problems. They were given a table of information which told them a serving of cereal contained 350 calories per 100 g. They were asked to calculate how many 30 g bowls of cereal they would need to eat to meet the daily requirement of 2000 calories.

Many of the children realised that the operation they needed to carry out was to divide but did not take care when they were deciding what to divide. Some also were looking for an answer that was exactly 2000, not realising that it would be OK to eat more than 2000 calories. So, for example, they answered:

- 5.714285714 (the answer on a calculator if you divide 2000 by 350). It would be difficult to eat such a precise amount of cereal, and five bowls of cereal would not really satisfy a growing child over a whole day.
- 67 (the answer if you divide 2000 by 30 and then round up to a 'whole' number of bowls). This is quite a lot of cereal!

There are three ways to support children in not just jumping to the first operation they see. Firstly, always ask if they think the answer is sensible and lead them back to the context – this does, of course, mean that you need to make sure the contexts are mathematically accurate. So, for example, if you are using prices try to be accurate. Children will have an understanding of the real costs of certain items and will be able to spot when you are just making things simple. Secondly, I often give children the answer to a multi-step problem and ask them to explain why this is correct. So in this case I would give them the same information but tell them that

- 19 bowls of cereal provide you with 1995 calories, which is very close to the daily requirement

and ask them to explain why this is correct. Another useful method is to present children with mathematical data and ask them to set each other multi-step problems, together with a solution. Getting children to pose their own questions is a very good way of teaching them to solve problems. This helps them to get inside the process of problem posing, and once they begin to understand how you set multi-step problems, they become more adept at solving them.

Teaching point 2: Not using a systematic approach to solve a problem

This area of difficulty is directly linked to the first one and I think it often arises from children thinking that the result of a problem-solving activity is a simple answer which the teacher knows and the child has to find out, as quickly as possible. For example, I set the following problem to a group of Year 4 children:

How many different ways can you arrange four different coloured cubes?

Say we are using red (R), blue (B), green (G) and yellow (Y) cubes. One way would be:

Another would be:

The group started to guess: '12' one group said, 'because it's 4 × 3'. Another group suggested 24, although they had no reason – they were just taking my non-committal response to mean that 12 was incorrect. So I gave the group boxes of different-coloured cubes and asked them to find all the different arrangements.

I recently asked my students to explore how many ways they could arrange four different coloured cubes in a line so that each arrangement is different. I asked them to use sketches to make sure they could convince each other that they had them all. One group came up with this solution:

R	Y	G	B		R	G	B	Y
R	Y	B	G		R	G	Y	B
R	B	Y	G					
R	B	G	Y					

The students' description was as follows:

> Here I have made sure that I have found all the arrangements that 'start' with a red cube. I also began by realising that if I place red, then yellow, there are two ways to arrange the blue and green cubes, and that this pattern repeats.

This is a good example of articulating mathematical reasoning, and it can be seen as a proof because it is convincing.

An effective way to encourage children to work systematically is to make sure the problem is complex enough that a system will be needed to keep track of all the possibilities. The problem we have been working on here demands a system as it is then easy to see the patterns. The most important question you can ask children to encourage them to work systematically is: 'Are you sure you have found all the arrangements?'

Teaching point 3: Difficulty explaining the thinking process ('I just did it')

One of the big ideas that I introduced at the beginning of the chapter was the ability to communicate mathematical reasoning. By the time pupils are leaving primary school we would hope they will be using sophisticated mathematical language to describe mathematical reasoning, as I mentioned in the progression section. However, this is not something that comes naturally. When I first ask a learner of any age how they have worked something out they often tell me 'I just did it'. This is not through an inability to describe their thought process. Until we start to try to remember how we are thinking mathematically it really does feel as though we 'just did it'. One way to get children to describe their thinking is to present a mental calculation – for example, working out how many children are in school today.

Say the numbers in school were:

Year 1	28	Year 4	22
Year 2	31	Year 5	25
Year 3	25	Year 6	30

Quickly calculate the total number in school. Now write down how you carried out the calculation. Two Year 6 children that worked on this told me:

> I added all the tens, so 20 + 30 + 20 + 20 + 20 + 30 and that gave me 140, then I added on 21 because that is what the units came to.

> I noticed that 28 and 22 made 50, and that 25 and 25 made 50 so that was 100, then I added on 31 and 30.

I got them to think more carefully about how they had worked it out by asking the first learner how they added the 10s. When they thought about it, they realised they had added all the 20s together first and then added 60 to get to 140.

The best way to 'teach' children how to explain their thinking is through your questioning. Look at the example in the Resource inspiration box below.

You will see that the text offers open questions, 'Can you use all the dominoes?', and asks the children to write about what they notice. The third question invites the children to try for other totals. You might want to support children in getting started on this by thinking about which totals are possible and which aren't possible. Always respond to an answer from one of your learners with a question. For example, if they say 13 isn't possible ask why, even

Resource inspiration

Domino totals

✱ Play a game of dominoes. Can you make a total of 6 each time? Can you use all of the dominoes?

✱ Play again. This time make totals of 5. Can you use all the dominoes?

✳ Try for other totals. Write about what you notice.

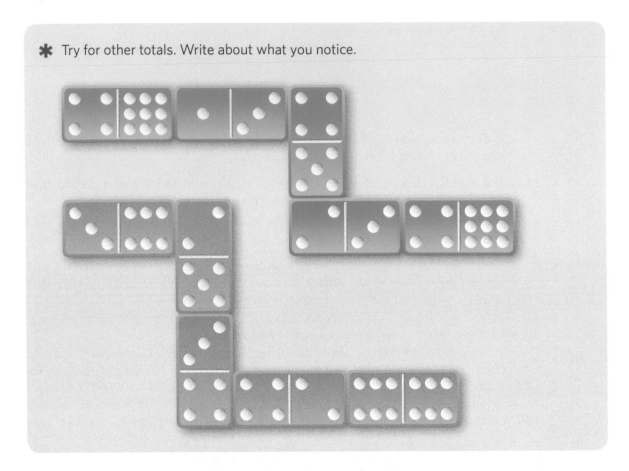

though it seems obvious. You might want to encourage different pairs to try different totals too – some will be easier than others and the pairs will then have an outcome to talk about.

Teaching point 4: Unwillingness to try to prove an assertion ('It just works')

A group of Year 2 children are making patterns with squares and equilateral triangles. Their teacher is trying to work with them to get them to 'prove' some of their findings:

> **Teacher: What if you made two rows of squares around your design; how many triangles will you need at the corner?**
> **Child: Two, I think. Oh no, look, it takes three.**
> **Teacher: And what if you made three rows of squares?**
> **Child: I don't want another row of squares.**

Earlier in this chapter I commented that many children did not immediately develop an 'inclination to solve problems'. It is often our younger learners who make this clearest to us. We can only work to develop the willingness of our learners to 'prove' their assertions

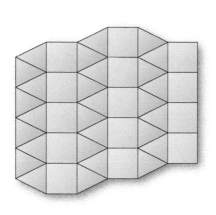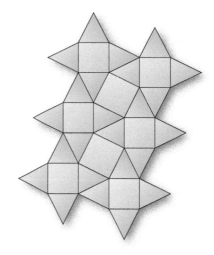

Squares and triangles

by modelling this expectation as the norm in our classrooms. Again this comes down to questioning. Several learners in classes I have taught have ended up frustrated with me as my usual response to an assertion they offer me is 'Why?' or 'Are you sure?' However, they quickly realise that 'being sure' of an answer is my measure of success and stop telling me the answer and begin to explain how they know it is the right answer.

Developing ideas of proof can be structured carefully. Look at the example in the following Resource inspiration box.

Resource inspiration

Pentominoes

✱ How many different ways can you arrange five squares so that two sides touch exactly?

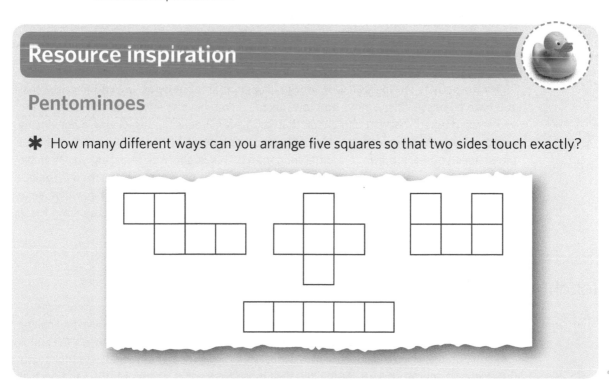

✳ How can you be sure that you have all the different arrangements?

✳ Sketch all your arrangements on squared paper. How many of these can you fold up to make an open cube?

✳ Is there a 'rule' you can write down which describes all the shapes which are nets of an open cube?

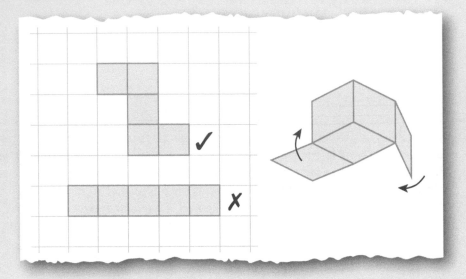

Try the activity for yourself. The activity is open at first but by asking you to check that you have all possibilities I move you towards proof. You have to introduce some system to your recording so that you can check that you have all possibilities. Giving a convincing reason why something is the case is the beginning of 'proof'. I then ask you to think about the shapes you have drawn in a different context. This is one way of asking you to make connections between different areas of mathematics. This time you can check your conjectures by cutting out the shapes and seeing if they will make an open cube. Then we move to trying to come up with a rule, or an 'algorithm' which allows you to 'generalise' from these special cases.

Teaching point 5: Not applying logical thinking

I will often find pupils looking back over correct answers they have written down and calling me over to ask me if they are correct. If I ask them what they think they will say – 'Well I think it's right but it seemed too obvious'. It is almost as if they expect mathematics to trick them. If something seems obvious, or logical, they must have got it wrong. Maths can't be that easy. This may be because they have just been taught a series of 'tricks' or routines rather than having been shown that mathematics is inherently logical and follows very predictable patterns. If I can add 7 to 15, I can follow exactly the same process to add 7 to anything. And any time I add 7 to a number with 5 'units' my answer will have 2 'units'.

One of my favourite problems to work on with young learners to help them see the importance of logical thinking and careful recording is the chessboard problem. I would like to ask you to work on this too. The question is very simple – How many squares are there on a chessboard? At first you will think the answer is straight forward – there are 64 squares on a chessboard. But if you look carefully there are many 2×2 squares, many 3×3 squares and so on, right the way up to an 8×8 square which forms the whole board. The next task is to find a way of counting these different squares. I will leave you to work on this. The solution is available on the companion website.

Many schools now use logical thinking activities, which do not necessarily draw on mathematics, to develop their pupils' problem-solving capacities. You can download many logic puzzles from the internet from sites such as **logic-puzzles.org**. Some of these are lateral thinking-type problems and some come with downloadable grids which your pupils can use to solve these puzzles. This gets you into the habit of reasoning things out logically. This is a very useful habit when it comes to working at more complex mathematical investigations

In practice

The following lesson plan was used to support a group of pupils beginning to develop their skills in 'Problem solving using mathematics'. The plan includes ICT to support the children's learning. The program described here is available on the companion website and you may wish to explore the 'number grids' program before reading the lesson plan. Following the plan is an evaluation of the lesson, which explores how successful the plan was in supporting the children to develop their knowledge, skills and understanding.

Topic: Odd and even numbers

Age group: Lower primary

Objectives

- To introduce the terms 'odd' and 'even' numbers
- To describe number patterns orally or using pictures

Key vocabulary	Context
Even, odd, pair	This is the fifth lesson in a series exploring counting on number lines and number tracks. Most of the children can count to 100 and can count backwards in 1s from 20. The previous lesson worked with the class on counting in 2s. All the groups could count in 2s from 0 but some found it difficult to start from any number other than 0. The higher-attaining group could count backwards in 2s from any number
	For this series of lessons I have grouped children according to their prior experience to provide support and challenge

Resources	Starter activity
Washing line and pegs, white socks (real!), 0–20 grid on the whiteboard, hoops, odd and even labels, multilink, 0–30 number cards	I will ask the whole class to stand in a circle. We will start by counting in 1s around the circle. Then I will ask every other child to clap rather than say their number, e.g. 1, clap, 3, clap . . . . We will then swap round: clap, 2, clap, 4 . . . . We will repeat this counting backwards starting at 28, which is the number of children in the class
	Next we will count feet around the circle – first counting everybody's feet, then counting in 2s. At this stage I will introduce the term 'even'

Main activity

	Ask the children to work in groups and give them all some socks (these should have been counted earlier and organised so that some groups have an even number of socks and some have an odd number)
	Each group have to calculate how many pegs they will need if they peg the socks on the washing line in 'pairs'
	Ask each group to come and peg their socks on the lines. I will ask each group if there is an 'odd' sock, or an 'even' number of socks which make 'pairs'. As each group pegs up the socks I will circle the even numbers in green and the odd numbers in red on the number square on the whiteboard

Group activity		Assessment
Group activity Children operating above expected levels	These children will work with the 0–30 set of cards. They will pick a card at random and have to decide if it is 'even' or 'odd'. I will focus on this group to encourage them to discuss how they know it is even or odd	**Assessment** I will ask the children to convince me how they know it is even or odd. They can draw pictures or use diagrams to convince me
Children operating at expected levels	These children will be using the multilink towers. They need to make some odd towers and some even towers and place these in the correct hoop	I will split this group into two so that they can check each other's towers at the end
	I will ask the children how they are deciding which are even numbers and which are odd numbers	

Children operating below expected levels	This group will continue working with socks on the washing line. This time they will work with 10 pairs of different coloured socks	I will ask the teaching assistant (TA) to support this group. She will ask them to peg up a number of pairs of socks and then count all the socks

Plenary

All the groups will come back together on the carpet area. I will set up a 10 × 2 number grid using the 'Number Grids' software. I will show the children the pattern and then hide all the numbers and move them around on the board so they are mixed up. I will ask the children to come to the front and pick a number to uncover. When they uncover it they will have to say if it is even or odd. The class will decide whether they are correct. All even numbers will be moved to the top left of the board and odds to the bottom right

Finally I will ask the higher-attaining group to describe how they decided whether a number was odd or even

1	2
3	4
5	6
7	8
9	10
11	12
13	14
15	16
17	18
19	20

Rationale and evaluation

The counting activity involved all the children. They were all successful too, which I was pleased about, although I could see Claire and Hannah mouthing the numbers when they were clapping. Rupa got a bit lost at one point so I asked him to use the number line on the classroom wall to count. He tapped the numbers as the rest of the group said them. This seemed to help as he could match his tapping to the rhythm of the clapping. Counting in 2s was a bit more difficult – I supported those who were having difficulty by circling all the even numbers on our number line. This allowed them to join in the activity, but I think they were simply reading the numbers off the line rather than coming to an understanding of their 'evenness'.

The children using the number cards really got into the idea of describing odd and even. Nasreen drew each number as a series of dots and circled pairs, so whenever there was an 'odd' dot outside her circles she knew it was odd. This showed that she was drawing on her learning in the socks activity.

The multilink towers worked well too. Both groups realised fairly quickly that by making towers that were two cubes wide they could very quickly decide which ones were odd and which were even. They finished this activity very quickly so I gave them number cards and asked them to label all the towers so they could see the odd and even numbers.

I was pleased that I continued with the washing line with the lower-attaining group. They labelled the numbers of socks on the line and this reinforced the idea of counting in 2s for them. During the plenary the rest of the children found Nasreen's suggestion about how to find out if a number was odd or even by using dots very helpful; they also liked the idea of odd and even towers. Both these images will help them consolidate the idea of odd and even. Finally, I asked if they could tell me how many socks there would be if I had 20 pairs of socks. They thought for a bit and then Michael told me, 'It's easy. They're all just doubles, so it's 40'. I was impressed – generalisation at age 6!

Audit task

For every chapter you will be asked to write your own lesson plan exploring an area covered in the chapter. You should focus on learning which is appropriate for a group of learners that you are working with and select an area of mathematics that has been discussed in this chapter. Construct a lesson plan using the proforma on the companion website or any planning proforma that is used by your course or by the school in which you work. Teach the lesson and then evaluate it carefully with a focus on children's learning and misconceptions.

Add this lesson plan and evaluation to your subject knowledge portfolio. This is a very important piece of evidence to show your developing subject knowledge. If you upload this lesson plan to the companion website you will be able to access lesson plans and resources which have been uploaded by other teachers using the site.

Observing 'Problem solving using mathematics'

You can access an example of a problem-solving activity on the companion website for this book. The activity uses the idea of a party and starts off with a table that seats six children: two at each side and one at each end. As more people arrive, tables are added to the end of the previous table. Watch the piece of video and work out for yourself what the pattern will be. Once you have a pattern that will allow you to predict the number of people seated at any number of tables, try to generalise the formula using an algebraic expression. Now explore other possible arrangements of tables. What would happen if you formed 'L' shapes with the tables? What would happen with tables which are different shapes?

Think carefully about how you would introduce this to a class you are working with. What questions would you ask to scaffold the activity? How would you leave the activity to be open enough so that your children move beyond simply filling in tables of results, and how would you encourage them to generalise?

Assessing 'Problem solving using mathematics'

When you wish to assess your learners to ascertain their skills in problem solving using mathematics you need to make sure you give your learners the opportunity to show evidence as to how they are approaching the problem that you have set them; the extent to which they are being systematic; their abilities in predicting possible outcomes and testing these; the effectiveness of the recording systems that they adopt; and, finally, the effectiveness of their communication of their reasoning process to others. As an example reflect on the activity described at the opening of this chapter and answer the following questions as honestly as you can.

1 How persistent were you at looking for a range of patterns? Did you explore a range of patterns or stop after you had found two or three?

2 Were you able to explain why the pattern appeared or did you just describe the pattern?

3 Did you use 'increasingly complex' mathematical vocabulary to describe these patterns?

4 How systematic were you in exploring whether every number appeared and in your search for 1000?

5 Did you have a convincing explanation for your answer to whether or where 1000 appeared?

Try this activity with the group you are currently teaching, or any of the other activities, and use these questions to assess your pupils. Be open with them about the criteria you are using to assess them so that they are clear about your expectations. It is important that your pupils become aware of what counts as 'success' in problem solving as this may be slightly different to previous success criteria.

Cross-curricular project

Learners respond very well to solving problems in their real world. This can also help them see the 'point' of learning new skills and motivate them to come to new understandings. A cross-curricular project offers you the possibility of working with mathematics over extended periods of time rather than in small chunks, often only an hour. Of course, when we solve problems outside school we don't limit ourselves to a single hour a day in order to find solutions.

A project focusing on developing a more sustainable school will both engage your learners and allow you to engage in a wide range of problem-solving activities. The most effective way to begin such a project is to ask your learners how they could explore this issue. Do some research for yourself first. How much waste paper is thrown away each day? How much does the school spend on paper and photocopying? What are the annual fuel bills? What are the implications for pollution for the ways that pupils travel to school? Some of the areas which learners have explored with me on this extended project over the years have included the following.

Car parking

What is the most effective way of redesigning the car park so that it uses a minimum of space and so that it can incorporate a bike shed to encourage cycling to school? This involves measurements of cars, the construction of scale models, and trying out different arrangements for parking spaces. The issue of ensuring there are sufficient parking spaces for those needing accessible parking is also important.

Travel to school

My pupils have always enjoyed surveying the whole school to find out how teachers and pupils get to school. They can then calculate the current carbon footprint. This has led to pupils exploring ways of lift sharing, of walking buses, of cycling schemes where pupils meet up and cycle to school together. The mathematics of it also involves exploring shortest routes to school, and possible 'pick-up' points.

Recycling paper

Again, a brief survey can ascertain which classes use most paper, which classes are best at recycling paper, and the money that can be saved through recycling paper internally as scrap paper, or in home-made exercise books. A trip to the recycling plant is always popular.

Energy bills

Sharing the energy costs within a school has always led to pupils becoming incredibly vigilant about turning off lights and thinking carefully about energy usage. In two schools where I have worked they have offered the school council a share of any money saved through cutting energy costs, and the school council has been able to make the decision about how they will spend this money.

Summary

The focus of this chapter has been 'Problem solving using mathematics'. This chapter is deliberately placed early in the book as the whole approach of the book in developing your subject knowledge is through a problem-solving or investigative approach. I hope that the chapter has given you insight into how you can learn mathematics through problem solving and that this in turn will enable you to teach children how to solve problems and investigate effectively. The key ideas of 'communication', 'reasoning' and 'enquiry and problem solving' were outlined early in the chapter as a set of key skills in this area. The Big ideas section also introduced you to ways in which 'specialising' and 'generalising' underpin any mathematical problem solving. The Portfolio tasks throughout the chapter and the exemplar activities within the teaching points will also give you a wide range of starting points with which you can explore mathematical problem solving with the children you teach.

Reflections on this chapter

There are several key points to take from this chapter. Firstly you should now feel able to make a start on an investigation that is open – and you should be able to support your learners in 'attacking' an investigation through questioning rather than through directing them too closely. Perhaps you will be able to work with the children you teach to explore mathematical problems with them so that you model 'being a mathematician'.

You should also have an understanding of how important it is to work with very young children on describing their thinking processes and realise that you can teach children to articulate their thoughts. You will have become more aware of the way you think mathematically when working at problem-solving activities. You can then share your thinking processes with the children you are teaching as a way of helping them understand their own thinking process.

You have been introduced to key concepts such as specialising and generalising. Just a reminder: specialising means looking at specific examples to look for patterns; generalising means being able to make a statement about all cases. The most important thing that you should take away from this chapter is that a problem-solving approach means teaching your children to act like mathematicians rather than simply follow rules that you have given them. If the children you are teaching are reflecting on their thinking, asking interesting questions about the problems they are working on and most importantly 'having an inclination' to solve problems, you will be succeeding.

Self-audit

You should carry out this self-audit and add it to your subject knowledge portfolio.
This offers evidence of your own learning and development in the area of 'Problem solving using mathematics'. Read through the problem several times before you try to make a start. Also re-read the description of rubric writing earlier in the chapter so that you can use this process to describe your thinking.

This task explores number patterns within a 100 square:

1	2	3	4	5	6	7	8	9	10
11	12	13	14	15	16	17	18	19	20
21	22	23	24	25	26	27	28	29	30
31	32	33	34	35	36	37	38	39	40
41	42	43	44	45	46	47	48	49	50
51	52	53	54	55	56	57	58	59	60
61	62	63	64	65	66	67	68	69	70

71	72	73	74	75	76	77	78	79	80
81	82	83	84	85	86	87	88	89	90
91	92	93	94	95	96	97	98	99	100

Look at a block of four numbers. For example:

| 15 | 16 |
| 25 | 26 |

If I add these numbers together I get a total of 82. This is $(4 \times 15) + 22$, as $4 \times 15 = 60$ and $60 + 22 = 82$.

Picking another block and looking at the number in the top left box

| 18 | 19 |
| 28 | 29 |

I notice that $(4 \times 18) + 22 = 72 + 22 = 94$ and $18 + 19 + 28 + 29 = 94$ too. This is an example of specialising – I have looked at two different blocks of four squares and explored the patterns in them.

In order to generalise I can write down

| n | $n + 1$ |
| $n + 10$ | $n + 11$ |

or

n	One more than the number to its left
10 more than the number above	11 more than the number in the top-left square

So, adding these 'numbers' together

$$n + (n + 1) + (n + 10) + (n + 11) = 4n + 22$$

This shows that if I take any section of four numbers from the grid and add them together I will always get a total which is four times the number in the top left corner + 22.

Now look at other patterns of numbers. For example:

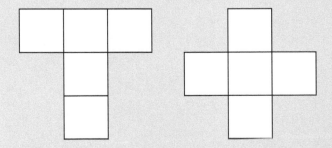

As you work at these problems jot down your thinking process at the side of the page. Use the rubric writing mentioned in the chapter. How do you get started on the problem? When are you stuck? What questions do you ask yourself to move forward? When are you specialising and when are you generalising? What 'aha' moments do you have? And finally, what have you learnt about this problem and yourself as a mathematical thinker?

Going further

The following books will help you explore the area of problem solving using mathematics in much more detail. The books also offer you a wide range of activities for both you and your pupils.

Transforming Primary Mathematics by Mike Askew
Mike draws on a huge body of research conducted in UK primary schools to argue that mathematics teaching in primary schools should be transformed to be based on problem solving and mathematical enquiry. He is clear that children should not be allocated to sets or groups to learn maths but should work together collaboratively on problem-solving activities, and that this will prepare them best for their futures.

Askew, M. (2011) *Transforming Primary Mathematics*. London: Routledge

The Elephant in the Classroom: Helping Children Learn and Love Maths by Jo Boaler
This book draws on Jo's research in both the UK and the USA exploring how children best learn maths. She has followed thousands of learners over several years and argues convincingly that problem solving through mathematics should be at the centre of the curriculum. The book includes examples of problem-solving activities that she has used or observed.

Boaler, J. (2009) *The Elephant in the Classroom: Helping Children Learn and Love Maths*. London: Souvenir Press.

Thinking Things Through: Problem Solving in Mathematics by Leone Burton
This book is another guide to the problem-solving approach in mathematics. Leone offers a schema which you can work on with your pupils and which will help you develop your own problem-solving activities. The book includes 30 problems for you to work on with your pupils.

Burton, L. (1984) *Thinking Things Through: Problem Solving in Mathematics*. Oxford: Basil Blackwell.

Thinking Mathematically by John Mason with Leone Burton and Kaye Stacey
In *Thinking Mathematically* the authors carefully describe the 'art' of problem solving which lies at the heart of mathematics. They demonstrate how you can encourage, develop, and foster this process both in your own thinking and in the children that you teach. They do this by carefully taking you through a series of problem-solving activities.

Mason, J., Burton, L. and Stacey, K. (1985) *Thinking Mathematically*. London: Pearson Education.

CHAPTER 4
COUNTING AND UNDERSTANDING NUMBER

Introduction

It is very difficult trying to remember how we learnt to count. It is one of those things many of us learnt before we can remember. You have probably either worked with or been with young children beginning to make sense of 'counting' at an early stage. Recently I was sitting with a three-year-old child of a good friend who had 'learnt' to count to 10. He did not have a sense of what 'counting to 10' meant but he had heard the pattern repeated many times. He counted carefully, saying each word accurately, 'one, two, three . . .' and so on. I wondered what would happen if I deliberately miscounted and so I jumped from six to eight missing out seven. For some reason he thought this was hilarious. 'No!' he shouted at me, so of course I repeated the 'joke'. He did not yet know that eight was two more than six, but he did know that you should always say seven immediately after six. This chapter will unpick the big ideas in learning to count and in understanding number. It will also engage you in activities which will allow you to reflect on how you learn 'Counting and understanding number' and will draw on research to illustrate how best to support children in their learning.

This opening activity helps you reflect on the skills you bring to 'counting' without really thinking about it.

Starting point

Portfolio task 4.1

You will need to work with a small group of friends or colleagues. Take it in turns to pick up a number of small cubes, between 5 and 12. Drop them onto a flat surface and cover them with a piece of cloth. Remove the cloth so that your friends can see the cubes but replace it before they have a chance to 'count' the cubes. Ask them how many cubes they saw. Then ask how they made their calculation. It is likely that the group will have counted in 2s, or 3s, or even larger groups depending on the arrangement of the cubes. Try this several times with increasing numbers of cubes to see how many cubes they can 'count' in this way.

This activity illustrates the basic principles of counting, which will be explored in more detail later in the chapter. Indeed those children who can quickly see the number of cubes are likely to have a well-developed 'number sense'. They are able see the cubes in a range of ways to help them count quickly and understand that the total of the count is the same as the total of the groups they are counting. They probably have a range of mental images attached to particular numbers. For example, they might see 5 as an arrangement of dots on a dice, as two dots next to three dots, or as a line of five dots. This means that when they see the number 5 they also see.

$5 = 2 + 1 + 2$ $5 = 3 + 2$

My guess would be that most of the parents of the pupils that you teach would say that counting and understanding number is at the heart of mathematics. The term 'numeracy' embodies 'number'. There are many counting games and traditional rhymes which show that counting and understanding number is a skill that is often developed outside the traditional classroom. There are also different traditions for finger counting – some cultures count each finger separately, some use knuckles so that each finger can represent a count of three, others use the thumb as a symbol for 5 or 10. Those who have grown up in European cultures tend to start counting with the thumb and assign 1 to the thumb. Finger counting systems that are still used in regions of Asia, and that you may well find in your classroom, allow you to count to 12 on one hand. In this case the thumb is used as a pointer and you touch each finger bone in turn. Occasionally the left hand is used to count and the right hand is used to tally the number of counts. So two completed counts on the left hand are shown by holding up two fingers on the right hand. This symbolises 24.

The big ideas that are explored in this chapter are 'counting', 'place value', 'fractions, decimals and percentages' and 'proportionality'. These terms will be defined in more detail later in the chapter. The next section shows the progression in counting and understanding number in terms of the key objectives within the framework.

Progression in 'Counting and understanding number'

Don't worry if you don't understand all of the ideas in this section. My aim is that you will understand what the area of 'Counting and understanding number' contains and will have been introduced to the key vocabulary. All of the ideas are discussed in detail later in the chapter.

Foundations for 'Counting and understanding number'

Initially young learners will learn to say and use number names in order in contexts that are familiar to them such as house numbers, or numbers of children in their group. They will start to understand that numbers identify how many objects are in a set and use this understanding to count reliably up to 10 everyday objects. They will be able to estimate how many objects they can see and check this by counting (the activity that opened this chapter would be a useful assessment activity to see how well this skill has been developed). They will become used to counting aloud in 1s, 2s, 5s and 10s and will have heard and developed language such as 'more' or 'less' to compare two numbers. They will use **ordinal numbers** (these numbers indicate position – first, second, third and so on) in different contexts and will be able to recognise the **cardinal numbers** 1 to 9.

⬇

Beginning in 'Counting and understanding number'

The next stage is for pupils to read and write numerals from 0 to 20 and beyond, and to use their knowledge of place value to place these numbers on a number track and number line. (Number tracks and number lines are used to support children in developing their counting skills. Number tracks have the numerals in the spaces. They can only represent positive whole numbers and must not include zero. Number lines have numerals on the lines and can therefore represent fractions and negative numbers at a later stage.)

Once pupils can count up to 100 objects they can learn to group them and count in 10s, 5s or 2s. They will also learn to explain what each digit in a two-digit number represents, including numbers where zero is a place holder. (0 is often described as a 'place holder' as it has no value. So, for example, in the number 40 there are no 'units' but we need to use the 0 as otherwise we would confuse 40 with 4.) When they understand the meaning of the digits in two-digit numbers they can be taught about **partitioning** two-digit numbers in different ways, including into multiples of 10 and 1. Partitioning is a very useful skill to develop in order to support the development of mental methods. For example, we can partition 47 into $40 + 7$. So if we are to add 47+15 we can see it as $40 + 7 + 10 + 5$ or $40 + 10 + 7 + 5 = 62$.

⬇

Becoming confident in 'Counting and understanding number'

Pupils can now develop their understanding of partitioning so that they can partition three-digit numbers into multiples of 100, 10 and 1 in different ways. They are also ready to be introduced to fractions. They should use diagrams to identify **equivalent fractions**. Examples of equivalent fractions are 6/8 and 3/4, or 70/100 and 7/10. Equivalent fractions have the same value. Children can also learn how to interpret **mixed numbers** and position them on a number line. An example of a mixed number is $3\frac{3}{4}$. It is a fraction which contains a whole number as well as a fraction.

Pupils can also begin to explain what each digit represents in whole numbers and decimals with up to two places, and partition, round and order these numbers. The rule to remember with **rounding numbers** to a particular decimal place is that if the next number to the right of that decimal place is 5 or more, you round the figure up to the next highest number, and if it is 4 or less it remains the same. For instance, if I were to round 4.72 to one decimal place I would write 4.7. If I were to round it to the nearest whole number I would write 5.

Towards the end of their time in primary school most learners should be able to express one quantity as a percentage of another (for example, express £400 as a percentage of £1000). You should also be working with them to see the connections between equivalent percentages, decimals and fractions.

Extending learning in 'Counting and understanding number'

The transition to secondary education will focus on developing children's use of **ratio notation**. Percentage notation is 30%, ratio notation is 30:100, and decimal notation is 0.3. Here the pupils you wish to extend can learn to reduce a ratio to its simplest form and divide a quantity into two parts in a given ratio. They will be able to use this understanding to solve simple problems involving ratio and direct proportion (for example, to identify the quantities needed to make a fruit drink by mixing water and juice in a given ratio).

The next section of the chapter focuses on the big ideas of 'counting', 'place value', 'fractions, decimals and percentages' and 'proportionality' which are at the heart of 'Counting and understanding number'. If you are confident with these ideas you will be able to teach children successfully throughout the primary school years and will have a clear understanding of the development of these ideas across the 3–11 age range.

Big ideas: counting

Many children will start school already able to count – but it is important to be aware of the principles of counting, both to support the children who cannot yet count and to recognise the processes that young children who have already learnt to count have mastered. The key research which supports us in understanding the process of learning to count was described by Rochel Gelman and Randy Gallistel in their book *The Child's Understanding of Number* published in 1986 by Harvard University Press. Gelman and Gallistel are both psychologists. They are married and work at Rutgers University in New Jersey, USA. Their book was seen as marking a huge development in our understanding of how children learn to count. Through careful observation of young children undertaking activities that they had planned they described five principles which underpin counting:

1 **The one-to-one principle:** a child who understands the one-to-one principle knows that we only count each item once.

2 **The stable-order principle:** a child who understands the stable-order principle knows that the order of number names always stays the same. We always count by saying one, two, three, four, five . . . in that order.

3 **The cardinal principle:** a child who understands the cardinal principle knows that the number they attach to the last object they count gives the answer to the question 'How many . . . ?'.

4 **The abstraction principle:** a child who understands the abstraction principle knows that we can count anything – they do not all need to be the same type of object. So we can count apples, we can count oranges, or we could count them all together and count fruit.

5 **The order-irrelevance principle:** a child who understands the order-irrelevance principle knows that we can count a group of objects in any order and in any arrangement and we will still get the same number.

Although there has been discussion as to whether such a rigid schema is innate or whether this view of the 'order' of skill development is a result of the teaching process, there is certainly evidence that children use 'subitisation' (the process by which very small sets are identified immediately – the process illustrated by the portfolio task which opened this chapter) but it is not clear if this is developed seperately from counting.

Portfolio task 4.2

Can you think of examples of children who do not yet understand these principles?
For example, a child who is asked to count seven multilink cubes laid out in a row and then count them again when you put them into a different arrangement to 'check' there are still seven would not yet understand the order irrelevance principle. Write your examples and enter this reflection in your personal portfolio.

Taking it further

In *Children and Number*, published in 1986 by Blackwell, Martin Hughes proposes a new perspective on children's early attempts to understand mathematics, suggesting that young children had well-developed understandings of number before starting school. This challenged the dominant Piagetian view of the stages of learning. He describes the surprisingly substantial knowledge about number which children acquire naturally before they start school, and contrasts this with the difficulties presented by the formal written symbolism of mathematics in the classroom. He argues that children need to build links between their informal and their formal understanding of number, and shows what happens when these links are not made. *Children and Number* describes many novel ways in which young children can be helped to learn about number. Martin Hughes shows that the written symbols that children often invent for themselves are more meaningful to them than the symbols that they are taught.

In the book *Mathematics with Reason: The Emergent Approach to Primary Mathematics*, published in 1992 by Hodder and stoughton and edited by Sue Atkinson, a number of authors explore the practicalities of adopting an approach to teaching mathematics in the early years which takes seriously the idea of children as 'emergent' mathematicians. This means that young children are encouraged to describe, both verbally and in written form, their emerging mathematical thinking. They are encouraged to develop their own ways of recording rather than being immediately directed towards formal recording methods.

Several chapters in the book draw on the work of Martin Hughes and define the emergent approach to learning and teaching mathematics which supports children in developing their own mathematical notation en route to a more formalised representation of mathematics.

The chapters in the book which draw on examples of children's own representations have particular relevance to the issues discussed in this chapter.

If you have a particular interest in the development of counting skills in the early years or are working on an assignment exploring this area these two books are Invaluable.

In this chapter I have separated the teaching points so that each set of teaching points is linked to each big idea. So the first three teaching points are linked to the big idea of counting.

Teaching points: counting

Teaching point 1: Inconsistent counting

Tony asks Holly how many ducks there are in the pond shown on the next page:

Holly says it's easy and counts 1, 2, 3, 4, 5, 5, 7, 8, 9, 10.

Here Holly has not grasped the one-to-one principle as she counts the big duck twice – perhaps in her mind she sees the size as important and so counts twice. She also misses 6 out of the count. This shows she does not yet realise that you always have to use the number names in the same order each time.

The best way to support children in overcoming this misconception is by giving them plenty of experience in counting. Try to use everyday objects that can be arranged in many possible ways for the children to count. Asking them to check each other's counting is a useful way of their supporting each other. Counting with the children is also important as you can model touching each object as you count it. Ask the children to count the same set of objects several times, arranging the objects differently each time.

This will help them come to an understanding of the order irrelevance principle. It is also important to teach the children lots of counting rhymes and songs. This supports the development of the stable order principle. There are many examples of counting songs and rhymes. It is well worth building up your repertoire. The songs take different forms. So 'Ten Green Bottles' and 'Ten in the Bed' count down from 10 to 1 by taking 1 away each time. Ten Fat Sausages counts

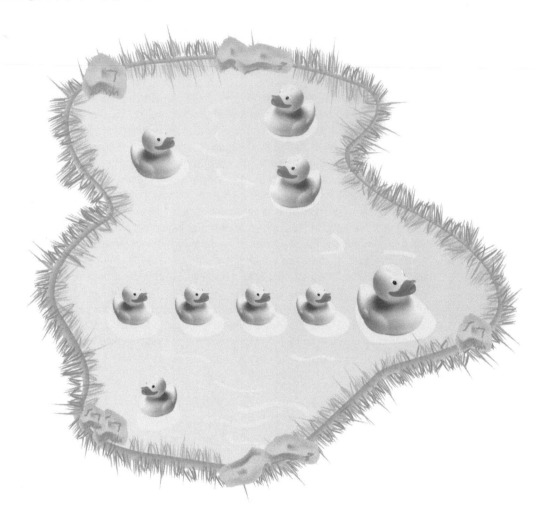

down in 2s. 'One, two, three, four, five – once I caught a fish alive' counts up in 5s. 'One, two, buckle my shoe' counts up in 2s. An internet search will provide you with lots of starting points. Even better, ask the children which songs they know and get them to teach you, or learn from the parents as that will ensure the songs you use reflect the cultures in the class you are teaching.

Teaching point 2: Miscounting on a number track

Sam is playing a game and he sometimes starts counting from the square that his counter is sitting on. This will cause a problem for him later when he uses a number line to support his mental calculations. This may be the reason why some children give incorrect answers for addition calculations. For example, they may write

$5 + 3 = 7$

| 1 | 2 | 3 | 4 | 5 | 6 | 7 | 8 | 9 | 10 |

This is because they counted 1, 2, 3, 4, 5 and then start on the 5 and count 5, 6, 7.

Again the best way to support children through this is to use number tracks regularly in many different contexts - frogs on lily pads, house numbers. It is particularly useful to ask young children to move on number tracks that you create in the classroom or the playground. Playing games which involve movement around a game board is also important. The children very quickly correct each other if they are counting incorrectly! Here I have used 'number track' to describe a representation of the number line which you can physically move along. A 'number line' represents numbers by points rather than spaces. We will use this later to support the development of mental methods of calculation.

Teaching point 3: Directed numbers

A directed number is one which has a plus or minus sign attached. This tells us whether it is a 'positive' or 'negative' number. So $^+7$ means 'positive' 7 and $^-3$ means 'negative' 3. A student of mine was researching **directed numbers** before planning a lesson for her Year 6 group. She remembered being told by a teacher in her secondary school that 'two negatives make a positive'. She had written $^-4 + ^-2 = ^+6$ and said to me, 'that can't be right'.

I illustrated the calculation using a number line - moving to the right on a number line represents addition and to the left subtraction. So I start with the arrow at −4. I am adding so I expect to move to the right; however, I am not adding 2, I am adding −2, so in this case the minus sign reverses the direction and the arrow moves to −6. So −4 + −2 = −6.

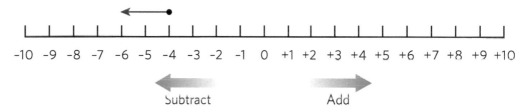

Primary age pupils should be using directed numbers to find the difference between positive and negative **integers** in context, or to count down in whole number and decimal steps extending beyond zero. An integer is a number which has no decimal or fractional part. We sometimes call them whole numbers. An integer can be either positive or negative. Integers should not be confused with 'natural' numbers. The **natural numbers** are all the positive integers, that is 1, 2, 3, 4 and so on. Pupils may also be expected to position positive and negative numbers on a number line and to be able to use the $<$ and $>$ symbols to state **inequalities**. (An inequality is a statement showing which number is greater or less than another: $<$ means 'less than' and $>$ 'greater than'. So $^-2 < ^+7$ and $^-4 > ^-9$.) This is helpful when pupils come to explore more complex equations at later stages of their learning.

The most appropriate way to support pupils with all of these ideas is to use a number line which extends beyond zero. I would suggest that it is appropriate that the number lines used for display, or used to support children's calculations in the later stages of primary school, should always extend above and below zero by the same number. This develops the pupils' visual representation of the number system to include negative numbers. One useful context to use in support of the pupils' understanding of negative numbers is temperature, as shown in the Resource inspiration box on the next page.

Resource inspiration

Measuring temperature

Jan	Feb	Mar	Apr	May	Jun	July	Aug	Sep	Oct	Nov	Dec
−2	−5	3	5	8	10	13	18	17	12	7	−8

✱ The table above shows the average temperature for each month in Otley. Which months do the thermometers represent?

✱ Shade in the blank thermometers to show the average temperatures in the other months.

This example shows how directed numbers can be illustrated using temperature. It is even better if you use temperatures for the local area in which you teach. To provide a wider range of temperatures use other contexts that are meaningful for the pupils. If your school is twinned with a school in Africa or another area with different climate this is ideal.

The thermometer provides an image of a number line for the learner, and the children are asked to draw their own thermometers to support them in developing their own use of number lines to model calculating using directed numbers. It is helpful to describe 'getting warmer' as addition and 'getting colder' as subtraction. The following Resource inspiration box shows how this activity can be developed to support children in developing their own use of a number line to come to understand directed numbers.

The next section of the chapter explores another big idea in counting and understanding, which is the concept of 'place value'.

Resource inspiration

Properties of number and number sequences

You will need:

✳ cards with numbers 1–20
✳ cards with numbers 10–20

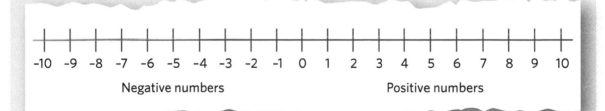

-10 -9 -8 -7 -6 -5 -4 -3 -2 -1 0 1 2 3 4 5 6 7 8 9 10

Negative numbers   Positive numbers

You will be creating number sequences with seven numbers.

Pick a card between 1 and 20 to get the size of the steps.

Pick a card between 10 and 20 to get the starting number.

The starting number is always the **fourth** number in the sequence.

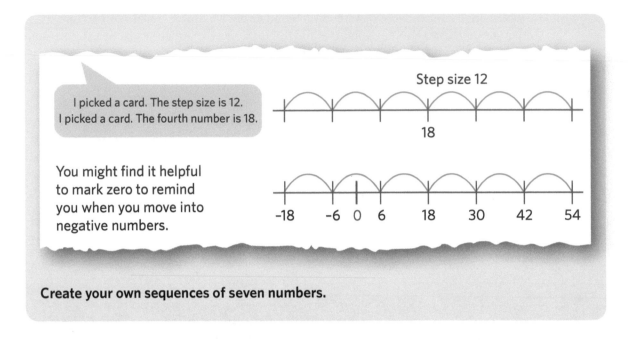

Create your own sequences of seven numbers.

Big ideas: place value

Place value refers to the value of a digit which is dependent on its location within a number, such as units, tens, hundreds. So in 352, the place value of the 5 is 'tens' and the 5 is worth 50.

The system of place value consistently used across Europe and in much of the Western world is described as the Hindu-Arabic method. It is based on the following key principles:

- There are 10 digits (0, 1, 2, 3, 4, 5, 6, 7, 8, 9).
- The column that a digit is placed in determines its value.
- A digit one place to left of another digit is worth 10 times its value.
- Zero is used as a place holder to represent an empty column.

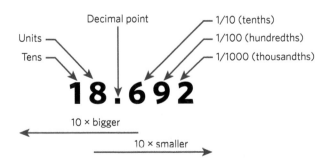

This place value system developed from the use of counting boards by traders. Beans or counters would be placed in each column on the board to represent a number. If 10 beans were placed in a column they would be replaced by a single counter in the column to the left.

As we saw in the previous section, many children begin their formal school already able to count. However, it is not always the case that they link the counting to the symbols which represent numbers. In the book *Children and Number*, which we referred to earlier, Martin Hughes suggested that children move through three stages when beginning to represent numbers. At first they will represent their counting pictorially, so they will record five sweets by drawing five sweets, then they move on to an iconic form of recording, so they might represent five sweets by drawing five sticks. Finally they use the symbol 5 to represent the count.

In 1989 Herbert Ginsburg, from Columbia University in New York, developed some of Piaget's ideas to suggest that there are three facets to understanding place value:

1 A child can write numbers but does not make the link between the symbol and the number they are counting.

2 A child can recognise when a number is written incorrectly.

3 A child understands the value of each digit in a number.

Teaching pupils to understand partitioning is a useful way to develop their understanding of place value. If you look back to the progression section which opened this chapter you can see that at the early stages children are encouraged to read and write numbers up to 20, which links to phases 1 and 2 in Ginsburg's schema.

Portfolio task 4.3

Can you think of examples of children who do not yet make the link between the numerical symbols and the results of a count? I have heard children ask how to 'spell' a certain number. They might count 15 ducks in a pond and ask, 'How do you spell 15?' Alternatively they may recognise particular numbers such as their age, the house number they live at, or the bus they catch to school, and not connect this to the numbers on a number line. Reflect on these experiences and add this to your portfolio.

There are several areas which often confuse learners when they are developing their understanding of place value. The following section describes some of these areas of misunderstanding and suggests how you can draw on these misconceptions as teaching points.

Teaching points: place value

Teaching point 1: Errors in writing numbers

Zeynab counts 19 sweets in the play shop. She writes down 91. Her friend Jasbir looks at the date written on the shopping list – she says, 'I can read that number, 2008, it is two hundred and eight.'

This is a common misconception and comes from children literally 'reading' the number. Zeynab sees the 9 digit first and knows she should say nine-teen. So she writes 9 and then adds the 1 to signal 'teen'. Similarly Jasbir notices the 200 and then the '8' so she sees 200 and 8.

Counting activities which involve children grouping objects in 10s and then finding the appropriate numeral on a number line will help these children. So, for example, you could give children 18, 23, 47 kidney beans – ask them to count them and then find the appropriate place on a number line and write a card which shows how many beans there are.

Teaching point 2: Confusion about the use of zero as a place holder

Some children become confused about the use of 0, particularly in decimals. For example, a child may think that 1.5 and 1.50 are different numbers. This can happen in the particular case when a child is using a calculator to work out money problems, as often calculators will 'remove' the 0 in £1.50 when it is entered. Many calculators will 'remove' the zero if you type in 1.50 when you press the 'operation' key. It is worth deliberately doing this with pupils so that they notice it happening. Using a resource such as arrow cards can support your pupils in coming to an understanding of place value, as they show the 'value' of each digit in a number when you remove the arrow cards. The next Resource inspiration box gives an example of an activity for you. The best form of the activity is to let your pupils have a set of arrow cards (you can download these from the companion website) and set each other challenges to make numbers. Once they have 'made' the number they have to be able to say the number. It is also helpful to make a series of numbers and ask the pupils to place them in order of size.

Resource inspiration

Place value

You will need:

* a partner
* place-value cards
* mini-whiteboards

Read the numbers below to each other. Then make them with your place-value cards. Read aloud the number from your cards to make sure it is the same as the one written in words.

The first one has been done for you.

1 twenty-four thousand three hundred and sixty-one

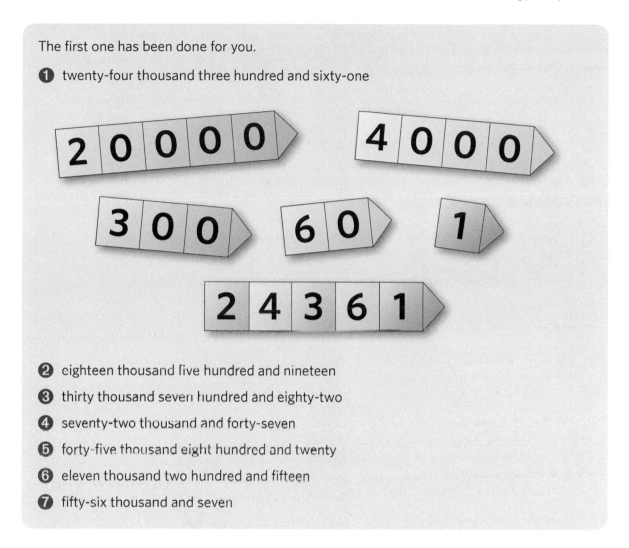

2 eighteen thousand five hundred and nineteen

3 thirty thousand seven hundred and eighty-two

4 seventy-two thousand and forty-seven

5 forty-five thousand eight hundred and twenty

6 eleven thousand two hundred and fifteen

7 fifty-six thousand and seven

Teaching point 3: Multiplication and division by powers of 10

A friend of mine questioned me when I suggested that teachers who told young children to 'add a zero' when multiplying by 10 were contributing to developing a misconception. I gave her the example of 1.7 × 10 and asked her what she thought the answer was. She came up with 10.7. The rule 'add a nought' was fixed in her mind from her time in school, but she realised that 1.70 was the same as 1.7 so couldn't be correct. However, 10.7 is approximately correct as 1 × 10 is 10. So 10.7 seemed a sensible answer even though the correct answer is 17.

A focus on moving the digits one place to the left when multiplying by 10 and moving to the right when dividing will overcome this misconception. The example described in the following Resource inspiration box shows how you can introduce the idea of moving 'digits' and not adding a zero to your group.

Resource inspiration

Multiplying and dividing by 10

1 Write a single digit in the middle of a page.

2 Multply this number by 10 and write this number above the first number. Repeat working up the page, until you have five numbers.

3 **a** Now divide your orignial number by 10. Write the new number below your original number.

  b Repeat, working down the page. What patterns can you see?

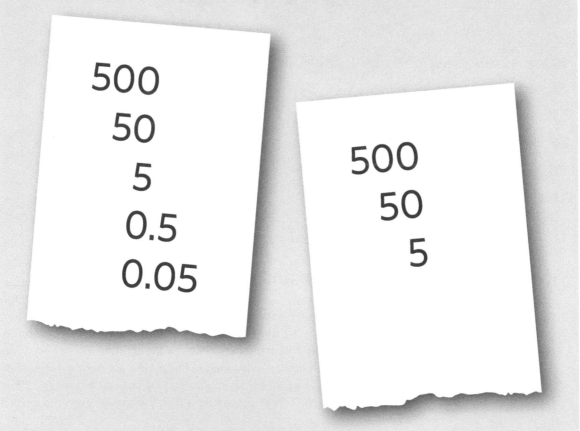

4 What happens when you dividde a whole number with up to four digits by 10 and then multiply the answer by 100?

Teaching point 4: Ordering decimals

Kev asks a group of children to order the following decimals:

1.7, 2.52, 1.65, 2.435, 0.812

One of the children writes:

1.7, 1.65, 2.52, 0.812, 2.435

The child has ignored the decimal point in ordering the numbers. So the child sees seventeen for 1.7 and two thousand four hundred and thirty-five for 2.435.

If children have this difficulty give them a place value grid to place the numbers on. For example:

Units	Decimal point	1/10	1/100	1/1000
0	.	8	1	2
1	.	6	5	0
1	.	7	0	0
2	.	4	3	5
2	.	5	2	0

Encourage the children to use the 0s as place holders and look for the patterns. When they write the numbers in ascending order outside the grid they can remove the 0s which are not needed and discuss when we need to write a '0' and when it can be omitted.

Teaching point 5: Rounding numbers

A pupil I was working with recently was asked to round 795 to the nearest 10. The pupil had written 800 and crossed it out and written 790. I asked why they had crossed it out and they told me it couldn't be right as they had been asked to the nearest 10 and not the nearest 100; they also knew that 810 was 'too many' so they had gone back to 790. Not recognising multiples of 100 as possibilities for multiples of 10 is an error that many pupils show.

A similar error with decimals would be a pupil who rounded 0.3 to 1.0 when asked to round to the nearest whole number. Here the pupil does not see zero as a whole number and so ignores the convention of rounding up from 5. So 0.3 to the nearest whole number is zero as it is nearer zero than 1.

An empty number line is a very useful resource to use when working with pupils on rounding numbers, and a useful strategy is to ask pupils to set each other challenges. They can write numbers down for each other to place on the number line and then round to an accuracy which either you or the pupils themselves decide. The following Resource inspiration box gives another example of an activity you could try with your pupils. This can be adapted for rounding to any degree of accuracy.

Resource inspiration

Rounding

1 When I round to the nearest 10 I get an answer of 130. What are four possible numbers that I might have started with? Place these numbers on the number line below.

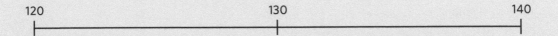

2 When I round to the nearest 1000 I get an answer of 12,000. Write down five possible numbers I could have started with and place them on the number line below.

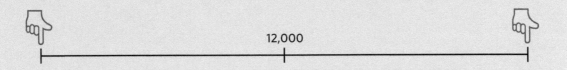

3 When I round to the nearest tenth I get an answer of 4.7. Write down six possible numbers I could have started with and place them on the number line below.

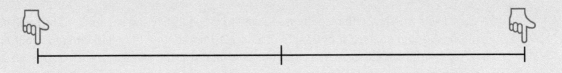

We will now move on to explore the next big idea in this chapter. That is the area of fractions, decimals and percentages.

Big ideas: fractions, decimals and percentages

Before you start this section I want you to try Portfolio task 4.4 as a way of you remembering all that you already know about fractions, decimals and percentages.

Portfolio task 4.4

Take as large a sheet of paper as you can get hold of. Write 1/2 in the centre. Now create a web diagram with as many different representations of 1/2 as you can think of. These might be diagrams with 1/2 shaded in different ways, they might be equivalent fractions, or they might be percentages. When you have exhausted this idea pick another fraction which is linked to 1/2 in some way. So you might choose 1/4 (which is 1/2 of a 1/2). Create another family of representations for a quarter. Carry on filling the paper with as many different fractions as you can think of.

This opening task shows how closely related fractions, decimals and percentages are. They are usually taught separately, which leads to children not making the link between the three ideas. In fact they are just three different ways of representing numbers. It is very useful to move between the three representations as this allows us to see mathematics as connected rather than separate. It also allows us to draw on our understanding of one area of mathematics to solve problems in another area.

Fractions are 'parts' of whole numbers. We need to be able to describe 'parts' of whole numbers for two reasons. Firstly, when measuring we can't be sure that a length or weight will also be a whole number. Secondly, when we 'share' or divide numbers there are many occasions when the result of the division is not an integer, so we need a way of writing an answer that is not an integer. We call this a fraction.

Terezinha Nunes and Peter Bryant have explored for many years the ways in which children understand fractions. In 1996 Blackwell published their book called *Children Doing Mathematics* and in this they suggest that understanding fractions is not simply a case of extending the knowledge we have of whole numbers. There are key differences. For example, a whole number can only be represented in one way: if we count three objects we will write 3. However, there are classes of fractions – 1/4 is the same as 2/8, 4/16 or even 25% or 0.25. Fractions are also used for different purposes, and appear to mean different things in different cases. So, if a fraction represents part of a whole, the **denominator** represents the number of parts into which the whole has been 'cut' and the **numerator** represents the number of parts taken. So in the fraction 5/7, 5 is the numerator and 7 is the denominator.

Nunes and Bryant suggest that children have to come to an understanding of two key ideas. Firstly, that for the same denominator, the larger the numerator, the larger the fraction – so 2/7 < 4/7 < 6/7. Secondly, that for the same numerator, the larger the denominator, the smaller the fraction – so 3/5 > 3/7 > 3/10.

Learning fractions is something we associate with 'rules'. For example, you may remember being told these rules when you were at school:

- You must multiply the numerator and denominator by the same number when making equivalent fractions.
- You must divide the numerator and denominator by the same number when making equivalent fractions.
- When dividing fractions you turn the second fraction 'upside down' and multiply.

It may be the case that you don't know 'why' these rules work, and the following section illustrates how sometimes children's misapplication of these 'rules' can lead to errors. I hope it will also support you in becoming more confident in your own understanding of fractions, decimals and percentages and in turn this will support you in teaching these closely linked concepts.

Teaching points: fractions, decimals and percentages

Teaching point 1: Fraction names and writing fractions

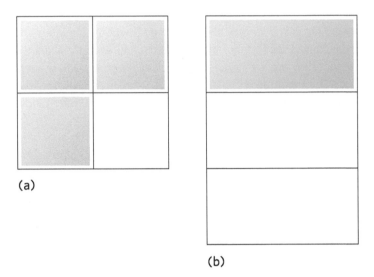

(a)

(b)

When faced with naming or writing the examples of fractions above, children may say many things. For example, a response to naming the fraction represented by (a) might be 'three-fourths'. Here the learner has remembered the convention for the denominator (number of parts in total) and the numerator (number of shaded parts), but has applied the convention of naming numbers that they are used to. Similarly I recently heard fraction (b) called 'a threeths'. It is important to listen carefully to the names that children give to fractions. In the examples above the children had an understanding of the ways in which the names are formed and so have understood the underpinning idea – they simply need help in selecting the appropriate language. This can best be done through the use of display, flash cards, and the repetition of key words.

Sometimes, however, the naming and writing of fractions may point to a deeper misconception. Another child looking at fraction (b) wrote 1/2. They also wrote 3/1 and then crossed it out to write 1/3 for fraction (a). Here they are noticing shaded and unshaded parts of the diagrams but are not seeing a fraction as a division of 'a whole'. So, in shape (b) they saw one shaded part and two unshaded parts. They knew that 1/2 is a common fraction and so wrote the fraction as shaded parts:unshaded parts. The same thinking led to their response for fraction (a). In this case, however, they saw the answer 3/1, coming from shaded parts:unshaded parts, but told me that this 'didn't look right', so they inverted the fraction to a fraction which they had seen before.

An understanding of naming and writing fractions is key to successful calculation. It is probably worth repeating that a fraction is made up of:

- The numerator: the number of parts of the 'whole'.
- The denominator: the number of fractional parts the 'whole' has been divided into.

It is often helpful to remind children that the line separating the numerator from the denominator refers to division. So in the examples above, (b) can be seen as 'one out of three' or 'one divided by/into three'. Similarly for (a) we can say 'three out of four' or 'three divided by four'.

Portfolio task 4.5

Write down all the errors that you can remember children making when they have named or written down fractions. For each example decide whether the children's misconception was based in a misunderstanding of the language of naming and writing fractions or a lack of clarity around what defines the numerator and denominator of a fraction. Add these notes to your portfolio.

Teaching point 2: Fractions as equal areas

I was observing a student teacher who had asked her learners to draw as many examples of 1/2 as they could by shading in a square. There were many imaginative and correct answers such as:

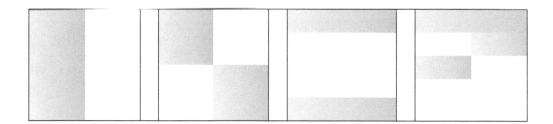

This showed me that both the student and the young learner understood that 1/2 could be represented by any four parts out of the eight that made up the whole; 1/2 does not have to be symmetrical, or obey a particular pattern. Other children had used diagonal lines which allowed her to show many more views of 1/2. However, one boy had drawn the following:

At first he was adamant that this was 1/2 as there were 'two out of four shaded in'. He was persuaded that this wasn't a half when I asked him if he would be happy to have the 'smaller half' if this was a bar of chocolate. This misconception often arises as informally we may call any sharing into two 'halving' – if we are splitting a cake, for example, we will ask our friend, 'Do you want half?', without thinking the two parts have to be exactly the same size. So when introducing fractions to children it is important to focus on the importance of equal areas. The example in the Resource inspiration box below gives you an activity which focuses on this. This activity is best carried out practically, as the pupils will take great care to make sure things are fair!

Another version of this activity is to place three chairs at the front of the class. Place one bar of chocolate on one chair, two bars on the next and three bars on the next. Ask 10 pupils to take it in turns to stand behind one chair, making their choice of chair one after the other. When all the pupils are standing behind the chairs they can divide the chocolate on the chair equally between the children at that chair. This activity leads to a great deal of discussion about fractions as equal areas. It can even make quite a good party game!

Resource inspiration

Fractions

1 The blue team has won this chocolate bar as a prize.

How many different ways can you break it into six equal pieces for the four team members? Draw each way.

2 Iqbal has 12 tulips in his garden. Half of them are red. One quarter of them are yellow. The rest are orange.
Draw a picture of Iqbal's tulips. What fraction are orange?

Teaching point 3: Fractions must be less than 1

Before exploring this teaching point in more detail try this task.

Portfolio task 4.6

Can you write down 2.75 as a fraction and a percentage? Can you do the same for 1.5 and 4.9?

When I ask my students to carry out this activity some find it difficult. Although they are used to seeing decimals greater than 1 they feel different about improper fractions (an **improper fraction** has a numerator larger than or equal to the denominator, such as 7/4 or 4/3) or percentages larger than 100%. This is probably because we are so used to thinking of fractions as simply a 'part' of a single whole rather than as a way of representing any part of a number between two whole numbers. So we can write 2.75 as $2\frac{3}{4}$; or even 275%.

It is important to use fractional number lines with children, and very important that these number lines extend beyond 1, and that you represent fractions and decimals together so that children begin to see how they can move between decimals and fractions in order to carry out comparisons and calculations.

Teaching point 4: Ordering fractions and decimals

Children often have difficulty ordering fractions. For example, they may think that 2/5 is larger than 2/3 as they notice that 5 is larger than 3 and they do not have mental images of the two fractions to fall back on. The most effective method I have found to support children in their ability to order fractions and decimals is to use an approach which uses multiple representations of fractions and decimals.

1/2	0.125		
3/4	0.4		
3/8	0.15		
1/8	0.5		
2/5	0.7		
7/10	0.75		
3/20	0.9		
9/10	0.375		

The activity described in the Resource inspiration box opposite illustrates a practical activity that will support pupils in coming to an understanding of fractions, their decimal equivalents and how to order them. Here children are encouraged to draw on their mental images of fractions and decimals to place them on an empty number line and draw on their current knowledge of fraction/decimal equivalents to calculate new equivalents. It would be even better to carry out this activity practically using a physical washing line in the classroom.

Resource inspiration

Fractions and decimals

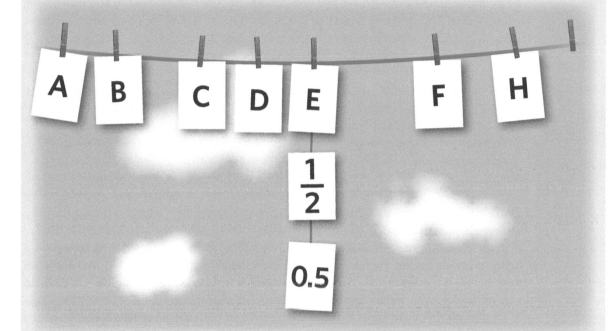

❶ Look carefully at the pegs on the washing line. Estimate which fractions they could represent. Copy the numbers onto a large sheet of paper.
Label the points A to H with their fractions and equivalent decimals.

❷ Working with your partner, look at the gap between peg B and peg C.
Think of a fraction that will hang on the line in the gap. Predict where it will hang.
Calculate the decimal fraction to check it will fit before you hang it on the line.

❸ Find a fraction to hang in each gap between pairs of letters.
Remember to calculate the decimal equivalent before you add it to your line.

❹ Look at the gaps between the pegs. Now find a space to add three more fractions that have a different denominator to any that are already on the line.

Teaching point 5: The meaning of percentage

I began my career teaching in secondary schools and I still clearly remember the following comment from one of my 15-year-old boys. He had arrived at my maths lesson fresh from a French test – he was beaming and said, 'We've just got the results of our French exam. I did really well, the teachers said. I got 85% – the only trouble is that I don't know how many it was out of.' As for fractions, children have intuitive understandings of percentages. More specifically they will have seen 50% and may know that this is equivalent to a half. They may well have come across 10% or 20% if they have been shopping with their parents, particularly at 'Sales' time. A good starting point for working with fractions is to explore children's current understandings of percentages. Look through the papers and magazines that they read – ask them to bring in examples of percentages so that you can set a real context for the exploration of percentages. By the time that percentages are introduced the children should have an understanding of the equivalence between fractions and decimals, so it is important immediately to make this link as well. Of course, a percentage is always 'out of 100', per meaning 'for every' and cent meaning '100'.

Another example of the misconceptions that can arise with percentages is confusing a percentage 'of' with the idea of 'out of'. So 20% *of* 60 = 12 because 20% is the same as 2/10, so we can write 2/10 × 60. This is a calculation I would carry out mentally as 1/10 of 60 is 6 so 2/10 is 12. It is best to explore the idea of *'out of'* with an example. If I get 15/20 in a test I have achieved a mark of 75% (15/20 can be cancelled down to 3/4 which is equivalent to 75%).

A good friend once telephoned me. He is a police officer and was having to submit a report on crime figures. He told me that he knew the old figures for burglary and knew the new figures were higher but 'couldn't remember which one to divide by 100' in order to convert this to a percentage increase. This is a good example of trying to remember a rule or an algorithm that we were taught at school but being unable to see how this applies to a real context. In this case the following calculation was appropriate.

Last year's burglary figures 124,000

This year's figures 142,000

This gives an increase of 142,000 − 124,000 = 18,000. So the percentage increase is (18,000 ÷ 124,000) × 100 = 14.5%. First you find the fractional increase by dividing the increase by last year's total, and then you find the percentage by multiplying by 100.

In order to change a fraction into a percentage you carry out the division to form a decimal from the fraction and then multiply by 100. You need to multiply by 100 to express the fraction as 'out of 100'.

Teaching point 6: Recurring decimals

As your pupils use calculators to carry out conversions between fractions and decimals or to carry out complex calculations they will discover recurring decimals. The most common recurring decimals are thirds, sixths and ninths. When we write recurring decimals we write enough digits after the decimal point to show the recurring pattern and insert a dot on the last decimal place to show it is a recurring pattern. For example, 1.3333 would be written as $1.\dot{3}$ or 1.214214214 would be written as $1.\dot{2}1\dot{4}$.

Portfolio task 4.7

Use a calculator to explore the following fractions in their decimal forms. What do you notice about the patterns that are formed?

(a) 1/3, 2/3, 3/3
(b) 1/6, 2/6, 3/6, 4/6, 5/6, 6/6
(c) 1/9, 2/9, 3/9, 4/9, 5/9, 6/9, 7/9, 8/9, 9/9

What other fraction families give you recurring decimals?

The final big idea we need to consider in this chapter is linked to fractions, decimals and percentages and is the area of 'ratio and proportion'.

Big ideas: ratio and proportion

Many of my students have come to me very worried when they have been asked to teach ratio and proportion. This has always interested me as it is an area of mathematics that we all have intuitive understandings about. In her book *Street Mathematics and School Mathematics*, published in 1993 by Cambridge University Press, Terezinha Nunes and her colleagues showed that street children in Brazil had well-developed ideas and strategies to work with ratio and proportion when they worked in the street markets, but that they could not transfer the methods they employed out of school to contexts that were introduced to them in school. For example, try to complete the conversion table below (this activity is most effective if you carry it out with some colleagues):

Pounds sterling	1	2	3	4	5	10	20	50	100
Euros	1.25								

When you have completed the table talk to your colleagues about the strategies that you used. Many people find that using 'doubles' is effective, so they will complete the 2 and 4 columns first. You can than find 3 euros by adding 2 + 1 pounds, or multiplying by 3. If you know 3 and 2 you can find 5. Once you have 5, doubling can allow you to complete the table. Try this sort of strategy to complete this table:

Euros	1	2	3	4	5	10	20	50	100
Pounds	0.8								

It is important to use the language of ratio and proportion from the early stages so that when the ideas are introduced more formally, later in primary school, children have the linguistic base on which they can build their understanding when they are introduced formally to ratio and proportion. A formal learning objective may be phrased as:

Pupils should use the vocabulary of ratio and proportion to describe the relationship between two quantities (for example, 'There are two red beads to every three blue beads, or two beads in every five beads are red.')

You can see how this vocabulary can be introduced at a day-to-day level across the school – perhaps at the beginning and the end of school days looking at things like school dinners and sandwiches, numbers of boys and girls, people who walk to school or come in the car, and so on.

Teaching points: ratios and proportion

Teaching point 1: Confusing ratio and proportion

One of my students asked this question at the end of the day: 'What proportion of the class are boys?' In her class of 25, only 10 were boys. One of the children replied 10/15. This response showed some understanding of the idea of ratio and proportion – the learner knew the answer should contain the numbers of boys and girls, and knew there was a link to fractions, but had confused ratio and proportion. Many adults find the difference between ratio and proportion difficult to remember. The definitions are given below.

Ratio

A ratio compares part with part. In the above example there are 10 boys to 15 girls, so the ratio is 10:15 or, by dividing each number by 5, we can cancel this down to 2:3. We might also say that for every two boys there are three girls. This is another way of remembering the difference between the two terms – if we use the language 'for every' we are describing a ratio.

Proportion

Proportion compares a part with the whole. In the above example there are 10 boys in a class of 25, so 10/25 or, by cancelling, 2/5 of the class are boys. The language we might use here is 'in every'.

You will see that we represent ratios by a colon, :, to represent 'to', whereas a proportion is represented as a fraction as it compares a part with a whole.

Teaching point 2: Adding rather than multiplying when increasing ratios and proportions

Another error you may come across when teaching ratio and proportion is children reverting to adding rather than multiplying when increasing ratios and proportions. For example, when given a recipe for soup that contains 2 onions for 3 people, and asked to work out how many onions are needed for 12 people, they realise there are an extra 9 people, and either add 9 onions or 18 onions (2 onions each). They do not see that the recipe is for 4 'times as many' people, or in a ratio of 4:1, giving 8 onions.

Carrying out practical cooking activities is a great way to 'practise' calculations involving ratio and proportion.

Portfolio task 4.8

Look back over the misconceptions you have explored in this chapter. Which of the misconceptions did you share? How do you think you developed this misconception? What might a teacher have done to support you in overcoming the misconception?
Before moving on to the case study section, try to write a convincing explanation to support a colleague in understanding why this misconception is incorrect. Add this to your portfolio.

In practice

The lesson plan which follows was used to support a group of children early in their understanding of place value. I wanted to introduce them to a number line as they have experience in moving along number tracks. I am also using a counting stick to support the children in developing mental images of number lines to help them develop mental methods for calculating.

The plan includes ICT to support the children's learning. The program described in the case study is available on the companion website which accompanies the book. You may wish to explore the 'Zoom Number Line' program on the website before reading the lesson plan. Following the plan there is an evaluation of the lesson which explores how successful the plan was in supporting the children as they developed their knowledge, skills and understanding.

Topic: Understanding place value

Age group: Lower primary

Objectives

- Explain what each digit represents in whole numbers and decimals up to two places, and partition, round and order these numbers
- Relate numbers to their position on a number line

Key vocabulary	Context
Equal to, ascending, descending, < , >	This is the second lesson in a series of five looking at place value, ordering and rounding. In the last lesson the pupils used digit cards to create numbers up to seven digits and named the numbers and wrote them down. All the group could recognise numbers up to four digits but found it difficult to name the numbers with five digits and above. One group worked with the TA naming the numbers, and she acted as a scribe for them. A particular difficulty was numbers containing zeros, such as 10,007 The children often work in numeracy partners, that is, one child achieving at expected levels or above paired with a child achieving below expected levels

Resources	Starter activity
Ten-sided dice, digit cards	I will use a counting stick. Initially we will count in 10s, starting at 0. Then we will count in 100s, then 1000s up to counting in 100,000s. I will then throw the 10-sided dice once to generate a number and we will count up in 10s from this number. I will repeat this with a two-digit number counting in 100s and then a three-digit number counting in 1000s and then 10,000s. I will use my 'numeracy partners' for this activity. They will take it in turn to count on

Main activity	Teacher	Pupil activity
	On the whiteboard draw _ _ _ _ _ < _ _ _ _ _ _ _ _ _ _ > _ _ _ _ _ Use a single set of 0–9 digit cards to generate a digit, one digit at a time. The pupils sit with their numeracy partners and have to place each digit to try to make the expression correct	Discuss placing each digit in pairs – understand the importance of placing the digits appropriately, showing an understanding of place value. Recognise the 10,000 column in order to name the numbers. Respond to my prompts in order to name the numbers
Group activity Children operating above expected levels	Children generate six-digit numbers using 10-sided dice. They place these in ascending order and write the numbers also in ascending order	**Assessment** I will point to digits and ask the children what the value of the digit is. I will write down numbers such as 120,002 and ask what the zeros represent. I will ask them to think what the values of some seven-digit numbers might be
Children operating at expected levels	I will give these children the digit cards 0, 2, 5, 6, 9 and ask them to make as many different five-digit numbers as they can. They should then place them in ascending order	I will ask the children how they make 'big' and 'small' numbers. What is their strategy for making the largest possible number?

Main activity	Teacher	Pupil activity
Children operating below expected levels	These children will use the digits 0, 3, 5, 8 to generate four-digit numbers and then order these numbers	I will ask the TA to support this group. She will pay particular attention to the naming of the numbers and the effect of zero in a column

Plenary		
I will use the Zoom Number Line software to create a number line from 0 to 10,000. We will generate any four-digit number using digit cards and I will ask individuals to come to the interactive whiteboard (IWB) and zoom in on the appropriate 1000 to locate the number on the number line		

Rationale and evaluation

The counting stick activity allowed most of the children to see the patterns although I did notice Helen and Rhupal watching rather than joining in. I made sure that I sat with them later. I repeated the activity and realised that they can count on in 10s and 100s but lose the pattern after that. The numeracy partners are effective I think. I heard very useful discussion. Martin said to Kerry, 'It's easy – you just put the biggest numbers on that end to make a big number.' When I asked Martin he knew that 'that end' was the 10,000 column.

The children operating at or above expected levels all found the ordering of the numbers relatively straightforward. It was important that I intervened, however, as they were more challenged when I asked about the values of the columns. I was pleased that Rob realised that 'all seven-digit numbers are millions'.

The group working with four digits still find the zero problematic – the TA told me that they all described 3058 as either thirty, fifty-eight or three-hundred-and-fifty-eight. I will devise more activities with a number line for this group. For homework I asked them to write down the names of these numbers: 358, 308, 3055, 3158, 3508, 3580.

The Zoom Number Line in the plenary supported the children in seeing the patterns in each 1000. So, for example, they could see that the numbers 6000–7000 followed the same patterns as 1000–2000. This should support them in realising the importance of zero as a place holder. I will use the Zoom Number Line with individual groups next lesson.

Audit task

Devise a lesson plan which is appropriate for a group of learners you are working with. The focus should be 'Counting and understanding number'. Construct a lesson plan using the proforma on the companion website. Teach the lesson and then evaluate it carefully with a focus on children's learning and misconceptions. If you can, use ICT to support the children's learning but only do this if the ICT enhances the children's learning. Give evidence for the effectiveness of the ICT in the evaluation.

Add this lesson plan and evaluation to your subject knowledge portfolio.

Observing 'Counting and understanding number'

On the companion website you can watch a session called 'Decimals forever' taught by Jonny Heeley, a teacher who is a previous winner of a Teacher of the Year Award. Although the session is put together specially for TV and described as a 'Master Class' there are lots of ideas that are directly transferable to most classrooms. The opening activity, for example, is a practical version of the activity suggested earlier in the chapter and helps pupils match decimals to their equivalent fractions and percentages. When you have watched this piece of the lesson think carefully about how you might organise this in your classroom. The key things to think about are which fractions you would choose and how you could differentiate the activity so that all your pupils could take part.

Focus on the opening five minutes of the session rather than watching all the way through and think how you could expand this for a full session. The first thing that I would do is work with the 'number families' so that they arrange themselves in ascending order. It would also be useful to ask your pupils to place themselves on a number line which you could place on the classroom floor or in the playground.

I was also very surprised at the decision to ask the pupils to explore recurring fractions by carrying out long division rather than using a calculator. If the purpose of a calculation is to explore the patterns which the results make, it is much more sensible to use a calculator to carry out the calculation.

Assessing 'Counting and understanding number'

For early learners it is most appropriate to assess their grasp of counting and understanding number through practical activity. For example, you can give 20 pupils in your class cards each with a separate number between 1 and 20 on it. Pick children in the class and give them instructions so that they are sorted into the correct order. Similarly you could ask children to stick numbers onto a picture of a street with house numbers, if you want to include odd and even numbers, or a block of flats if you simply want to order whole numbers. Ask the children to stick the numbers on the doors so that the post(wo)man can find the correct houses to deliver to.

Matching equivalent representations of fractions, decimals and percentages is an excellent assessment activity too. To assess pupils' understanding of finding equivalents leave some of the equivalence cards blank so that the pupils have to fill them in for themselves. It is important to ask learners to order these numbers as a part of this activity so that they come to see how useful it is to move between different representations. Many pupils will find it difficult to order fractions but much easier to order decimals or percentages. Having this understanding can also help if your pupils still have difficulty in ordering fractions by looking at the numerator and denominator.

Cross-curricular project involving 'Counting and understanding number'

Almost any planning for a class or school event will involve the pupils in counting and applying their understanding of number. Children of any age can be involved in planning and organising events in the classroom or for the wider school community.

If you are working in an early years setting there will be many occasions when you wish to invite parents and carers into events in the classroom. The children can be involved in making sure there are enough seats and enough hangers for their parents' coats, and if you are serving food making sure that there are enough places set so that everyone has a knife, fork and plate. You can even involve the children in making refreshments. Making buns with a cherry on top leads to lots of counting activities – particularly if you cut each cherry in half to make the buns look even better.

As the pupils get older they can get much more involved in making the refreshments. You can use recipes for smaller numbers of people and use ratio and proportion to ensure that you have enough ingredients to make sure everyone has enough to eat. If you are buying pizzas the pupils will need to think about what fraction of each pizza everyone will want and then use this to calculate how many pizzas to buy.

You may want to divide your class up into separate groups, each with different responsibilities. One group can organise the invitations and make sure the class knows how many guests to expect. Another group can be in charge of refreshments, both buying and making sufficient for all the guests, and a third group will need to organise hospitality during the event and make sure there is enough space for the event to take place. Finally one group will need to be in charge of the budget for the event.

Summary

The aim of this chapter was twofold: to support you in understanding how children learn to count – something it is hard to recall from our own experience – and to offer a range of activities which will support you in teaching young learners this most basic of skills. I would also hope that these activities will allow you to observe young learners coming to an understanding of counting. The big ideas of 'Counting', 'Place value', 'Fractions, decimals and percentages' and 'Ratio and proportion' have also been explored with teaching points to accompany each of these big ideas. I hope that by exploring each of them holistically you are able to make the connections between and within them. That is, you can see how fractions, decimals and percentages are all simply different ways of writing numbers and that choosing the most appropriate representation can make calculating simpler.

Reflections on this chapter

I opened the chapter by suggesting that 'Counting and understanding number' is an area you may find difficult to teach as it is something we cannot remember learning ourselves. If I had to pick a key idea from this chapter it would be the five principles underpinning counting. These principles are observable when we watch learners beginning their journey to counting confidently and support us in deciding how to structure the learning experience. The more you observe children at these early stages, the more you will be able to see these principles in practice. This is also an area in which we may bring our own misconceptions from our own experiences. How many of us were told to 'add a 0' when multiplying by 10, or that 'two minuses make a plus' when we were introduced to directed numbers? Our teachers who used these stock phrases were showing that they were not confident in their own mathematical understanding. I would hope that the teaching points within the chapter have offered you alternative ways to describe these processes – explanations that won't lead to misconceptions.

Self-audit

1 This question allows you to develop your use of number lines to explore ideas of rounding and estimation.

   Each of these numbers is the answer to a question asking you to round a number. You should draw a number line to show the range of possible numbers you could have started with. For example, 2300 has been rounded to the nearest 100 so the smallest number I could have started with would be 2250 (we always round up from 5) and the largest number I could have started with could be 2349 (as I would round 2350 up to 2400):

2250 _____ 2300_____ 2349

   (a) 570 has been rounded to the nearest 10.
   (b) 3000 has been rounded to the nearest 100.
   (c) 7.8 has been rounded to the nearest tenth.
   (d) 10.75 has been rounded to the nearest hundredth.
   (e) 0 has been rounded to the nearest whole number.

2 These questions explore your skills in expressing numbers as decimals, percentages and fractions. It is important that you feel comfortable moving between these three representations of numbers. Children who can move easily between fractions, decimals and percentages are better able to carry out complex calculations, and have a clearer sense of number.

   (a)

20%	5/8	0.25
9/10	2.8	2/3
5/9	75%	1/3
30%	1/2	0.7

Use the fractions, percentages and decimals to make questions with the following answers (for example, 75% of 12 is less than 10 and 0.7 × 20 is between 10 and 25):

(i)	< 10		**(vi)**	= 15
(ii)	> 25		**(vii)**	= 0
(iii)	between 10 and 25		**(viii)**	= 0.5
(iv)	between 5 and 6		**(ix)**	= 20%
(v)	< 1		**(x)**	= 4/5

(b) Draw this number line:

Add the following numbers to the appropriate place on the number line:

5/8, 0.9, 1/3, 0.66, 75%, 65%, 8/9, 15%

The next question introduces proportionality. This is the final key idea within counting and understanding number.

3 Look at the following information about a group of students on a teaching training course:

There are 25 students on a teacher training course: 20 are female; 10 are from minority ethnic groups; 5 have a mathematics A-level; 8 are living with their parents; 4 are mature students.

I can write the following statements from this information: One out of five of the students has mathematics A-level; the ratio of students from minority ethnic groups is 2:5; 32% of students are living with their parents.

Write down ten more statements using this information. Use fractions, decimals, ratios and proportions.

Going further

The following books have been referred to in this chapter. Here is a brief overview in case you want to explore these areas in more detail. I have also included the full Harvard reference for the book.

Children and Number: Difficulties in Learning Mathematics by Martin Hughes

Reading this will give you a new perspective on young children learning number, and in particular the skills of counting and understanding number. Martin Hughes shows how young learners bring a wealth of knowledge about counting and understanding number with them when they start school. He argues that it is important for teachers to support children in making links between their own informal understandings and the more formal language of school mathematics. He includes lots of ideas for activities which teachers can draw on to make this possible.

Hughes, M. (1986) *Children and Number: Difficulties in Learning Mathematics*. Oxford: Blackwell Publishers.

***Mathematics with Reason: The Emergent Approach to Primary Maths* edited by Sue Atkinson**
This is a very practical book which aims to support teachers in connecting their teaching with the ways that children learn mathematics outside the classroom. As with the Martin Hughes book it takes the approach that children develop understandings of number at a very early age and that it is the teacher's role to draw these understandings out and to develop them. There are contributions from a wide range of teachers and other mathematics educators who describe how they put these ideas into practice in their classrooms.

Atkinson, A. (ed.) (1992) *Mathematics with Reason: The Emergent Approach to Primary Maths.* London: Hodder and Stoughton.

***Teaching and Learning Early Number* by Ian Thompson**
This has been described by the *Times Educational Supplement* as a radical and influential book. Although solidly based in research it is very accessible and offers lots of practical ideas which teachers of young children can use to support young learners in the early states of learning about number and counting. It includes chapters exploring learning and teaching number through play and assessing pupils' knowledge of number skills through interviews.

Thompson, I. (2008) *Teaching and Learning Early Number*. Maidenhead: Open University Press.

CHAPTER 5
KNOWING AND USING NUMBER FACTS

Introduction

Mathematics is about much more than knowing facts. However, there are some facts that are very useful as they support us in carrying out calculations quickly and in being able to check that our answers to problems are accurate.

You may have played 'Guess my Number' with classes that you have taught. This is when you think of a number and the children in your class have to guess the number by asking questions. You can only answer 'Yes' or 'No' to their questions. The following exchanges probably ring true too:

> Tony: **OK, I've written my number down on this piece of paper. Tom, you start asking the questions.**
> Tom: Is it 57?
> Tony: **It might take quite a long time if you just guess numbers. Michelle, have you got a question?**
> Michelle: Is it even?
> Tony: **Well done, that's a great question. No it's not even. Megan, you next.**
> Megan: Is it odd?

Just as with the games where we ask people to guess famous people, the game above relies on good subject knowledge, here knowledge of number facts, for success. It also relies on good questioning. My class got much better at questioning, and very quickly. After each game we talked about what the best questions were – that is, which questions narrowed down the choices best. I asked the children to work in pairs to come up with good questions before we started the next game. As an extension we tried to use the minimum number of questions possible. We also had a 'number of the day' and during the day, in a spare moment, children wrote down any number facts they could about this number.

Starting point

The story above is an illustration of 'knowing number facts', and, of course, we need to know number facts before we can use them. One of the most useful ways we can use number facts is to 'derive' new facts. This is sometimes referred to as having good 'number sense'. When we look at a number we get a 'sense' of that number. So I might look at 36 and see a number that has a lot of factors, that is a square number, that is divisible by 12, and so on. If we see numbers in this way we are better able to work with the numbers, calculation becomes more straightforward, and estimation comes easily.

Most importantly this chapter emphasises how important it is to be able to use the facts that we can remember to work out new facts. For example, if I can remember that $2 \times 6 = 12$ I can work out that $4 \times 6 = 24$ and $8 \times 6 = 48$ by doubling and that $9 \times 6 = 54$ by adding another 6, and so on.

I want to emphasise that your pupils do not have to memorise a huge range of facts while they are being taught by you. Rather they have time to make sense of the number facts they have been previously introduced to and you can work with them to use the facts that they already know to derive new sets of facts.

Taking it further

The term 'number sense' was introduced by A. McIntosh, B.J. Reys and R.E. Reys in 1992 in their article 'A proposed framework for examining basic number sense' in *For the Learning of Mathematics*, 12 (3), 2–8. They explored the link between informal methods and the formal calculation procedures. This issue is analysed in detail by Ian Thompson in the paper 'Narrowing the gap between mental computational strategies and standard written algorithms' presented to the International Convention on Mathematics Education in Denmark in 2008 and available online at **http://tinyurl.com/bh9f8n8.**

The idea of 'number sense' has been discussed widely, and is an important area for further exploration if you wish to develop your understanding of how children draw on their own informal methods to come to an understanding of formal written methods.

There has been debate about how much children should commit to memory. Having rapid recall of number facts allows us to derive new facts more quickly. Memory is developed by using particular facts regularly – so we can help our learners by regularly asking them to draw on their knowledge of number facts. The 'Guess my Number' activity I opened this chapter with is one way of doing this. As you can see from the progression section below you can introduce 'new' facts gradually throughout a pupil's time in primary school so that the teacher can focus on specific facts in a range of displays to support the children in recalling them rapidly.

Developing an ease with numbers is what 'Knowing and using number facts' is about. Sometimes our learners seem to treat numbers with suspicion – as if they can't be trusted. This happens if mathematics is presented to them as a series of tricks and rules to be learnt. If they can be presented with mathematics as inherently logical they may begin to trust numbers, to see that they always behave in the same way. This chapter gives a wide range of examples of how mathematics is logical – and how you can convince yourself and your learners that it is logical.

The next section shows the development of children's knowledge of number facts as learners move through primary school. It also shows you what you might expect the learners in your class to have experienced before they meet you. These are the number facts that you can build on, the facts you can draw on as you encourage your learners to deepen this knowledge. Of course, the easiest way to see what 'facts' children bring with them is to have conversations with your learners which allow them to demonstrate what they already know before you move on to teaching them 'new' facts.

Progression in 'Knowing and using number facts'

Foundations for 'Knowing and using number facts'

At the early stages you should work with young children to help them observe relationships and patterns in numbers they see in their everyday environment, like house numbers, the numbers in blocks of flats, numbers on classroom doors, numbers in nursery rhymes, and so on. In particular you could work with them on finding one more or less than a number, at this stage only working with numbers up to 10. So they will know that one more than five is six, and one less than nine is eight. In addition to this, through using number lines, they will begin to see how the process for finding one more or less remains the same whatever number you start with. This is the beginning of seeing mathematics as logical and consistent.

↓

Beginning in 'Knowing and using number facts'

At this stage you will be introducing children to all pairs of numbers that total 10. You should also look at addition facts to at least five and be able to use this to work out the corresponding subtraction facts. Drawing on this pupils can begin to count on and back in

1s, 2s, 5s, and 10s and through this notice the patterns in multiples of 2, 5 and 10. Eventually they will be able to remember all the doubles of numbers to at least 10.

The next step is to learn how to derive and recall addition and subtraction facts up to 10, all pairs with totals up to 20 and pairs of multiples of 10 up to 100. So they will notice the patterns when you add

$$20 + 20 = 40 \text{ or } 50 + 50 = 100$$

and make the links with this pattern and the patterns of pairs up to 10 ($2 + 2 = 4$; $5 + 5 = 10$).

At this stage pupils will be making the link between halving and doubling and remembering their times-tables for the 2, 5 and 10 times-tables. They will also be beginning to use this knowledge to estimate and check their answers are sensible.

Becoming confident in 'Knowing and using number facts'

Your next aim would be for pupils to be able to derive and recall all addition and subtraction facts to 20, sums ('sum' means addition, although many teachers use it as a generic term for 'calculation'; try to avoid using 'sum' unless you mean addition - sums of multiples of 10 would be $30 + 30 = 60$ and so on) and differences of multiples of 10 and number pairs that total 100 ('difference' is found by subtraction or adding on, so the difference between 50 and 60 is 10).

Once pupils have developed their ability to recall multiplication and division facts for the 2, 3, 4, 5, 6, 10, 11 and 12 times-tables (you will see that this is different from simply being able to recite their times-tables) you can work with them so that they 'know their times-tables' up to 12. This means being able to derive multiplication and division facts of all the tables up to the 12 times-table, up to the 12th multiple. Pupils at this stage should also recognise the patterns which allow them to recognise multiples of 2, 5 or 10 up to 1000.

Drawing on their prior knowledge pupils will be able to derive sums and differences of pairs and multiples of 10, 100 or 1000. As previously they will see how these patterns build on patterns they have been introduced to earlier. So if $3 + 3 = 6$, then $30 + 30 = 60$ and $300 + 300 = 600$ and so on. Similarly, if $70 - 30 = 40$ then $700 - 300 = 400$. This is the way in which the consistency within mathematics begins to become clear.

Other facts that should be introduced at this stage include the doubles of two-digit numbers and using these to calculate doubles of multiples of 10 and 100 and derive the corresponding halves (so 52 is $26 + 26$ which tells me 520 is $260 + 260$ and that half of 520 is 260).

This will help pupils develop their knowledge of fractions to identify pairs of fractions that total 1 (for example, $1/2 + 1/2$ and $1/4 + 3/4$).

All this prior experience will enable your pupils to derive sums, differences, doubles and halves of decimals. For example, if I know $38 + 25 + 637$ then I know $3.8 + 2.5 = 6.3$, and I can work out that $6.3 - 2.5 = 3.8$; or because I know 19 is half of 38, I also know 1.9 is half of 3.8.

By the end of their time in primary school learners will be able to recall their tables facts quickly and draw on this to multiply pairs of multiples of 10 and 100 ($7 \times 50 = 350$ and

$70 \times 50 = 3500$ and so on). They will be able to identify **factors** of two-digit whole numbers and use this knowledge to find **common multiples**. Factors of a number are the numbers that divide into that number. So the factors of 12 are 1, 2, 3, 4, 6 and 12. A common multiple is a multiple which is shared by two or more numbers. So a common multiple of 3 and 6 is 12 as 3 and 6 are both factors of 12. A common multiple is in the times-tables of both of the numbers.

Building on the understanding of decimals pupils will use their knowledge of multiplication facts to derive related number facts linked to decimals. (So, if I know that if $5 \times 9 = 45$ I can derive the following facts: $0.5 \times 9 = 4.5$, $4.5 \div 9 = 0.5$.)

The pupils will also be able to derive **square numbers** (a square number is the result of multiplying a number by itself, so 9 is a square number because it is 3×3 and 25 is a square number because it is 5×5) and use this ability to derive squares of multiples of 10. (For example $80 \times 8 = 640$ and $80 \times 80 = 6400$.) They will also be able to recognise **prime numbers** less than 100 and use this to find **prime factors** of two-digit numbers. A prime number is a number with only two factors, itself and 1. So 13 is a prime number because its only factors are 1 and 13. Another way of explaining this is that a prime number doesn't appear in any times-tables apart from its own. The first 10 prime numbers are 2, 3, 5, 7, 11, 13, 17, 19, 23; 1 is not a prime number as it has only one factor. A prime factor is a factor of a number which is also a prime number. For example, the factors of 18 are 1, 2, 3, 6, 9, 18. However, if you were asked to write 18 as a product of its prime factors you would write $2 \times 3 \times 3$.

Extending learning in 'Knowing and using number facts'

The current expectation is that by the time pupils progress into secondary school they have a good grasp of all the number facts they will need to draw on during their time in secondary school. A new idea you can introduce to extend your pupils would be the recognition of **square roots** of **perfect squares**. The square root of any number is the number which, if squared, would give you that number. So the square root of 16 is 4, and the square root of 100 is 10. A perfect square is the square of a whole number, so 36 is a perfect square as it is 6^2 or 6 squared.

The aim of this section is to support you in seeing how a child's knowledge of number facts gradually builds over seven or more years, and how it forms a coherent and consistent landscape in which numbers behave as we expect them to. We can use this consistency and our current knowledge to derive new knowledge.

Big ideas

I have called the two big ideas in this section patterns and rules. In the opening to the chapter I wrote about developing a 'number sense' in pupils. This sense of number develops with an understanding of the patterns that exist within the number system and the rules which our number system obeys. Noticing patterns allows us to derive new facts quickly from those which we know, and applying rules appropriately allows us to use the facts accurately. This skill is vital when we begin to develop our algebraic thinking. The word 'algebra' is derived from the Arabic 'al-jebr' which means, literally, putting back together broken parts. Being able to see and notice patterns, seeing individual numbers in terms of their properties all support us when we need to create and solve equations.

There is a story of two famous mathematicians, G.H. Hardy and Srinivasa Ramanujan, who whenever they met used to pick numbers and see who could find the most interesting facts about them. On one occasion Hardy had travelled to meet Ramanujan in hospital in a taxi which had the number 1729. Hardy picks up the story:

> I remember once going to see him when he was ill at Putney. I had ridden in taxi cab number 1729 and remarked that the number seemed to me rather a dull one and that I hoped it was not an unfavorable omen. 'No', he replied, 'it is a very interesting number; it is the smallest number expressible as the sum of two cubes in two different ways.'

We should not expect to know everything there is to know about every number, but being able to see numbers in many different ways allows us to manipulate them and to explore and understand pattern.

Patterns

The most important resources to support children in noticing pattern are number lines and 100 squares. At the early stages of learning we are encouraging children to notice what happens when we add or subtract 1 from a number. At this stage they will be using a number line to see that they move one digit to the right to add 1 and one to the left to subtract.

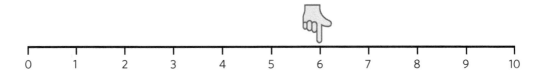

This image will support them as they explore more complex ideas but they have already learnt an essential image – we add and subtract by moving up and down a number line. This is the beginning of algebraic understanding. If I can see this pattern I will be able to solve the equation

$x + 1 = 9$

For learners in the primary school we would substitute a 'cloud' or a box for 'x' but the question remains the same. If I add 1 to a number and get the answer 9 what is that number?

Portfolio task 5.1

Describe the following operations on a 100 square:

Adding 10

Subtracting 11

Adding 27

Try to describe the 'move' you make: for example, to add 11, 'I move down one row and one column to the right.'

Add these notes to your personal portfolio.

1	2	3	4	5	6	7	8	9	10
11	12	13	14	15	16	17	18	19	20
21	22	23	24	25	26	27	28	29	30
31	32	33	34	35	36	37	38	39	40
41	42	43	44	45	46	47	48	49	50
51	52	53	54	55	56	57	58	59	60
61	62	63	64	65	66	67	68	69	70
71	72	73	74	75	76	77	78	79	80
81	82	83	84	85	86	87	88	89	90
91	92	93	94	95	96	97	98	99	100

The patterns that we see are all linked to the idea of place value which was explored in the previous chapter, and a good understanding of place value is key in helping learners see the underlying reasons for the patterns that we see. You can see from the 100 square that all multiples of 10 end in a 0 and multiples of 5 end in 5 or 0. Whenever you are introducing new ideas linked to number facts draw on these resources to give children images they can use to help them memorise the facts, but also for them to realise how the 'facts' link to the number system.

Other patterns that are introduced are square numbers. These are also easily represented pictorially, as

The first square number is 1, the second is 4, and so on. We write

$1^2 = 1,$ $2^2 = 4,$ $3^2 = 9$

and say 3 squared is 9.

There are also the triangle numbers. 1, 3, 6 and 10 are triangle numbers:

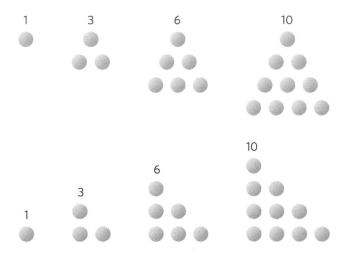

Portfolio task 5.2

Explore the link between square numbers and triangle numbers. If we call the square numbers S1, S2, S3, S4, and so on, so that

   S1 = 1, S2 = 4, S3 = 9, S4 = 16 . . .

and the triangle numbers T1, T2, T3, T4 so that

   T1 = 1, T2 = 3, T3 = 6, T4 = 10, . . .

try to represent any square number as the sum of two triangle numbers. Try to illustrate your answer with a picture.

Rules

The rules that are important to help children in applying their number facts appropriately are the commutative property of numbers, the distributive property of numbers and the associative property of numbers. These sound complicated, but you will have been using them all your life, and they make absolute sense.

The commutative property

This means that for some operations it does not matter which order the numbers come in. The numbers can 'commute' or change places. You may have already realised that addition and multiplication are commutative – if I am asked to add 15 and 12 I can either work out 15 + 12 or 12 + 15. Similarly, if I want to know 32 multiplied by 13 I can either work out 32 × 13 or 13 × 32. This property is useful as it means we can immediately halve the facts we need to learn! It is also helpful as we can encourage children to rearrange calculations so they can carry out mental calculations. We would use this property if we were to be asked to carry out the following calculation:

15 + 7 + 14 + 3 + 5

as we could rearrange the numbers in the following way:

15 + 5 + 7 + 3 + 14 = 20 + 10 + 14

to make it easier to add the numbers.

It is the commutative law that teachers are using when they suggest to pupils that they start counting on from the largest number first, when carrying out an addition by counting on a number line.

The commutative property does not hold for subtraction or division; the order of numbers cannot change. You will see that, for example,

15 − 8 is not the same as 8 − 15

and

28 ÷ 7 is not the same as 7 ÷ 28

The distributive property

The best way to illustrate the meaning of the distributive property is through an example. Often when we carry out mental calculations for multiplication we rely on this distributive property. For example, the figure below illustrates the calculation 13 × 8 graphically:

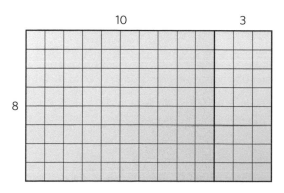

so rather than calculate 13×8 I can calculate 8×10 and then add 3×8.
Then I could write

$$13 \times 8 = (10 \times 8) + (3 \times 8) = 80 + 24 = 104$$

Similarly, if I want to work out 28×7 I could write

$$28 \times 7 = (30 \times 7) - (2 \times 7) = 210 - 14 = 196$$

Being able to draw on the distributive property is very helpful in order to develop your mental calculation skills. There are some examples below for you to try out in your portfolio. Always encourage the pupils you are working with to describe how they are carrying out their mental calculations. This will help all your learners come to terms with the distributive law.

Portfolio task 5.3

Use the distributive property to carry out the following calculations mentally – draw a sketch to illustrate the calculation:

18×8

34×7

29×14

48×6

Check with a calculator to convince yourself!

The associative property

As with the distributive property the best way to describe the associative property is through examples. Whenever we carry out a calculation we always begin with pairs of numbers. So if I ask a child to calculate the sum of 22, 14, 6, 3, 18 and 5 they have to decide which pair of numbers to begin with. For addition it does not matter which pairs of numbers we begin with. The same applies to multiplication. For example,

$$8 \times 5 \times 2 = (8 \times 5) \times 2 = 40 \times 2 = 80$$

or

$$8 \times 5 \times 2 = 8 \times (5 \times 2) = 8 \times 10 = 80$$

However, subtraction and division are not associative; for example,

$$18 - 7 - 3 = (18 - 7) - 3 = 11 - 3 = 8$$

but

$$18 - (7 - 3) = 18 - 4 = 14$$

so we have to carry out subtraction and division in the order the numbers are given.

These rules are very helpful in reorganising calculations to make them easier but can lead to some confusion as you will see later in the chapter. This is why it is always important for children to be checking that answers are sensible – then they will know if they have misapplied a rule.

The next section of this chapter explores common errors that you might notice children making and suggests how you can use these errors as teaching points.

Teaching points

Teaching point 1: Confusion in definitions of properties of numbers

You will probably have seen questions in test papers which ask children to sort numbers according to their properties either using a Carroll diagram or a Venn diagram. (Examples of Carroll diagrams and Venn diagrams are shown below.) For example, children were asked to sort 2, 7, 8, 9, 17, 20 using this Carroll diagram:

	Even	Not even
Prime		
Not prime		

The main confusion here involved 2 and 9. Children are introduced to odd and even numbers early in Key Stage 1 and so have a good sense of 'oddness' and 'evenness', but prime numbers are not introduced until much later. Because all prime numbers are odd, apart from 2, children often make the mistake that all odd numbers are prime, forgetting that 9 has three factors (1, 3 and 9) and so isn't prime. Similarly, many children don't see 2 as a prime number even though it has only two factors, 1 and 2.

Games like 'Guess my Number' which opened the chapter are very useful for helping children become familiar with the wide range of properties of numbers.

Another activity which is useful as a starter is to give children number cards – a different number for each child. Ask them to move around the room and form groups of three. The three in the group then have to find a property that is shared by all the numbers in their group. Another activity which can be repeated as often as you like is to draw a large Venn diagram on the board. One of the class comes up to the front and writes numbers in the appropriate part of the Venn diagram. As they are doing this the rest of the class have to guess what the properties are that are being used for the sort.

Sometimes these misunderstandings can be used directly by asking questions that the children may think are impossible:

Tell me an even number that is also an prime number.

Tell me a multiple of 3 that is even.

Tell me a multiple of 10 that is in the 3 times-table.

And so on.

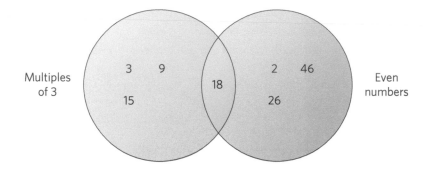

Teaching point 2: Errors in remembering times-tables

Most of us can remember that every number in the 5 times-table ends in a 0 or a 5 and that every number in the 10 times-table ends in a 0. You will also probably remember that all the even numbers are in the 2 times-table. This sometimes leads to confusion for children who can overgeneralise. They notice that every even number is in the 2 times-table and so invent a new rule – 'every odd number is in the 3 times-table', which sounds plausible, but unfortunately isn't true.

It is very useful to try to discover the 'rules' that children are following so that you can ask them to find examples that show their 'rule' doesn't work. It is also helpful to introduce them to the patterns that do exist in the other times-tables. For example, let's look at the 3 times-table:

3, 6, 9, 12, 15, 18, 21, 24, 27, 30

If I add up the digits of any number in the 3 times-table, and repeat this until I get a single digit, I always get 3, 6 or 9.

So, 15 gives me $1 + 5 = 6$, and 27 is $2 + 7 = 9$.

I can tell you that 4341 is divisible by 3 ($4 + 3 + 4 + 1 = 12$ and $1 + 2 = 3$). Check it on a calculator if you don't believe me.

Asking children to explore the patterns in numbers in the times-tables is a good way of encouraging them to get a feel for the properties of numbers.

Portfolio task 5.4

Explore patterns in the 4 and 9 times-tables. Are there rules that you can find so that you know if a large number is divisible by 4 or by 9?

Taking it further

For an example of how a Year 1 teacher explored number patterns using posters see Jill Russell's article 'Interactive pictures' in *Mathematics Teaching* 182, March 2003, available online at http://www.atm.org.uk/mt/archive/mt182files/ATM-MT182-28-29.pdf.

She describes how she used sets of posters to support the children in 'telling stories' about the numbers, which in turn developed their understanding of number patterns. There are also examples of the posters in the article. One poster is called 'Animal fields' and has pictures of a wide range of animals in fields. Jill Russell asked her class to make up questions based on the poster. One child came up with the following story:

> Seven rabbits were just finishing their breakfast when they spotted five sheep in the next field. Four of them ran away frightened so then there were only three of them left.

It is a great idea to ask your learners to make up their own 'number stories' based on illustrations or photographs that you give them. This helps them become at ease with numbers, and also helps them when they come to interpret number problems that are set for them by other people.

Teaching point 3: Errors in estimation when deriving new facts

Sometimes the children I'm working with get very excited when they realise they can derive a huge number of new facts with the knowledge that they have. I had asked a Year 6 group, many of them high attainers, to jot down as many new facts as they could given their knowledge that $8 \times 7 = 56$. This is the list that one group gave me:

$8 \times 7 = 56$ so $80 \times 7 = 560$ and $80 \times 70 = 56,000$ and
$800 \times 700 = 560,000$ and $8 \times 0.7 = 0.56$ and $0.8 \times 0.7 = 0.56$

I asked them if they were sure they were all right and they looked at me blankly – I think they had forgotten that they were looking for genuine new facts in their excitement and speed and had just been jotting down numbers that 'looked' right. I asked them to look at $80 \times 7 = 560$. They agreed this was correct because '80 is less than a 100 so the answer should be less than 700'. So then I asked them to apply the same logic to 80×70. 80 is still less than 100 so the answer should be less than 7000, as 100×70 is 7000. They spotted their error and checked the rest. You might like to do the same.

A useful strategy to get children to look carefully for accuracy is to give them lists like the one above with errors in them and ask them to find the errors and explain why the incorrect answers are wrong. If they can notice the sorts of errors that can be made they are less likely to make them themselves.

Teaching point 4: Children misapplying the commutative and associative laws

My son Sam once brought home the following calculation from school:

$$\begin{array}{r} 584 \\ -376 \\ \hline 212 \end{array}$$

He said to me, 'I know it's wrong, the answer should be 208, but I've done it right.' Mentally he had counted on; he knew that 576 was 200 more than 376 so if he added another 8 he would get to 584, but frustratingly for him, using the method he thought he had been taught gave him the wrong answer. This is an example of why some children seem to see maths as fraught with confusion: you can do the right thing and still you get it wrong.

What had happened is that Sam had followed an instruction he may have been given by a previous teacher: 'You always take the smaller number from the larger number'. This works when you are trying to find differences between numbers, but not for column subtraction! Similarly he may have been told '4 take away 6 doesn't go', so here he was trying to find a way to make it 'go' and so he subtracted the 4 from the 6 giving him the answer 2. We need to be very careful with the way we describe mathematical rules so that we don't unwittingly add to children's confusion.

He may also have remembered the commutative law and thought that it applied to subtraction as well as addition. If you remember, the commutative law says that it doesn't matter which order you carry out a calculation. This is fine for addition and multiplication but not for subtraction or division. At least he had the knowledge to be able to carry out the calculation mentally and realise that something was going wrong.

Teaching point 5: Mental calculation errors in partitioning

The previous chapter introduced you to 'arrow cards' or 'place-value cards'. You can use them to support learners in developing their mental methods by using partitioning. The example in the following Resource inspiration box shows how place value 'arrow' cards can be used to support learners in using partitioning to develop their skills in mental calculation.

It is important that children working on this activity are given the cards to manipulate. The overlapping of the cards is a vital part of coming to an understanding of the concept of partitioning. So, for example, as the learner makes 256 by using the cards, they must be able to overlap the card so that they read 256 and not 200, then 50, then 6. This can lead to their developing misconceptions around place value and around partitioning.

Because children realise that partitioning offers them a powerful way of calculating mentally, they sometimes see it as a first port of call rather than one strategy to choose when appropriate. This can lead to the following misconception. A class I was working with had been looking at partitioning as a way of carrying out multiplication calculations mentally the previous week. This week, however, they were looking at division. I had asked

Resource inspiration

Partitioning numbers

Use these place-value cards.

2 0 0   **3 0 0**   **7 0**

5 0   **9**   **6**

❶ How many different numbers can you find by combining these cards?

❷ Find all the numbers using just two cards each time.

❸ Find all the numbers using just three cards each time.

Here are some examples:

200 + 50 = 250

50 + 6 = 56

200 + 50 + 6 = 256

them to use any strategies they wanted to calculate 280 divided by 14. Sohm had written this in her book:

280 ÷ 14 = 20 + 20 = 40

I asked her how she had done this. She said she had partitioned 280 into 200 and 80 and 14 into 10 and 4 and so 200 ÷ 10 was 20 and 80 ÷ 4 was 20 giving her the answer 40. The fact that both answers were 20 seemed to have convinced her even more that it must be right (there's something about round numbers in maths that feels right, isn't there?).

To encourage her to check, I asked her what 40 × 14 was; if her answer was correct this should have been 280. Very quickly she answered 560. I asked her how she had worked this out. Again, she had used partitioning, where she had calculated and 40 × 10 and added 40 × 4. This time she had partitioned correctly. She then realised that 280 ÷ 14 couldn't be 40, and should be 20 (because 20 × 14 = 280). The examples below unpick this in more detail:

280 ÷ 14

Partitioning 280 into 200 + 80 doesn't help as neither of these is easily divisible by 14; and as we saw above, splitting this calculation into

200 ÷ 10 and 80 ÷ 4

gives us a different calculation altogether. For this calculation it is easiest to notice that 28 is double 14 so 280 ÷ 14 = 20. This is an example of how 'memorising' our doubles can help us with mental calculations.

However,

40 × 14 = (40 × 10) + (40 × 4) = 400 + 160 = 560

As I mentioned before, the best way to work with the rules of number is always to question your learners about the strategies they are using, whether they are correct or making errors. This way they will talk to you about the methods they are using; you can pick up the misconceptions and work with them. Very often children are giving you correct answers, they just aren't carrying out the calculation that you asked them to.

Teaching point 6: Not understanding the use of a symbol for a variable

With older learners you may wish to ask them to generalise their solutions to an investigation or to solve simple equations. On many occasions I have asked pupils to solve equations such as:

$$\star + 5 = 15$$

$$\star + 7 = 22$$

$$\star - 5 = 12$$

They have looked at me and asked, in a very frustrated way, 'Yes – but what does the star stand for?'

The issue for the pupils is that they do not understand the concept of a variable. That means that the value of $\star$ 'varies' depending on the set of the equation. If you ask your pupils to read the equations as: 'Something plus 5 equals 15' and 'Something plus 7 equals 22' and 'Something minus 5 equals 12' they will be able to solve the equations by drawing on the knowledge of number facts.

While it is appropriate for learners in primary school to be 'finding the missing numbers' in equations such as these, it would be inappropriate to move on to solving more complex equations by balancing each side of the equation. However, by developing their concept of a variable you will help them when they come to solve equations in secondary school.

In practice

The following lesson plan was used to draw on a group's current understandings of number bonds to 10 to develop an understanding of place value in decimals. I did this through asking them to find pairs and triples of numbers that total 10 or 100 including decimals. This allowed them to use the knowledge that $45 + 55 = 100$ to deduce that $4.5 + 5.5 = 10$. The plan includes ICT to support the children's learning. The program described in the case study is available on the companion website to this book. You may wish to explore the 'Number Boards' program on the companion website before reading the lesson plan. I used the Number Boards program as it allows me to differentiate the activity to provide appropriate challenge and later gives the pupils control over their learning. Following the plan is an evaluation of the lesson which explores how successful the plan was in supporting the children to develop their knowledge, skills and understanding.

Topic: Numbers totalling 10 or 100

Age group: Lower primary

Objectives

- Use knowledge of place value and addition and subtraction of two-digit numbers to derive sums and differences, doubles and halves of decimals

- Explore properties of numbers and propose a general statement involving numbers. Identify examples for which the statement is true or false

Key vocabulary	Context
Units boundary, tenths boundary, addition, plus, pattern	This is the first lesson in a series of five. This lesson supports children in finding pairs and triples of numbers that total 10 or 100. Future lessons use this understanding to carry out calculations arising from word problems. This lesson should support the children in devising mental strategies so that they can carry out the calculation effectively

Resources	Starter activity
0–9 digit cards, 6 × 4 grid	I will use the interactive whiteboard and the program 'Number Boards'. This provides a 6 × 4 grid of pairs of numbers which add to 10. The first run-through uses whole numbers. I will ask the children to work in mixed-ability pairs and give them one minute to find as many pairs as possible which add to 10. They will record this on mini-whiteboards. After a minute I will ask each pair to come up to the board and select a pair of numbers to check if they are right. I will repeat the activity using numbers to one decimal place
	Finally I will use the two versions of the program again – this time one of the children will come up and select a number and I will then pick someone to tell them what the 'complement to 10' is.

Main activity	Teacher	Pupil activity
Group activity Children operating above expected levels	The children will work in pairs. Each member of the pair creates a 'pairs' and 'triples' board so that it contains sets of numbers that add to 10. This should be decimals. They will then give them to a partner who will shade in the pairs	Pupils will list pairs and triples of numbers and decide how to make the board 'challenging'. The TA who is working with this group will ask the children to explain their thinking and to describe the patterns they notice when they are finding pairs and triples of numbers
Group activity Children operating at expected levels	The children will work in pairs. Each member of the pair creates a 'pairs' board so that it contains 12 pairs of numbers that add to 10. This should include some that are decimals. They will then give them to a partner who will shade in the pairs on the number grid	Pupils will list pairs and triples of numbers and decide how to make the board 'challenging'. I will work with this group and will ask the children to explain their thinking and to describe the patterns they notice when they are finding pairs and triples of numbers
Group activity Children operating below expected levels	This group will continue to use the program on the laptops. I will use the program which asks the children to find pairs of numbers that sum to 100	The children will record the pairs of numbers that they find sum to 100. They will organise this list so that they can report back on any patterns they have found

Plenary

The group who were summing to 100 will report back on the patterns that they have found. I will ask the other two groups if these patterns are reflected in the patterns that they have found. Hopefully they will notice, for example, $45 + 55 = 100$ and $4.5 + 5.5 = 10$. We will then revisit the activity from the starter. This time we will only use the decimal grid. As a child finds a pair they will describe to the group the mental process they are using

Rationale and evaluation

I realised very quickly that pairs to 10 in the introductory activity was not challenging any of the pupils so I reset the grid for pairs to 100. This was a little more challenging and I noticed that some of the children were making the mistake of just adding the 10s digit. This was a useful teaching point. When we moved into the decimal numbers I was very pleased that Philippa noticed that 'the decimals are just the same as the normal numbers – if you just pretend the decimal point isn't there you can do them just the same.' I explained that we were dividing by 10, which is why the answer was 10 and not 100. I set her and Christine the challenge of finding three-digit numbers that sum to 1000. They went away on their own and very successfully completed this task. I was also very impressed by the way they explained their thinking to the rest of the class in the plenary.

I wonder if the activities were challenging enough – each group was very successful. It seemed that once they had found the pattern they managed to complete the task relatively easily and without problems. However, the pupils seemed to be engaged and motivated by the task. They were also very articulate in the plenary and were able to describe their thinking process well. For example, Hannah said:

> If I've got 3.4 (three point four), that means I need another 0.6 (point six) to make 4 and then 6 to make 10. So that means 3.4 + 6.4 = 10. I can check this because 34 + 64 = 100.

At that point Philippa chipped in, 'And that means that 340 + 640 = 1000.'

Audit task

Devise a lesson plan which is appropriate for a group of learners you are working with. The focus should be an aspect of knowing and using number facts that is appropriate to the age group you are working with. Use the proforma that is available on the companion website. Make sure you think carefully about the context and evaluate the lesson. Try to use ICT to support the children's learning.

Add this lesson plan and evaluation to your subject knowledge portfolio.

Observing 'Knowing and using number facts'

Watch the video *Using a Counting Stick* on the companion website which shows a counting stick being used to support the learning of multiplication tables. A counting stick provides a powerful mental image which can support children in both learning multiplication tables and retaining these facts. They are easy to make either by buying a metre-long piece of dowelling rod, or by using a metre stick. Use coloured tape to define 10cm-long sections on the stick.

While you watch the video try to learn the multiplication table yourself by putting yourself in the place of a learner. Reflect on the following questions:

- How does the counting stick support learners in memorising new facts by drawing on facts they already know?

- How might you use the counting stick to model other aspects of the number line? (For example, how could you use it to model decimals between 0 and 1, or multiples of 100,000 between 0 and 1,000,000?)

Assessing 'Knowing and using number facts'

The most effective way of assessing your learners' knowledge of number facts is on a day-to-day basis. Playing the 'Guess my Number' game, as in the example which opened the chapter, is one way to get a sense of which pupils are at ease with properties of numbers.

Similarly you can choose a 'number of the week'. This can be an individual, group or whole-class activity. Simply select a different number each week and during the week the pupils have to list as many properties or facts as they can about the number.

'Loop Cards' are a great way of assessing your pupils' current knowledge of number facts as well as supporting them in learning new number facts (through noticing patterns and hearing other children's responses). You can also see how they are using current facts to work out new ones by stopping the game and asking pupils how they arrived at an answer. Loop cards are a set of cards on which the answer to the question on one card leads to the next card. So, for example, one card might read, 'I am 15% of 200'; another card will have the answer '30' written on the top of the card and a new question on the bottom of the card.

There are examples of loop cards and a blank set on the companion website to this book. Alternatively you can go to http://www.loopcards.net/ which is a website devised by Adrian Pinel. This gives many examples of loop cards. For a more formal assessment you could ask individuals to create their own sets of loop cards, having given them a specific set of number facts.

Cross-curricular project

The idea of these extended cross-curricular projects is to draw on the key ideas within the chapter to develop a cross-curricular project which you can explore with your learners over a series of lessons. This allows you and your class to develop your subject knowledge together.

Boxes for stock cubes

This investigation asks children to explore cuboids with constant volume. This involves them in looking at prime numbers, factors and multiples. It is most effective for children to work in small groups. Give each group enough multilink cubes to construct a range of cuboids made from 36 cubes. You will need to encourage the children to keep a record of the cuboids they make and so on. They will probably notice that cuboids with the same dimensions look 'different' in different orientations.

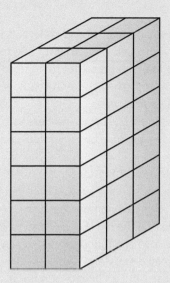
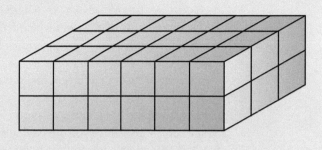

Ask groups to explore the range of cuboids that can be made from different numbers of cubes; you could suggest they work systematically on this, starting with one cube, then two cubes, then three, then four, and so on. They can then decide what 'sort' of numbers give the largest number of different cuboids. They will discover that numbers which have a large number of factors can be made into a large number of cuboids, and prime numbers can only make a single cuboid.

This leads them into exploring boxes of stock cubes. Bring a range of stock cube boxes into the class. Ask the groups to decide which cuboid they would use if they were packaging 36 stock cubes. They should create the packaging for this and prepare a 'bid' for the rest of the class to argue for their design. The whole class can judge the best designs as a concluding activity for the investigation.

Summary

The chapter opens with a discussion of 'number sense'. The development of this number sense is an underpinning theme for the chapter and I describe it as being 'at ease' with numbers, or trusting the internal logic of the number system. The progressions section outlines which 'facts' are appropriate for each stage of learning, but the chapter also focuses on techniques you can use to support children in using the facts that they already know to learn new facts. Using patterns to remember and predict number facts is illustrated, and the rules which underpin the number system are carefully outlined. You will also have seen how this supports pupils in coming to an understanding of algebra. The teaching points illustrate how you can use children's misconceptions around number patterns and the rules of number to bring them to a better understanding of how the number system works. If they trust the number system they will also trust their memory!

Reflections on this chapter

I hope that this chapter has helped you see how you gradually build children's knowledge of number facts over seven years of primary education. Learners do not have to memorise a huge range of facts immediately; they have time to make sense of the number facts associated with their stage of learning, and most importantly they come to see how they can use the facts that they already know to derive new sets of facts.

You should now understand which facts you should help your learners to memorise and which you should be working towards. I hope you have also consolidated your own understanding of these key facts.

In terms of 'using number facts' this chapter has aimed to explain 'why' certain rules work – I hope you understand the commutative, associative and distributive properties of numbers, and how the misapplication of these rules can sometimes lead to errors. Finally, most importantly, I hope you are beginning to see that the number system makes sense, and that it is feeling less mysterious and more logical. In the foundation stage you teach your learners how to add 1 to a number below 10, so they understand that every time you add 1 to 8 you get 9. Armed with this knowledge you can carry out an infinite number of calculations – eventually you know that because $1 + 8 = 9$, then $100 + 800 = 900$, $0.1 + 0.8 = 0.9$ and $28.01 + 3.08 = 31.09$. What could be more logical than that?

Carry out the following self-audit to examine how your learning has progressed as a result of working on this chapter. Include your results in your portfolio.

Self-audit

This activity asks you to use your knowledge of place value and multiplication facts to multiply 10 by 10 to derive related facts involving decimals.

I know that $8 \times 7 = 56$ so I can derive the facts $56 \div 7 = 8$ by rearranging the number sentence; $28 \div 7 = 4$ by halving 56; $2.8 \div 4 = 0.7$ by dividing by 10.

Start with 12×10 and write down 10 other number facts you can work out from this starting point. Explain how you derived each new fact.

1
2
3
4
5
6
7
8
9
10

Going further

Numbers: Facts, Figures and Fiction **by Richard Phillips**
This is a useful book for giving you lots of facts about individual numbers. It isn't a research book, but you will find it useful as a resource book.

Phillips, R. (2004) *Numbers: Facts, Figures and Fiction*. London: Badsey Publications.

The Number Mysteries: A Mathematical Odyssey through Everyday Life **by Marcus de Sautoy**
This is a book to engage and challenge you in learning more about number facts for yourself. It is a very accessible text and hopefully will fascinate you. You will be able to draw on much of what you learn from this book in your own classroom and it will certainly make you much more confident – and excited – about the properties of numbers.

De Sautoy, M. (2011) *The Number Mysteries: A Mathematical Odyssey through Everyday Life*. London: Fourth Estate.

Numbers: Their History and Meaning **by Graham Flegg**
I once drew on this book to write a complete course for one-year-olds. It is a 'history' of the development of numbers through their spoken and then written form. You will come to understand how calculation developed and realise that counting and number properties have developed differently across different cultures.

Flegg, G. (2003) *Numbers: Their History and Meaning*. Harmondsworth: Penguin Books.

CHAPTER 6
CALCULATING

Introduction

I often ask children to think of someone they know who is 'good' at mathematics. Then I ask them what this person can do that makes them 'good' at mathematics. One child said recently, 'They can't just do additions, they can do subtractions too'; another said, 'They can do really hard things like long divisions.' An answer that I am regularly given is that 'they can work things out really quickly, in their head – and they don't even need to use a calculator.' Although the main thrust of this book is to illustrate that mathematics is much more than simply calculating, this suggests that for many of us our image of mathematics is linked predominantly to calculating.

This chapter will explore how you can develop your capacity to 'do it really quickly in your head'. Developing your own mental methods in order to help you teach your pupils to calculate 'in their head' can be challenging, as you were probably not encouraged to do this when learning mathematics. Some of my students also remember being taught a particular method that seemed to work most of the time but there were always times when the method didn't seem to work. Because they had only one method to fall back on, they were unable to carry out the calculation, particularly in high-pressure situations like tests or exams.

You will be introduced to the idea of 'appropriate methods'. This is a move away from teaching one method for all calculations. What is more efficient is reaching a stage where you have a range of methods to draw on and you can select the most appropriate method for the particular calculation you are working on. You will also come to accept that the method which is most appropriate for one person may be different for another person. Through discussing our own methods we can expand the range of methods we have to draw on.

You will also see how addition, subtraction, multiplication and division all connect. If you can add, you can subtract; if you can multiply, you can divide. Hopefully by the end of the chapter you will feel confident that you are a 'good' calculator – perhaps this will go a long way to convincing you that you can be 'good' at mathematics too. This will give you the confidence to use your calculating skills in solving problems – an important functional skill.

Starting point

Work out the answers to the following calculations mentally. Avoid writing anything down at this point:

$11 + 6 =$
$28 - 9 =$
$20 \times 5 =$
$57 \times 3 =$

Now ask yourself, 'how did I carry out the calculation?' You may think 'I just did it', but let's think more deeply. Did you just know that 11 and 6 made 17, or did you add 6 and 1 to make 7 then add that to 10? Did you partition 9 into $8 + 1$ so you could take 8 away from 28 to get 20 and then take away another 1 to give 19? Did you multiply 10 by 5 and then double the answer to get 100, did you add $20 + 20 + 20 + 20 + 20$, or is this a fact you know? And, finally, did you work out 3×50 and 3×7 and then add $150 + 21$ to give you 171, or did you use the **algorithm**, or rule, you were taught in school? In your head you might have said something like '$3 \times 7 = 21$; put the 1 down and carry 2; 3×5 is 15, add 2 is 17. So the answer is 171'. This models the written algorithm.

When you carried out these calculations you were making decisions about what was the most effective strategy for you. It is unlikely that you drew on one formal written method for any of these calculations. In Chapter 5 you were introduced to the idea of 'number sense' and it was this 'number sense' that you drew on to decide how to come to an answer. The only time this 'number sense' might have deserted you is if you drew on the formal algorithm to carry out the multiplication. You may have lost sight of the value of the numbers – saying something like 'add 2 to give me 17 and then 1 gives me 171'. This describes the patterns of the numbers rather than their values, which can lead to confusion.

It is significant that in November 2011 Ofsted chose to release a report called *Good Practice in Primary Mathematics: Evidence from 20 Successful Schools* which focused on calculation. The key findings in this report included the following:

- Children should focus on practical activities and developing mental methods in the early stages of their time in primary school.

- A good understanding of place value and the ability to recall multiplication tables and number bonds supports effective calculation. (This area has been covered in the previous chapter.)

- Your learners' confidence and 'fluency' in calculating will be improved if you place a strong emphasis on problem solving and make the most of any cross-curricular links.

- A focus on misconceptions will make sure that these do not develop and impede next steps in learning.

These schools did not teach 'chunking' as a method of division, nor did they teach the long-division algorithm. The teachers in these schools had realised that neither of these approaches help children become efficient at calculations which involve long division. (You will read more about chunking and the long-division algorithm later in this chapter.)

As you can see, there is much more to calculating than just knowing the written methods for adding, subtracting, multiplying and dividing – the message is clear: mental methods first, then a range of written methods to allow children to develop 'efficient, reliable and effective' methods when it is not possible to use mental methods. Chapter 12 looks at the use of calculators in detail and describes how you can introduce these to your learners so that they are supported in developing their mental methods and know when it is appropriate to use them. In this chapter you will read about the importance of developing a range of calculating methods so that your learners can make sensible choices over their methods when they are faced with a calculation to carry out.

Taking it further

In Chapter 4 you were briefly introduced to *Children and Number: Difficulties in Learning Mathematics* (1986, Blackwell) by Martin Hughes. It is worth revisiting this research at this point. There is an important section exploring calculation strategies and the way in which children invent their own forms of recording when carrying out calculations. Hughes suggests that, left to their own devices, children go through a series of stages in their responses. An initial stage is the 'pictographic' response. At this stage children literally 'draw' the calculation. So if they are adding three multilink cubes to four multilink cubes they will draw the cubes in two groups and then count them up to add them together. Another stage is described by Martin Hughes as the 'iconic' stage. Here children represent the cubes by 'icons'. So for the calculation above a child might draw three sticks in a circle and four sticks in a circle and then add them. Again there is a direct correspondence between the drawing and the physical act of counting. Both of these stages precede the use of formal symbols – here a child would write the symbol '3' and the symbol '4' to represent the calculation.

I have seen children using the number symbols as icons – for example, when working out

$3 + 4 =$

they will count each point of the 3 by tapping their pencil on the points and then tap each point of the 4 to carry out the calculation. They count the taps and reach 7. You may have seen children doing this – you may even remember doing it yourself!

Be sure to spend some time with early learners in your setting as they start to record their calculating process. Encourage them to use individual whiteboards to 'jot' down their 'working out'. It is likely that you will notice them developing in the way that Martin Hughes suggests.

Progression in 'Calculating'

Foundations for 'Calculating'

Counting is at the heart of calculating and initially you will be working with your learners on counting objects and using language such as 'more' and 'less' to introduce them to ideas of addition and subtraction. You should compare different groups of objects to find out how many more or less there are in each group and start to explore sharing by splitting groups of objects into equal parts.

Beginning in 'Calculating'

The next step is to introduce your pupils to the idea of **counting on**. That is, that if you are adding 5 and 3 you point to 5 on a number line and count on saying, 6, 7, 8. You can teach that addition can be carried out in any order and that you can carry out subtraction by finding the difference between two numbers through 'counting up'. This also shows them how addition and subtraction are inverse or opposite operations, and the two operations should be taught together. You may introduce the number symbols to record practical activities but should ensure pupils are secure in their understanding before you do this.

You should develop children's understanding of division by combining groups of 2, 5 or 10 objects and by sharing into equal groups.

At this stage you can begin to introduce children to the four symbols $+$, $-$, $\times$ and $\div$ as well as $=$. This will help children find unknown numbers in number sentences such as $20 - 8 = 12$, which is the early stages of algebra. Mentally they will be able to add and subtract one-digit numbers or multiples of 10 from two-digit numbers and they could use practical or informal methods to add and subtract two-digit numbers. Children should understand that addition and subtraction are inverse operations, and should represent multiplication as an array – for example,

4×3 is the same as

Becoming confident in 'Calculating'

At this stage you can support your pupils to add or subtract mentally one- and two-digit numbers and introduce them to practical and informal methods to multiply and divide two-digit numbers (these informal methods are described later in the chapter), teaching them that multiplication and division are inverse operations. Your pupils will also start to find unit fractions.Unit fractions have 1 as the numerator. So they will be able to find 1/2 of 5 metres or 1/6 of 18 litres, for example.

You can develop your pupils' use of written methods to record and explain multiplication and division of two-digit numbers by single-digit numbers, and teach them to use written methods to add and subtract two- and three-digit whole numbers, including working in the context of money. You should expect your pupils to multiply and divide by 100 and 1000, and they will have developed their understanding of fractions to find fractions of quantities and shapes. You will explore the use of a calculator to help them carry out one- and two-step calculations involving all four operations, including understanding the meaning of negative numbers in the display.

The next stage is to develop calculation skills so they can use efficient written methods to add and subtract whole numbers and decimals up to two decimal places. You will have helped them extend their mental methods for whole number calculations, including multiplying one-digit numbers by two-digit numbers; multiplying by 25; and subtracting near multiples of 1000. You will ask them to draw on their understanding of place value to multiply by 10, 100 or 1000 and be able to draw on a range of written methods to multiply and divide three-digit numbers by single-digit numbers. They will be able to find fractions and percentages by division including using a calculator.

By the end of primary school, children will be calculating mentally when appropriate and will be able to use a range of written methods for those calculations which cannot be carried out mentally. You will expect them to use a calculator to solve multi-step problems and find fractions and percentages of whole-number quantities.

⬇

Extending learning in 'Calculating'

With these learners you can teach them to apply the commutative, associative and distributive laws that were described in Chapter 5, as well as using their understanding of inverses to calculate more efficiently. Look at these examples:

$$12 \times 13 = 156$$
$$13 \times 12 = 156$$
$$156 \div 12 = 13$$
$$156 \div 13 = 12$$

For example, multiplication and division are **inverse operations**; this means they are the opposites of each other. By knowing the answer to one of the above problems you can work out all the others.

The children will have developed their mental methods to include fractions and decimals and will be able to calculate percentage increases and decreases.

Big ideas

To introduce the big ideas in calculating try this activity:

Portfolio task 6.1

Work out 48 + 36 and record your solution using a pencil and paper method.

When I use this activity with teachers the most common response is

```
   48
 + 36
   84
```

When I ask them 'how' they calculated the answer a common response is, 'I added 40 and 30 to give me 70 and then added on 14'. What is interesting here is that this calculation is not represented by the method they record. The written method records the question and the answer but does not 'represent' the method used. When I work with children they are more likely to use an empty number line to record the calculation. For example,

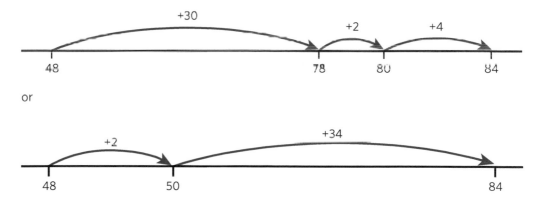

or

The big ideas in calculating are how children develop mental methods, which support them in understanding and developing formal written methods at an appropriate stage.

Children's development of mental methods

The reason why we encourage pupils to develop mental approaches to calculation is that it is much more efficient to work things out 'in our heads' if we can, rather than immediately reverting to a pencil and paper or a calculator. If we are fluent in mental methods we carry this confidence over into other areas of mathematics. The reason for developing rapid recall of number facts is to help us become fluent in mental calculation – not so that we can pass our weekly times-tables tests. It is interesting that the poet Ted Hughes and the writer Jeanette Winterson both advocated the memorising of poems and other classic literature. Ted Hughes even put together poetry collections just for that purpose. They argue that having access to these memorised texts gives them easy access to a wealth of examples of great literature to support them in their writing. In the same way, having access to a wealth of number facts and key relationships between numbers means that we can quickly manipulate numbers in our heads. It is interesting that Ted Hughes describes how important it is to be able to draw on images in order to memorise text. This is just the same for number facts and mental calculations. The most appropriate strategy to support children in developing their mental methods is to use a wide range of images and models which children can draw on to enable them to 'see' calculations in their heads. Using number lines, number squares and empty number lines all support the development of mental methods.

Activities such as 'Guess my Number' or 'loop cards', discussed in the previous chapter, give you plenty of opportunity to ask individuals how they are calculating mentally and also support your pupils in developing effective mental methods. You should join in these activities too and make you own thinking overt; share it with your learners. In this way you will make sure that you develop your own mental capacity too.

Children's development of written methods

There has been a long-held belief that young children cannot carry out calculation activities until they reach what Piaget called 'concrete operational thinking' at around age 7. Martin Hughes, who carried out the research explored earlier in the chapter, challenged this view, suggesting that very young children can begin to explore the underlying processes of calculating. He developed a 'box task' – in this task he worked with children aged between 3 and 5. With some children he asked them to count a number of bricks into a box which he would then close – he would either add additional bricks to the box, or remove bricks, and ask the children how many were in the box now. The young children could understand and succeed on the task so long as the numbers were very small. When working with one child he counted five bricks into the box, then removed three and asked the child how many were left. The young boy told him 'two'. Martin Hughes then records the following conversation (see page 27 in his 1986 book *Children and Number*):

> MH: **I want to take three bricks out of the box now.**
> Richard: **You can't can you?**
> MH: **Why not?**
> Richard: **You just have to put one in, don't you?**
> MH: **Put one in?**
> Richard: **Yeah, and then you can take three out.**

This suggests that Richard was capable of carrying out two successive mental calculations before he was 5. Asking children to represent activities such as this early in their experience in school will help them see written methods as supportive of mental calculation rather than simply a record of the question and the answer. They should be given the opportunity to develop pictographic recording of their calculations when the activities are predominantly practical; they will move on to iconic representations during the early years, but it is unlikely that formal written methods will be helpful until Year 3.

The following sections of the chapter draw heavily on a series of articles written by Ian Thompson for the Association of Teachers of Mathematics (ATM). These appear in *Mathematics Teaching*, issues 202, 204, 206 and 208 and explore in detail an approach to calculation which has been drawn on by many effective schools. These are available from the ATM, which can be found on the internet at **http://www.atm.org.uk/**. The articles and many others are also available at Ian's own website **www.ianthompson.pi.dsl.pipex.com**.

Addition

An initial approach to written calculation is the empty number line which I introduced you to at the beginning of this 'Big ideas' section. The empty number line is a useful 'record' of a mental strategy as you can use it to support any addition or subtraction calculation.

The next stage which is introduced by the strategy is the use of 'partitioning'. So, for example,

$$39 + 52 = 39 + 50 + 2 = 89 + 2 = 91$$

or

$$39 + 52 = 30 + 50 + 9 + 2 = 80 + 11 = 91$$

Can you see that only the first example of partitioning builds on the use of an empty number line? If you draw a number line you can sketch the calculation on that line. The second example changes the order of the numbers so that an empty number line would not model the calculation, as you need to conserve the order of the calculation to sketch it in a number line.

In order to move towards formal written methods it is important to offer children practice in the second form of partitioning. This can then be represented in a more formal way as

$$\begin{array}{rl} 39 & = \ 30 + 9 \\ +52 & \underline{\quad 50 + 2} \\ & \ 80 + 11 = 91 \end{array}$$

This leads children into the 'expanded column method' – this method would record the calculation above as either

```
  39 (adding 10s first, that is 30 + 50)
 +52
  80
  11
  91
```

or

```
  39 (adding 1s first, that is 9 + 2)
 +52
  11
  80
  91
```

It is helpful to work your examples both ways so that your pupils can see there is no difference between adding 10s first or 1s first. The final strategy to be taught to children is the column method involving 'carrying' with the 'carry digits' recorded below the line. In order to make sure that children make the links back to place value it is suggested that they are encouraged to say 'carry 10' or 'carry 100' rather than carry 1' as may have become a habit.

Subtraction

We can view subtraction in two ways: subtraction as take away or as difference. Sometimes children will model a subtraction calculation such as 15 - 6 by placing 15 objects in a box, taking out 6 and then counting how many remain. This will give them 9. They may represent this by a jotting like this:

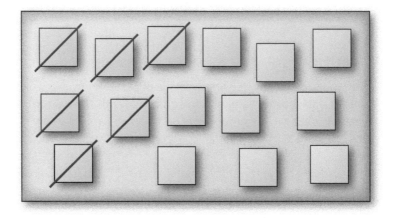

Subtractions as difference can be calculated on a number line. Here the pupil will start at 15 and count back 6 ending up on 9.

The stages for developing written methods to support subtraction also employ a progression through the empty line to partitioning before moving on to column methods. The first stage in the strategy involves counting back on an empty number line. So, for example, to calculate 74 - 27 we might write:

or combine steps by initially subtracting 7 and then 20. It is important that children see the calculation can be carried out in any order:

An alternative is to begin with the 27, and ask the children how many they would have to count up to get to 74. This can be recorded on an empty number line as follows:

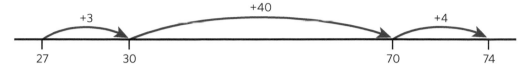

Ian Thompson suggests that if children can use the empty number line in this way there is no benefit in using partitioning to support subtraction. In fact children are effectively partitioning if they are using the empty number line efficiently.

The final stage in moving towards a formal algorithm is the expanded layout. An example of this is 653 − 289:

$$
\begin{array}{r}
600 + 50 + 3 \\
-200 + 80 + 9 \\
\hline
\end{array}
\qquad
\begin{array}{r}
500 + 140 + 13 \\
-200 + 80 + 9 \\
\hline
300 + 60 + 4
\end{array}
$$

In moving from one calculation to the other I have partitioned:

$$
\begin{aligned}
600 &= 500 + 100 \\
50 &= 40 + 10 \\
3 &= 3
\end{aligned}
$$

So 653 can be written as 500 + 140 + 13.

Taking it further

In his article 'The same difference' in *Mathematics Teaching* 202, published by the ATM in May 2007, Ian Sugarman describes a mental strategy for subtraction developed by children he was working with which does not appear in the National Strategy. He argues that this method is more appropriate for carrying out subtraction calculations than the decomposition method described by the strategy. He worked with Year 4, 5 and 6 children and the activity he used with them involved transforming numbers that would be difficult to work with using the column method to a pair of numbers that could be subtracted mentally. So, for example, rather than trying to calculate 563 − 278 the pupils transformed this to 565 − 280 and then 585 − 300 by initially adding 2 to each number and then another 20. The children described this as the 'same difference' method. They realised that if you add the same number to each number in the calculation, the 'difference' remains the same, and so the answer to the calculation is unaltered. This can be extended to four-digit numbers: for example,

2038 − 1757
2040 − 1759 (adding 2)
2000 − 1719 (subtracting 40)
2081 − 1800 (adding 81)
= 281

Multiplication

Ian Thompson suggests it is important to let children develop their own informal methods to record multiplication as with addition and subtraction. The first formal stage therefore would be the grid method. This approach is supported by the 2011 Ofsted report mentioned earlier in this chapter. The schools which were visited, all of which were successful in supporting their pupils in becoming effective at 'calculating', used the 'grid' method to introduce the pupils to the ideas of 'long multiplication'. It is worth spending some time becoming secure with this method yourself so that you are able to introduce it confidently to your learners. It will also help you see why the more traditional long multiplication method 'works'.

You record the grid method as follows. We would write 38×7 as

$\times$	7
30	210
8	56
	266

The next step would be recording this as:

```
   38
×   7
  210
   56
  266
```

because it develops naturally from mental methods and the grid method shown above. The grid method can be extended to multiply a two-digit number by a two-digit number. For example,

$\times$	20	9	Total
30	600	180	780
7	140	42	182
			962

It is important to remember that by the end of primary school the most complex calculation that pupils would be expected to carry out is a two-digit by three-digit one. There are three ways to carry out this calculation. Firstly, consider:

286 × 29

×	20	9	
200	4000	1800	5800
80	1600	720	2320
6	120	54	174
			8294

or writing the same calculation in columns

286 × 29		
	200 × 20	4,000
	80 × 20	1,600
	6 × 20	120
	200 × 9	1,800
	80 × 9	720
	6 × 9	54
		8294

or finally

```
   286
 × 29
 5720    (286 × 20)
 2574    (286 × 9)
 8294
```

Division

When I talk to people about why they do not feel confident about teaching mathematics they often describe 'long division' as a hated memory. This is not something that many pupils should be exploring before Year 6. It is interesting that not a single school that Ofsted identified as being effective in teaching calculation expected their pupils to use the long-division algorithm which you probably remember.

It is important to allow children to explore mental methods and also their understanding of division as the inverse of multiplication. It is also important not to rush into any formal recording of division. The written algorithm or rule for short division will be recognisable as:

$$\begin{array}{r} 27 \\ 3\overline{)8^21} \end{array}$$

I still hear children in schools, or my students, describing this process in the following way: '81 divided by 3. So 8 divided by 3 goes 2 carry 2; 3 into 21 goes 7. So the answer is 27.' The problem with this form of calculation is that the actual place value of the numbers is forgotten: 80 becomes 8 and 20 becomes 2. This can lead to children not noticing if answers are incorrect as they do not return to think if 27 is a sensible answer to 81 divided by 3. Estimating first can help this process. I would expect the answer to be less than 90 because 90 divided by 3 is 30. I would also expect it to be more than 25 as 75 divided by 3 is 25. The answer should therefore be between 25 and 30, so 27 seems about right!

Towards the end of their time in primary school you can introduce your pupils to the short division method – for most children this will be early in Year 6. This is the method you will probably be familiar with. So, to calculate $291 \div 3$ we can write:

$$
\begin{aligned}
291 \div 3 &= (270 + 21) \div 3 \\
&= (270 \div 3) + (21 \div 3) \\
&= 90 + 7 \\
&= 97
\end{aligned}
$$

This same calculation can be shortened to:

$$
\begin{array}{r}
97 \\
3\overline{)29^{2}1}
\end{array}
$$

Teaching points

Teaching point 1: Misapplying algorithms

I often tell teachers that children very rarely make mistakes – they can come up with an answer that doesn't seem quite right but when you ask them what they have done, they have answered a question correctly – it just isn't the question you have asked them. For example, Sam, aged, 9 had been asked to calculate:

$$
\begin{array}{r}
85 \\
-48 \\
\end{array}
$$

and gave the answer 43. He was irate when his teacher suggested this was 'wrong'. 'It isn't,' he said, 'I took away 8 from 5 by "finding the difference" so I put 3 down and 80 take away 40 is 40 so that gives me 43.' Whenever you are asking children to calculate using a formal algorithm it is useful to have them 'talk it through', sometimes at the front so that the rest of the group can see the approach, and sometimes in a one-to-one situation with you. This way you will begin to understand whether your learners understand the mathematics behind the algorithms or whether they are simply following, or misapplying, a rule. This is where having secure mental methods is helpful: this can help the pupils see when they have misapplied an algorithm, as they will have a good sense of what the answer should be. In this case Sam could work out that the answer should be 37. (He counted on, 48 + 30 is 78, 78 + 2 is 80, and another 5 is 85. So the answer is 30 + 5 + 2 = 37.)

Teaching point 2: Not checking calculations

We all remember putting our hands up to tell a teacher we had finished our calculations, or completed a test paper, only to be told by the teacher to check our answers carefully. Be honest with yourself – did you always check carefully? It is important to try to get children into the habit of checking as a first step. So when Helen came up to the board and wrote:

$3 \times 142 = 126$

I said, 'I don't know what the answer is but I know that it isn't 126.' She looked at me and then said, 'Oh no – it should be more than 300, shouldn't it?' She was then able to find her mistake and carry out the calculation. Sometimes when pupils are following algorithms they lose track of the numbers they are working with and so forget to estimate and use this estimate as a check. By encouraging pupils to estimate as a first step you will help them get into this habit.

In the activity described in the following Resource inspiration box the pupils are being encouraged to look for errors by drawing on their knowledge of odd and even numbers. It is important that the pupils are not asked to carry out the calculation.

Resource inspiration

Checking calculations

1 Will the results of these calculations be odd or even?

a 4861 + 3758	**b** 7052 − 507	**c** 34 × 57
d 711 − 296	**e** 72 × 28	**f** 461 + 836

2 Which of these are incorrect? Use rules for odd and even numbers to check.

a 30 × 91 = 2730   **b** 9072 − 978 = 8272

c 826 + 7095 = 7922   **d** 68 × 47 = 3196

❸ Which of these are incorrect? Use rules for odd and even numbers to check.

a   76 + 128 = 204   b   241 − 129 = 111

c   97 − 38 = 58   d   50 + 503 = 553

❹ Will the results of these calculations be odd or even?

a   419 + 282   b   174 − 86

c   347 + 63   d   70 − 47

Teaching point 3: Not understanding written symbolism

The research by Martin Hughes described in some detail earlier in the chapter suggests that often children's errors in calculations are not because they do not understand the mathematical concepts, rather they get confused with how the written symbolism relates to the calculations they are carrying out. It is a problem of 'translation' rather than a problem of mathematics.

The best way to support pupils in making this translation is to work with the pupils as they say number sentences and to write it down for them. In this way they will begin to see the + sign as simply shorthand for saying 'add'.

Other activities which can help children begin to understand the use of the multiplication sign '×' is to introduce them to **arrays**. An array is simply an 'orderly arrangement of objects'. Arrays can help us understand multiplication by lining up objects in rows and columns. So, for example, 4 × 3 can be shown as

When I look at a box of six eggs I can see both 6 and 3 × 2. Similarly for a box of a dozen eggs I see 12 and 2 × 6.

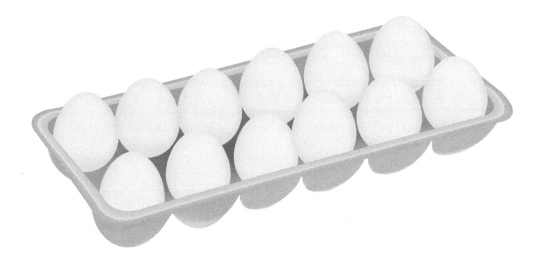

If I buy a book of stamps arranged in the way they are below I see both 15 and 3 × 5.

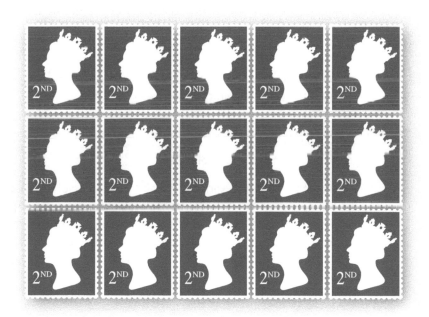

This sense of multiplication as an array helps me both with multiplication and with rapid recall of number facts. It is worth drawing on the many examples of arrays that your pupils will see around them every day: the milk bottles in the crate; desks if you organise them in rows on occasions; lining up in pairs. Making physical arrays is a great activity. Get a group of 12 of your class, or 24, and see how many different arrays they can form. Ask the pupils to make sketches of these arrays.

Teaching point 4: Carrying out the wrong operation when solving number problems

I recently picked up a greeting card from my local farm shop. It is headed 'Rural Maths' and contains the following text:

'Jack,' said the teacher, 'you have 30 sheep in your field, two escape through a hole in the wall, how many are left?'

'None,' Jack replied instantly.

'No Jack, it's 28!' the teacher replied, sounding cross, 'I thought you knew your maths!'

'Yes Miss, I know my maths alright, it's you that doesn't know sheep.'

This is a great example of a child solving a mathematics problem in their 'actual', real world rather than the pseudo-reality of a maths problem. Children who are successful solvers of word problems realise that these are very rarely 'real' problems but are mathematics problems set in a context. The first skill for your learners to develop is to decode such problems so that they apply the correct operations to solve the problem and then check the answer. Many teachers use the acronym RUCSAC to help their learners solve such problems. This acronym stands for:

R - **R**ead the question carefully

U - **U**nderstand the question – what do you have to find out?

C - **C**hoose the correct operations to solve the problem

S - **S**olve the problem

A - Find the **A**nswer

C - **C**heck your answer – is it sensible?

It is helpful just to focus on a series of questions without solving them to teach your pupils to select the operation which will solve the problem. Spend some time simply underlining key pieces of information in questions in order to help pupils see through all the extraneous information that is contained in word problems. Focusing on selecting the correct operation without having to carry out the calculation allows your pupils to see the importance of this step.

Another useful classroom activity is to provide your pupils with a sketch or an image from which they can devise their own word problems. For example, an image of a pot containing six pencils with two pens lying by the side of the pot will allow learners in the early years to devise several different word problems. The answers might be $6 + 2 = 8$ or $8 - 2 = 6$ or even $2 + 2 = 4$. (There are two pencils outside my pot. I take another two out, how many are outside the pot now?) If you visit **http://www.oxfam.org.uk/ education** you will find many images illustrating global issues which can be used for your learners to devise number problems with the added bonus of developing their global awareness.

Portfolio task 6.2

The grid method

Calculate the following using the grid method. Before you carry out the calculation estimate the answer. Which two numbers do you think the answer should be between?

358 × 34

×	30	4	
300			
50			
8			

Then use the expanded method shown on page 115.

In practice

The following lesson plan and evaluation describe a lesson taught to a group of pupils who have been introduced to pencil and paper procedures. The particular focus was developing skills in multiplying and dividing using mental methods to support their use of pencil and paper methods for more complex procedures. The program 'Grid Multiplication' was used to introduce the idea of multiplying by partitioning to the whole class. This program is available on the companion website to this book.

Topic: Multiplying two-digit numbers

Age group: Upper primary

Objectives

Develop and use written methods to record, support and explain multiplication of two-digit numbers by one-digit numbers

Key vocabulary	Context
Digit, multiply, product, estimate	This is the second lesson exploring the grid method for multiplication. The group worked on differentiated examples using the grid method in the last lesson. The children who needed extra support found the concept of the grid difficult although they were able to carry out the individual calculations

Resources	Starter activity
Set of 1–9 digit cards	Working in pairs use any operation with one two-digit number and a one-digit number to make 100

Main activity	Teacher	Pupil activity
	Use the 'Grid Multiplication' program to explore multiplying through partitioning. Use the examples 13 × 6; 18 × 4; 24 × 7 and 32 × 5. Partition using the 10s. So 24 × 7 = 20 × 7 + 4 × 7 and so on	Before carrying out the calculation ask pairs to estimate to the nearest 10 using individual whiteboards
Group activity Children operating above expected levels	This group can work with four digits and carry out TU × TU as well as HTU × U	Pupils should estimate before carrying out the calculation. They should try to explain why a particular arrangement of digits gives the largest answer, drawing on their understanding of place value
Group activity Children operating at expected levels	The group should pick any three cards from the set of 1–9 digit cards and write down all the multiplication calculations that can be formed from these numbers. Working in pairs within the group they should carry out these calculations and see which gives the largest product	Pupils should estimate before carrying out the calculation. They should try to explain why a particular arrangement of digits gives the largest answer, drawing on their understanding of place value
Group activity Children operating below expected levels	This group should be supported by the teacher. The group should just work on two-digit multiplied by one-digit numbers. The teacher should model each calculation on a whiteboard	Estimate which calculation will give the smallest answer and which will give the largest. Pupils should 'tell' the teacher how to proceed throughout the calculation

Plenary
Each group feed back one of their calculations – the core group and the extension group explain why the particular arrangement of digits gives the largest answer

Rationale and evaluation

My aim was that, by presenting this as an investigation into which arrangement of digits would give the largest product, I would encourage the pupils to estimate first. This worked very well – it also encouraged them into checking as they went through the grid multiplication. The extension and the core groups didn't share out the different multiplications as I suggested – rather they took it in turns to calculate while the others in the group watched to see what the answer would be. This was actually a useful way of organising the activity as those who weren't carrying out the calculation were checking as they went along.

I worked alongside the support group so that I could model the process for them carefully. This group still aren't making the connection between the grid method and the numbers they are working with. So, for example, Parmjit carried out the calculation

23 × 4

×	4	
2		
3		

and Jay wanted to put a '2' instead of '20' and was quite happy with the answer 20 as a result: $(4 \times 2) + (4 \times 3) = 20$. This was despite the group agreeing that the answer should be bigger than 80. As a result I have suggested that she uses the 'Grid Multiplication' program with this group in the next lesson so that they can have an image of how partitioning works to support the grid method. I am also going to focus on multiplication of multiples of 10 by single-digit numbers with this group before coming back to the grid multiplication with them.

Troy seems to be understanding how the grid method can help, though – in the plenary he showed everyone how you can write it 'without the grid'. He wrote:

```
  27
× 4
  80 (saying 'that's 4 times 20')
  28 ('and that's 4 times 7')
 108 (so that's all together which is right cause it's a bit more than 100 and 4 times 25
      would be 100')
```

Observing 'Calculating'

On the companion website find the clip called 'How Many Peas Fill The Classroom'. This is a fascinating activity in which the teacher works with her class to try to calculate how many peas it would take to fill the classroom. As well as developing and practising children's calculation skills it also develops the idea of very large numbers in a real context. Children often find it extremely difficult to visualise very large numbers. The task also requires the pupils to break down a complex problem into small steps.

Although this clip is from a Year 7 group I have carried out very similar activities with learners in primary schools. Focus particularly on the segment from four minutes onwards, which focuses on the teacher taking feedback from the groups. What might you do differently as a result of observing this section of the lesson? One concern might be that the large numbers they were working with did not carry very much meaning to the children as they didn't break the task down into chunks which they could visualise. Perhaps dividing the classroom up into more manageable 'chunks' to start with would have allowed the learners to make more sense of the answers they were coming up with.

Imagine you are feeding back to the teacher. What are three things that you feel were strengths in the lesson, and what is one key thing that you would suggest the teacher does differently?

How would you adapt this activity for the group that you are currently working with?

Assessing 'Calculating'

The 2011 Ofsted report mentioned earlier in this chapter describes 'Problem Solving' as at the heart of learning arithmetic. This supports the argument presented to you in Chapter 3 and suggests that the ability to solve problems should also be central to assessing your pupils' calculating skills. This can be carried out in a wide range of contexts. It is helpful if these contexts are genuine 'real life' contexts rather than the pseudo-reality I referred to earlier in the chapter. Examples that you can use could include:

- Calculating the best value purchase. Bring in a range of cereals, or drinks in different sized containers. The pupils have to calculate which size offers the best value.

- Calculating the costs to redecorate the classroom. Include the costs of paint for the walls and carpet for the floor.

- Calculating costs of fruit for younger pupils. Make sure you let the pupils devise their own ways of recording their calculations at this stage. It is likely that these learners will begin with repeated addition and will sketch the fruit they want to buy and 'attach' a price to it.

- Ask very young learners to work out how many raisins there are in a packet. Observe how they group the raisins. Some may choose to count in 2s or 3s or even 5s.

Cross-curricular teaching of 'Calculating'

The idea of the extended project is to draw on the key ideas within the chapter to develop a cross-curricular project which you can explore with your learners over a series of lessons. This allows you and your class to develop your subject knowledge together. The examples given above in the assessment section all offer cross-curricular routes into calculating. I have found that developing the assessment activity around redecorating the classroom is a very fruitful cross-curricular activity which involves all learners in developing their calculation skills.

You need to begin this investigation in an open space. Ask 24 pupils to come to the centre of the space. The rest of the pupils stand in pairs. They take it in turns to tell the 24 pupils how to arrange themselves in an array, for example 2 × 12 or 3 × 8. Keep going until you have exhausted all the possibilities. Repeat for a range of other numbers – some that give a large number of possibilities and some that only offer one.

Return to the classroom and ask the pupils to explore how many different 'arrays' you can make for each number from 1 to 36. At this stage you can ask pupils to identify other arrays that they notice around them, such as carpet tiles on a floor, or panes in a window.

This allows you to begin to think through different ways of organising the classroom. How many ways could the desks be arranged – what is appropriate in the space, and which arrangements work for which parts of the curriculum? Depending on the time you have you can develop scale models in either 2D or 3D.

Summary

The key focus for this chapter is the link between the mental methods we employ as a first choice and how these can be formalised into written algorithms when the calculations become too complex for us to hold in our head. You have read how the four operations link together and how you can use your knowledge of one of the operations to support calculations using another operation. Our aim for children leaving school is that they have a good understanding of the four operations and that they can carry out calculations mentally, when possible, and can employ a range of written methods, making sensible choices depending on the calculation they are carrying out.

I have emphasised the importance of children approaching calculation practically and through activity – this allows you to support them in developing their vocabulary of calculation. They should also be encouraged to develop their own informal records for calculations. The key to understanding the more formal algorithms is to build carefully on previous understanding so that your pupils understand the reasons why the algorithms 'work' and don't just apply them unthinkingly. Most of the misconceptions come from losing sight of the value of the numbers in the calculation so that children don't notice they have an answer that doesn't make sense.

Work your way carefully though the progression of written methods – the grid method may be an idea that you are not used to. If the written methods make sense to you, you will be able to share these with your learners.

Reflections on this chapter

My guess would be that many of you have found this chapter the most challenging in the book – not because the ideas are more complex but because the methods of calculation may well be different from those that you were taught. My hope is that you can see the rationale for teaching these methods of calculation and that pupils will be able to see why the methods are effective, and will begin to move away from simply trying to remember how you carry out a calculation to understanding why a 'rule' works. If you understand how the calculation is carried out you can make effective decisions about which method to use, and are also more likely to notice when you have made a mistake.

I also hope that you have become able to notice the choices that you are making when you carry out calculations, whether mentally or on paper. In a sense you have 'relearnt' the algorithms for the four operations, noticing, maybe for the first time, why you carry out calculations in a particular way. This process of revisiting your own learning should support you in explaining 'Calculating' to your learners.

Self-audit

Carry out this audit to explore how your learning has progressed as a result of working on the ideas in this chapter. Include the results in your portfolio.

1   Make a copy of the following table:

Just know it	Need to think a bit	Need to work it out on paper

Using the digits 1, 3, 5, 7, 8, 9 make up a range of addition and subtraction calculations. Make sure you have some calculations that you would place in each column. Write the calculations in the appropriate column, together with a rationale for your choice.

2   Set yourself the following questions:

A column addition involving decimals.
An addition involving decimals you would calculate mentally.
A column subtraction involving decimals.
A subtraction involving decimals you would do mentally.
A short multiplication involving decimals you could do mentally.
A multiplication involving decimals you would do using pencil and paper.
A short division involving decimals you could do mentally.
A division involving decimals you would do using pencil and paper.

Complete the calculations and write a commentary outlining your thought processes and the points at which you think pupils may make a mistake.

3   Spot the mistake: these three long multiplication calculations have got mistakes in them. Write down the mistake that the pupils have made, then complete the long multiplication correctly.

135	270	452
× 62	× 30	× 18
270	710	324016
710		452
980		324468

Going further

Issues in Teaching Numeracy by Ian Thompson
This book contains a very useful section on calculation which outlines progression in written and mental calculation in much greater detail than there was space for in this chapter. There is also a very helpful chapter on using the empty number line which you will find invaluable in supporting your learners in developing mental methods.

Thompson, I. (2010) *Issues in Teaching Numeracy in Primary Schools*. Buckingham: Open University Press.

Teaching and Learning Early Number by Ian Thompson
This book is the forerunner of the text above. It is important for all teachers, not just those who teach learners in the early years, as he outlines in detail the ways in which early learners begin the progress of learning to calculate. These two books will expand the research base on which you can draw to develop your pracice as well as offering lots of practical approaches to learning and teaching calculation skills.

Thompson, I. (2008) *Teaching and Learning Early Number*. Buckingham: Open University Press.

Good Practice in Primary Mathematics: Evidence from 20 Successful Schools by Ofsted
This offers useful small-scale case studies on how to teach calculation. There are several vignettes from classrooms which are enlightening as well as evidence from children. This is particularly helpful in seeing how learners can develop their own written methods for calculating.

Ofsted (2011) *Good Practice in Primary Mathematics: Evidence from 20 Successful Schools*. Manchester: Ofsted.

CHAPTER 7
UNDERSTANDING SHAPE

Introduction

I remember working in a mixed-age class in a small school in North Yorkshire. There were children aged from 7 to 11 in the class and the teacher was working on an activity I had suggested which involved visualising whether or not a range of nets of cubes would 'fold up' to make a cube. The children had created the nets by drawing all the different arrangements of six squares they could think of. Once they had decided which they thought would fold up into cubes they cut them out to check their conjectures.

At the end of the session the teacher said to me, 'What was interesting to me was that some of the less able children did best on that activity.' I often question the unproblematic use of the word 'ability'. If someone has been successful in a mathematical activity linked to shape surely they are 'able', even if their achievements in other areas of mathematics are not at similar levels. Some of you will be more comfortable with this area of mathematics, and for some of you it will present a challenge. I hope that this simply illustrates the breadth of the mathematics curriculum and how there will be areas of mathematics in which we feel comfortable and areas in which we struggle. The important point is that we are able to make connections between all areas of mathematics so that we become a confident mathematics teacher and learner.

Starting point

Close your eyes. That may seem a strange request to someone reading a book so let me expand. Firstly, find a friend, then ask them to read the next section while you have your eyes closed. If we are going to think about how you teach and learn 'Understanding shape' we need to begin with a visualisation.

Create a large red rectangle that you can see clearly in your mind's eye. Stand it on its end so that you can see it standing on its shortest side. Then slowly rotate it so that it is lying on one of the longest sides. Now rotate it again so that it is balancing on a corner. Move the rectangle round and round in your mind's eye and make a decision about which way round you want, finally, to picture the rectangle and stop it in that orientation. Now imagine a small, blue right-angled triangle that will fit inside the rectangle. Picture it inside the rectangle and slide it so that the right angle fits exactly into one corner of the rectangle. Imagine another small, blue right-angled triangle, which can be a different size from the first one you thought of. Slide into one of the other corners of the rectangle. Notice the red shape that is left inside the rectangle. Open your eyes and sketch what you see.

Talk to your friend about the shape you have sketched. How many different properties can you describe? What do you notice about its properties? Are there **parallel lines** (like railway lines) or **perpendicular lines** (lines at 90° to each other)? What can you say about the angles: are they **acute** (less than 90°), **obtuse** (between 90° and 180°) or **reflex** (more than 180°) **angles**? Do you know what the shape is called?

This simple activity embraces two of the key skills you need to teach children to help them understand shape. They need to be able to visualise the shapes that we are working with and they need to be able to describe them so that someone else can 'see' the same shape. We do this by having a clear understanding of the properties of different shapes.

These are both skills that we can teach – although visualisation is not always a skill that we will have been taught. As I suggested in the opening of the chapter the interesting thing is that sometimes those learners who have not excelled when working with numbers will be able to visualise and manipulate shapes very quickly. These learners are good at maths too!

You will have noticed that you are having to draw on language that you may not have used for a while. There are the names of the shapes (all provided in the answers at the end of this chapter) and perhaps, more importantly, ways to describe their properties. We have already used parallel and perpendicular. Other vocabulary you may have drawn on for the activity above is **congruent shapes** (two shapes which will fit perfectly on top of each other) and **similar shapes** (these are shapes whose sides and angles are all in the same ratio).

For example, the two right-angled triangles below are similar as one has each side three times bigger than the other one. This also means that the corresponding angles in each triangle are the same size.

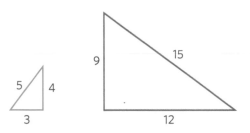

Portfolio task 7.1

Look at the polygons below:

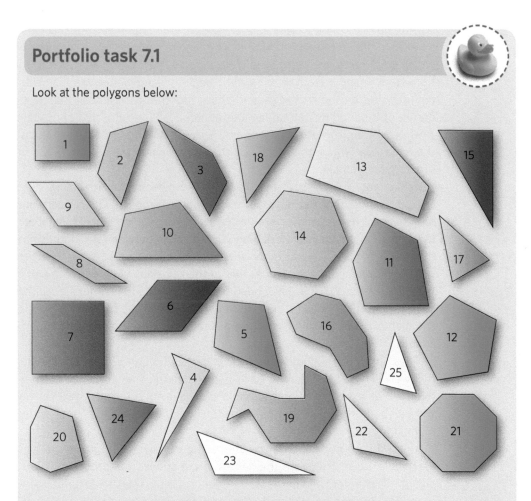

Classify them in any way you like, into as many groups as you like. When you have completed this task explain your classification to a friend. Then classify them in a different way. Finally name as many of the polygons as you can. Answers are on page 154. (This activity is taken from many of the free online resources provided by the National Council of Teachers of Mathematics in the USA. This activity can be found at **http://illuminations .nctm.org/LessonDetail.aspx?ID=L277.)**

Taking care to develop children's vocabulary of shape is vital, so make sure there are plenty of displays utilising the vocabulary and also that there is plenty of opportunity to talk about the shapes we are working with.

In the 1950s Pierre van Hiele and Dina van Hiele-Geldof, two Dutch mathematics teachers and husband and wife, identified five levels of understanding that help us appreciate how children come to understand shape. These are described in their article 'Developing geometric thinking through activities that begin with play' in *Teaching Children Mathematics*, published in February 1999. It is useful for us to explore these levels in some detail before exploring how progression is described by the strategy:

Level 0: Visualisation - at this stage learners can name and recognise shapes by their appearance. They cannot yet describe properties or use properties to sort shapes.

Level 1: Analysis - at this stage children identify properties related to shapes and use these to classify them.

Level 2: Informal deduction - at this stage learners can use the properties that belong to classes of shapes to problem-solve. So they will be able to talk about regular and irregular shapes, and about triangles in general, or specific types of triangle. This is the furthest we would expect most learners to progress within primary school.

Level 3: Deduction - at this stage learners use their understandings about shape to construct geometrical proofs. That means that they can use their understanding and knowledge about the properties of shapes to convince others that new understandings are true.

Level 4: Rigour - At this final stage students would be constructing rigorous proofs about the geometrical properties of shapes. These proofs will follow mathematical conventions rather than the more informal proofs at Level 3.

This research suggests that the visualisation and analysis stages of learning are key to understanding shape. This has become the focus of most of the teaching throughout the early and primary years of education. The teaching points later in the chapter emphasise the importance of the development of the vocabulary to allow children to be able to talk about what they are noticing at the visualisation stage. You will notice that many children will move between the visualisation level and analysis level as their vocabulary develops to describe particular concepts within 'Understanding shape'. As with many 'schemas' for learning, this can be seen as dynamic rather than a stepladder. That is, children do not rigidly move through the five levels - rather, they will move backwards and forwards through the stages depending on the particular idea they are exploring.

Taking it further

Penny Coltman, Dinara Petyaeva and Julia Anghileri have explored how adults can best support young children using 'building blocks' to carry out problem-solving activities which help them come to an understanding of three-dimensional (3D) shape. In an article 'Scaffolding learning through meaningful tasks and adult interaction', published in the *Early Years Journal*, 22 (1) in 2002 by Carfax, they suggest that young children between 3 and 6, although operating at the first of the van Hiele levels, are limited by their experience and language and that through careful adult intervention children can learn effectively. The children were given 'poleidoblocks', a set of wooden 3D shapes and toy animals and cardboard models to produce 'playful' contexts which made sense to the young children. Children were allowed to become familiar with the blocks through free play and constructed their own stories using the blocks and the other resources. However, after this free play the researchers then used practical activities to support the children's learning. For example, children were introduced to cylinders and cuboids. The children were told a story about cylinder birds loving to roll – the children could use this idea to see the difference between cylinders and cuboids and to begin to sort them according to this property of 'rolling'.

This research emphasises the importance of exploring properties of shapes by manipulating the shapes themselves. Shapes are dynamic, they move in space: 2D shapes move so that we can see them in any orientation, 3D shapes can roll and slide and build and balance. By working practically with shape, children are much more able to 'see' their properties.

The next section outlines the development of children's understanding about shape as they move between Foundation Stage and the end of their time in primary education. You should keep in mind the advice from the research above that as much of this should be explored actively and dynamically as possible.

Progression in 'Understanding shape'

Foundations for 'Understanding shape'

The initial focus should be to provide children with common objects and shapes so that they can make and re-create patterns, build models and talk about what they are doing to begin to develop the language of shape, size and position. You can then start asking children to visualise common 2D and 3D shapes and use them to make patterns and models.

Children should be introduced to ideas of whole, half and quarter turns as an introduction to angle. They can be introduced to the difference between things that turn about a point (like a pair of scissors)

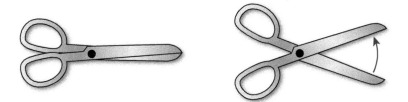

or about a line (like a door). You can help them develop their use of language to describe position, using vocabulary like 'in front of', 'behind', 'next to', 'on top of', and 'underneath'.

Later you can teach children to recognise shapes in different orientations and use their properties to classify them. This will help them notice reflective symmetry in patterns and draw lines of symmetry on 2D shapes. Teach them to give instructions using the language of position and understand the difference between clockwise and anti-clockwise. By this stage children will understand that a quarter turn is equivalent to a right angle.

Becoming confident in 'Understanding shape'

At this stage children will be able to match 2D and 3D shapes to drawings of them. They will also be able to use mirror lines to draw reflections and use compass directions to describe movement about a grid. Pupils will be able to draw and classify polygons and describe their properties. The children will visualise **nets** of 3D solids. A net is the 2D shape that you can 'fold up' to make the 3D shape. They will know that angles are measured in degrees, that a whole turn is 360°, and they will be able to compare and order angles of less than 180°.

Pupils at this stage will read and plot coordinates in the first **quadrant** (see below), and recognise parallel and perpendicular lines. They will use their understanding of symmetry to complete patterns and draw positions of shapes after reflections and rotations. They will also be able to estimate, draw and measure angles and calculate angles on a straight line using their understanding that angles on a straight line add up to 180°.

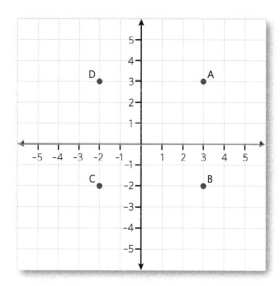

Here A is in the first quadrant, B in the second quadrant, C in the third quadrant and D in the fourth quadrant.

Extending learning in 'Understanding shape'

Pupils at this stage will recognise **vertically opposite angles**, use this to find 'missing angles' and will be operating in all four quadrants with coordinates.

Below are vertically opposite angles, made where two lines cross. The angles have the same value.

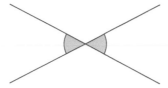

The children will be able to transform images using ICT and to construct a triangle given two sides and the angle between them.

Big ideas

Properties of shapes

A young man in a lesson I was observing about algebra once said to his teacher, 'That's what maths is all about, isn't it Sir? It's about saying complicated things very simply.' Being able to classify and order sets of objects fits this perfectly. And we classify and order shapes using their properties. A property of a shape is something that doesn't change. It might be **2D** (having length and width but not depth) or **3D** (having length, width and depth); shapes can be **closed** (all sides join together) or **open** (there is a gap between two corners); they may have sides which are all straight or some curved sides; shapes can be **convex** (all the interior angles are less than 180°) or **concave** (at least one interior angle is greater than 180°); or they may be **regular** (all sides the same length and all interior angles the same size) or **irregular** (having sides and angles which are different lengths and sizes).

Closed shapes with straight sides are called polygons and these are listed below.

Number of sides	Name	Regular	Irregular
3	Triangle		
4	Quadrilateral		
5	Pentagon		
6	Hexagon		
7	Heptagon		
8	Octagon		
9	Nonagon		
10	Decagon		

| 11 | Hendecagon | ◯ | ⟨shape⟩ |
| 12 | Dodecagon | ◯ | ⟨shape⟩ |

It is important to use both regular and irregular versions of the polygons with children, otherwise they only link the name to the regular version of the shape.

Portfolio task 7.2

Look at the shapes you sorted earlier in the chapter. For your portfolio sort them into groups using the vocabulary you have been introduced to above – so you may sort into concave and convex, regular and irregular, and so on – and draw them.

Within the set of polygons there are further classifications. So, for example, triangles can be:

- **Equilateral**: All angles are 60° and all the sides are the same length.
- **Right angled**: One angle is 90°.
- **Isosceles**: One pair of sides are the same length.
- **Scalene**: All sides are different lengths.

A triangle can be right angled and isosceles or right angled and scalene.

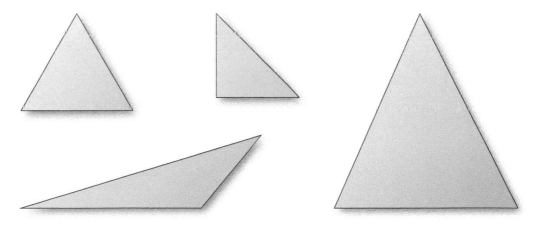

Similarly, several quadrilaterals have special names:

- **Square**: A quadrilateral with four equal sides and four right angles.
- **Rhombus**: A quadrilateral with four equal sides; the angles do not all have to be 90° (so a square is a specific version of a rhombus).
- **Rectangle**: Any quadrilateral with four right angles. An **oblong** is a rectangle that isn't a square.
- **Parallelogram**: A quadrilateral with opposite sides parallel.

- **Trapezium**: A quadrilateral with only one pair of parallel sides.
- **Kite**: A quadrilateral with adjacent sides (i.e. sides that are joined at a point) of equal length.

Portfolio task 7.3

Try this activity – the folding helps you understand ideas of symmetry, and the surprises when you unfold the shape support you in 'noticing' the properties of the shapes. Children find it motivating too; it develops their skills of visualisation as they have to try and 'picture' the shape that will emerge when they unfold the paper. Take a piece of A4 paper and make one fold anywhere – you do not have to fold it in half. Make a cut so that you form two shapes out of the piece of paper. Sketch the two shapes that you have made and name them. Can you find ways to fold and cut the paper so that you make a square, a rhombus, a rectangle, a parallelogram, a trapezium and a kite?

The 3D shapes can also be classified in several ways. **Prisms** and **pyramids** are sometimes confused. I remember a 14-year-old pupil of mine describing the difference as 'a prism is where you find naughty people and a pyramid is where you find dead people.' The difference

Examples of prisms

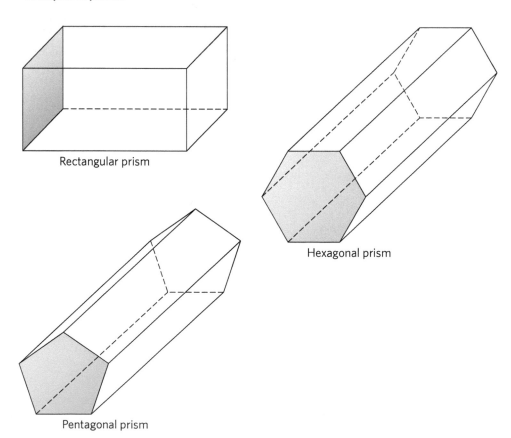

Rectangular prism

Hexagonal prism

Pentagonal prism

is to do with the cross-section. You can slice a prism at any point, parallel to the face at the end, and you will always get the same cross-section, whereas if you slice a pyramid you will different sizes of the same shape.

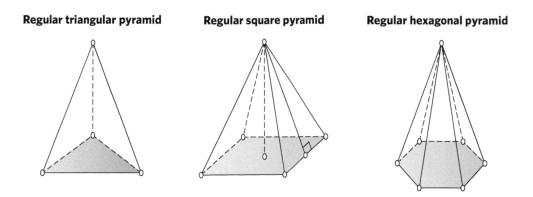

Two prisms you might recognise are a **cube** and a **cuboid**. The most common 3D shapes are shown below.

One way of classifying 3D faces is by the numbers of **faces**, **edges** and vertices (singular **vertex**). The faces of a shape are the flat regions. The edges are where two faces meet and a vertex is a point at which two or more edges meet.

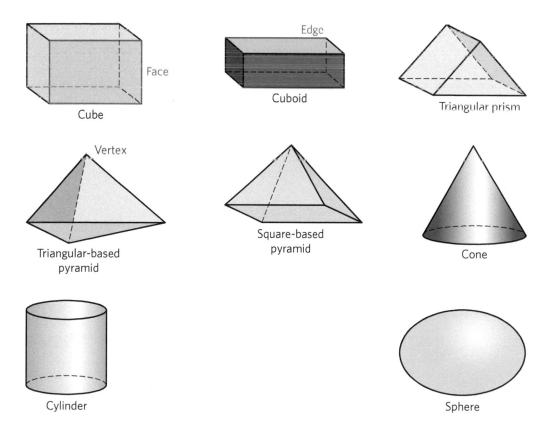

Position

When we want to define, or locate, a point mathematically we use **coordinates** on a pair of **axes** (you pronounce this 'axees' – not like the implement you chop wood with). These axes cross each other at what is known as the **origin**, which has coordinates (0,0). The four areas created by the axes are known as the four **quadrants**. The best way to explain these terms is by a diagram. In the diagram below the x axis is the horizontal axis and the y axis is the vertical axis.

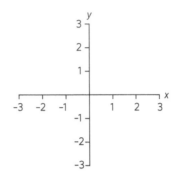

The two axes are labelled x and y. We write coordinates as a pair of numbers in brackets separated by a comma, for example (2,3) or (21,4). The first number always refers to the x coordinate and the second number refers to the y coordinate.

Primary pupils are also introduced to defining direction by compass points.

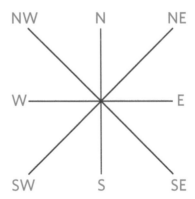

There are four points of the compass: north, south, east and west. The direction halfway between north and west is described as north-west. Similarly, the direction halfway between south and east is described as south-east, the direction halfway between south and west is south-west, and the direction halfway between north and east is north-east.

Once we have placed a shape on a grid we can change its shape through a **transformation**: this is the process of moving a shape on a grid. The three transformations are **translation**, **reflection** and **rotation**.

A translation leaves the shape's dimensions and its orientation unchanged. In other words, it is the same as sliding the same shape across the grid. Here is an example from a Year 6 girl.

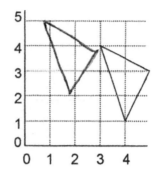

The shape has moved −2 in the *x* direction (i.e. backwards along the *x* axis) and +1 in the *y* direction (i.e. upwards on the *y*-axis),

$$\begin{pmatrix} -2 \\ 1 \end{pmatrix}$$

A negative sign in front of the number would represent a move backwards along the *x* axis or down the *y* axis.

A reflection moves the shape using a mirror line, as below.

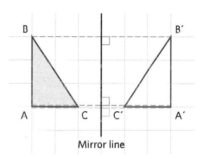

Mirror line

When reflecting in a mirror line you need to take care to check that all points are the same distance from the mirror line. So, in the example above, points A and B are three squares from the mirror line and C is one square away. You must always measure at right angles to the mirror line.

Finally we can rotate shapes. When we rotate shapes we have to define the point we are rotating about, called the **centre of rotation**, and say the angle we are rotating through. So, for example, if we rotate this triangle about the origin the dimensions of the triangle will stay exactly the same. It is as if we have fixed a 'stick' to the corner 'A' and moved it through *x* degrees.

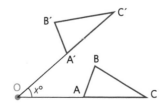

Symmetry

The use of the mirror line gives us a link into the idea of **symmetry**. The form of symmetry you will use is called **reflective symmetry**. The best way to explore line symmetry is through folding shapes. If you can fold the shape in half so that the pieces fit exactly on top of each other you have found a **line of symmetry**. For example,

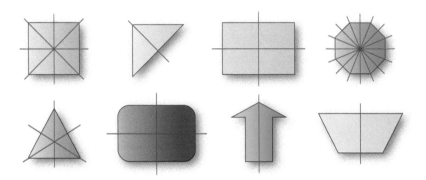

A shape can also be described as having **rotational symmetry**. This means that you can rotate the shape and it will look the same before you have rotated the shape through 360 degrees. The **order of rotational symmetry** is the number of times the shape is repeated before it makes a complete turn and the **degree of rotational symmetry** the amount of turn you must make for a repeat to take place.

© TP / Alamy Images

For example, the image on the Manx flag has an order of rotational symmetry of 3 and a degree of rotational symmetry of 60 degrees.

Portfolio task 7.4

Draw the regular polygons given in the table earlier in this chapter. Find all the lines of symmetry for each shape. What do you notice about the result? Why do you think this is the case?

Teaching points

Teaching point 1: Issues with language – describing properties; positional language

Find a couple of friends – or phone a couple of people up. Ask them to find a scrap piece of paper and draw a triangle. My prediction would be that they draw an equilateral triangle.

I have tried this out with very large groups of students, teachers and children and this is always the case. Of course, there is a huge range of triangles to choose from (isosceles, scalene, right angled) but it appears as though the default option is equilateral. Indeed many young children find it difficult, initially, to see a shape like this:

This looks very 'different' from the shape they were first introduced to as 'triangle'. This reminds me of my daughter Holly when she was young. We had a dog called Henry, a small skinny mongrel. One day Holly saw a cat crossing the road and said to me, 'Oh look, there's a Henry.' For her Henry was a small animal with four legs and a tail, so it made absolute sense that all animals with four legs and a tail should be 'Henrys'.

When introducing shapes to children it is very important that they see the whole range of shapes. So rather than offering one example of a triangle, offer a whole range and ask children what all the shapes have in common. In this way they will see that what makes a triangle is that it has three straight sides all joined together.

Similarly, when introducing vocabulary which may have a range of meanings, such as **face** or **edge**, take time to find out the children's meanings before imposing a new definition on them. A simple activity to help with this is to ask children to draw or write a definition for a set of key words. These might be face, edge, vertex, corner, line, straight. You can then use the children's definitions to help explain the mathematical definition.

Teaching point 2: Orientation of 2D shapes

I once carried out some work for an examination board looking at GCSE scripts. One of the criteria which were used to help decide borderline cases was whether or not the pupils could use Pythagoras' theorem effectively. It was clear from looking at the scripts that if a triangle such as this:

appeared in the question most pupils realised that they should try to use what they knew about right-angled triangles. However, when faced with a triangle such as this:

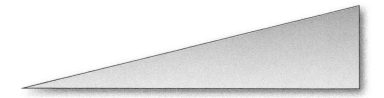

pupils seemed not to recognise the shape as a right-angled triangle. This is a similar issue to the one mentioned in teaching point 1. Children get used to seeing a single representation of a shape and cannot transfer their learning when faced with an unfamiliar version.

An activity such as 'Shapes in a bag' can help with this. Get yourself a cloth bag and a set of large shapes. Gradually and slowly reveal a shape. When the children can see only a small portion of the shape, ask what different shapes it could be; slowly reveal a little bit more and ask again. As you reveal the shape it will become clear what the shape is, but the children's focus is on noticing the properties of shapes rather than simply remembering names.

Teaching point 3: 2D representations of 3D objects

Try to sketch a sphere. Did you draw

rather than something like this?

Children find it very difficult to sketch 3D shapes. It is difficult after all – in trying to draw a 3D object using only two dimensions we will often draw representations such as a square for a cube. This can lead to difficulties when working with more complex shapes, and the ability to sketch 3D objects supports us in visualising.

The activity in the Resource inspiration box on the next page introduces isometric paper as a way of sketching 3D cuboids. It also raises the importance of orientation. We need to look at 3D shapes such as this in different ways if we are to be able to reproduce them exactly. I often find that the children who can quickly grasp sketching on isometric paper may not have as quick a grasp of other areas of mathematics. This is an important skill, so it is good for these children's views of themselves as mathematicians to see themselves as the experts in this particular area. A helpful extension of this activity is to draw the plan view and the two side elevations of each shape. These are the two-dimensional views that you get if you look directly down onto the shape and directly at the front and the side.

Resource inspiration

Building shapes out of cubes

You will need:

* inerlocking cubes
* dotty paper

There may be some hidden cubes

1 Build each of these shapes using the numbers of cubes shown.

   a 8 cubes   **b** 10 cubes   **c** 9 cubes

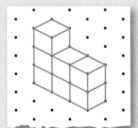 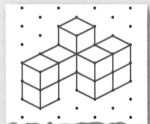 

2 Can you find more than one way to build each shape?

3 **a** Make this shape.

    b Add a cube to make a new shape.

    c Draw your new shape on dotty paper.

    d How many different shapes can you
       make using the extra cube?

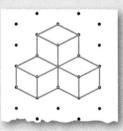

4 **a** Make this shape.

    b Add a cube to make a new shape.

    c Draw your new shape on dotty paper.

    d How many different shapes can you
       make using the extra cube?

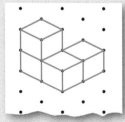

Teaching point 4: Errors in not seeing angle as dynamic

One of the early activities I work on with children is asking them to order angles intuitively in terms of their size. This follows discussion of angle as a measure of turn using strips of card pinned at a corner of angle measurers made from two strips of different-coloured card.

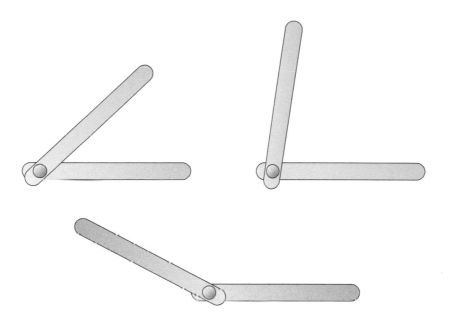

Alfie was looking confused the last time I worked with his group on this.
He looked at this angle

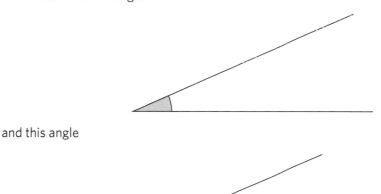

and this angle

and said, 'the first angle is much bigger but it's the same size'. He was confused as he was noticing the length of the lines and equating that with the 'size' of the angle as well as realising that angle is a measure of turn. I was able to convince him that they were actually the same angle by extending the 'lines' on the second angle so that it appeared identical to the first angle.

Teaching point 5: Estimating and measuring angles

There are two common mistakes when using a protractor to measure angles. The first error is using the wrong scale to measure the angle. The two scales are often referred to as the 'inner scale' and the 'outer scale'. Asking children to estimate angles before measuring them will help them decide which scale they need to use.

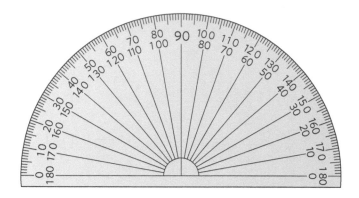

So if we were measuring an angle of 63° using this protractor we would know that we should be looking for 'about' 60° rather than using the wrong scale giving an answer of 117°.

The second error to look out for is when children place the bottom of the protractor on the vertex rather than the point where the '0–180' line and the 90 line cross.

The first angle that most children are introduced to is a right angle or 90°. Using this fact we can help children estimate many other angles. They will be able to see that two right angles, which make a straight line, are 180°. Similarly, half a right angle must be 45°. Also, if they divide a right angle into three they will get an angle of 30°. It is helpful to ask children to sketch as many different angles as they can, using multiples and combinations of 30°, 45° and 90°. They can then classify these angles as acute and obtuse. If they get used to having a sense of angle this will help them when they are using protractors to measure angles to 1° of accuracy.

Teaching point 6: The language of coordinates

I have heard many teachers remind children to 'go along the corridor and then up the stairs' as a way of reminding children to write down the x coordinate first and then the y coordinate. Many children remain unconvinced that it really matters in which order you write the coordinates and so seem to forget. I once observed a teacher convince children that order matters, and that the plus and minus signs are important when working in four quadrants. He drew a set of axes on the board and marked a point A in the first quadrant. He then asked the group, 'what shall I call the point A?' One of the group immediately shouted out 'Alisha'. Rather than show any irritation the teacher asked another pupil to come up to the front, drew another set of axes and asked them to draw 'Alisha'. The pupil said, 'but it could go anywhere'. The teacher then asked for other ways to describe the point. Pupils responded with answers such as, 'It's 2 along and 3 up', or 'Its x coordinate is 2 and its y coordinate is 3.' This allowed him to draw up all the possible ways of 'naming' the point, illustrating the importance of coordinates as giving information.

Teaching point 7: Confusions with mirror lines

There are a number of errors you may notice pupils making when using mirror lines to explore symmetry. Earlier in the chapter I suggested asking children for their own definitions of key terms as a way of finding out what their current understandings are. I recently asked a group of Year 3 pupils what 'mirror line' meant to them. Ben suggested that 'it is something that splits a shape in half'. This was accepted by the group. So I asked them to draw me the lines of symmetry on the following rectangle.

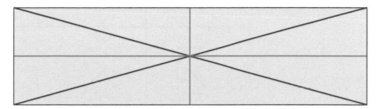

Again they were all happy that this showed a rectangle had four lines of symmetry. It was only when I asked them to try to fold the rectangle along the diagonals so that the halves 'matched up' that they agreed these were not lines of symmetry. (Try it if you don't believe me!)

Similarly, if a shape is to be reflected in a mirror line and the original shape is placed some distance away from the line, children often place the reflection flush to the line. It is simply a matter of reminding them that the 'reflected' shape should be the same distance from the mirror line as the original shape.

While I usually suggest using practical materials in this case I would advise against actually using a mirror to explore line symmetry. Mirrors are often very difficult for children to use effectively – I would avoid using mirrors at this stage and reinforce the importance of reflections being equidistant from the mirror line. Pupils benefit from plenty of practice in drawing shapes and their 'mirrors'.

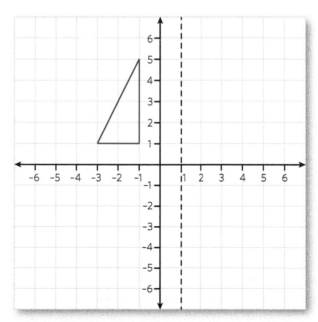

As well as providing pupils with a starting shape and a mirror line in which to reflect it, it is helpful to give pupils an initial shape and a reflected shape and remove the mirror line. The task is to find the mirror line. This helps reinforce the notion of equal distance.

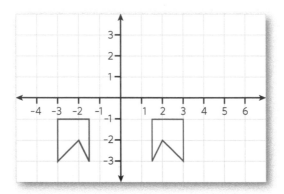

Teaching point 8: Rotations about vertices and centres of shapes

As with all areas of understanding shape it is important to focus on the dynamic. If I want to explore 'rotation' with a group of learners they need to rotate a shape about either the centre of the shape or one of its vertices, and then sketch the result. In that way they will be able to describe what is happening for themselves rather than simply trying to remember 'rules' they have been told. A useful strategy is to ask the pupils to work in pairs or groups so they can check each other's answers. They very quickly see if they are getting the same results, and, with encouragement, support each other in identifying their errors.

In practice

The following lesson plan and evaluation describe a lesson taught to a group of pupils who have some understanding of the language of shape. I was wanting them to develop their language in order to be able to identify and describe the properties of shapes in greater detail. I was also wanting them to become increasingly sophisticated in their use of technical vocabulary. The particular focus for this lesson was developing skills in visualising and naming 2D shapes and describing their properties. I used the program 'What's Hiding?' to explore the children's knowledge of properties of the shapes as it was the first time I had worked with this particular group on this area. The open questions I could ask meant that I was able to see what their current understandings were and could model more sophisticated vocabulary in my 'interpretation' of their answers. The 'What's Hiding?' program is available on the companion website to this book.

Topic: Exploring 2D shapes

Age group: Lower primary

Objectives

Visualise and name common 2D shapes and describe their properties

Key vocabulary	Context
2D Property Circle Triangle Square Rectangle	This is my first lesson with this group of pupils exploring their understanding of shape. My aim was to discover the pupils' prior knowledge to support me in developing their skills

Resources	Starter activity
Collection of miscellaneous shapes – regular and irregular Mini-whiteboards	Using the 'What's Hiding?' program to assess the pupils' current knowledge of shape properties and shape names. I placed the pupils with their 'talk partners' and as I gradually revealed each shape I asked the talk partner to discuss what the shape might be. When I asked a pair for their response they had to justify their guess by describing a property of the shape they were guessing. On each occasion we explored all possible shapes as well as shapes that it couldn't be. For example, 'That cannot be a square because squares don't have curved lines,' or 'That can't be a rectangle as that isn't a right angle'

Main activity	Teacher	Pupil activity
	With the group sitting in a circle with a range of shapes in the middle I asked one of the group to sort the shapes in any way they wanted. Others in the group had to guess the criteria that were being used to sort the shapes. If they guessed correctly they had the next go. They showed they had guessed correctly by placing a new shape in the correct group	Sitting in a circle observing the sorting and deciding on possible criteria
	Asking the pupils to sort the shapes in a number of different ways allows me to point out that there are many different properties that describe shapes. We can look at the number of sides, the properties of the angles, parallel and perpendicular lines and so on	

Group activity Children operating above expected levels	For this activity I decided it would be appropriate to use all attainment groups – this would allow those pupils with less experience to hear a wide range of the vocabulary of shape
Children operating at expected levels	The groups continued to play the game that had been introduced above until each person in the group had a turn at sorting the shapes. The next activity involved one of the group hiding a shape. They had to describe the shape so that the others in the group could draw it on their mini-whiteboards

Children operating below expected levels	As I moved around the groups I made a note of the range of vocabulary that I heard being used. I was able to share this with the class at the end of the lesson and construct a vocabulary display that we referred to in future lessons.

Plenary

On the whiteboard I sketched a square and an irregular quadrilateral with one right angle. In pairs the children had to say in what ways they were the same and in what ways they were different. I then shared my list of vocabulary with the class and asked the group for an example of a shape with this property and an example of a shape which did not have this property

Rationale and evaluation

My aim was to discover the pupils' current knowledge and I was pleased that I left the lesson with a clear understanding of the range of prior experience. Some of the pupils are secure in their knowledge of triangles, squares and rectangles – Bartek even knew the difference between isosceles and equilateral triangles. However, Malc thought that the scalene couldn't be a triangle because it was 'all wonky'. I will introduce a group to the different sorts of triangles next time through a classification exercise.

Most of the group found the irregular shapes difficult to work with – they are obviously more used to working with regular shapes. I will start every day this week with an example of an irregular shape and a regular shape so that they get used to seeing irregular shapes.

I was particularly pleased with the way that the all-attainment groups operated. The pupils listened carefully to each other and I could see that some of the children who had a more developed vocabulary were using it – almost to show off – but I was pleased that the other pupils were exposed to a wide range of vocabulary. I made a rule that if anyone didn't understand a word they had to ask – and that the person who had used the word had to explain what it meant by drawing an example. My TA and I made sure that we asked pupils what they meant when they introduced some new vocabulary.

The pupils were very impressed with the long list of vocabulary I shared with them at the end. You could see a sense of pride in their knowledge of the vocabulary of shape.

Observing 'Understanding shape'

On the companion website there is a video which shows a teacher working with her class of 7-and 8-year-olds in describing and constructing three-dimensional shapes from two-dimensional drawings (http://www.tes.co.uk/teaching-resource/Primary-Maths-Shape-and-Space-6044810/).

I would like you to focus on the section from 4 minutes 30 seconds into the video. This is the point at which the children are hiding 3D shapes behind a board and describing them to a friend who then has to guess which shape has been hidden. Listen to the extract and jot down all the technical language that the pupils are using to describe the shapes.

If you were planning this activity which shapes would you use in order to maximise the vocabulary that could be developed? What do you see as the teacher's role in this sort of activity?

A useful way of adapting this activity is to ask the children what the shape could be after each question so that they begin to notice the sorts of properties that shapes have in common. So, for example, if a shape has eight vertices it may be a cube, or another kind of cuboid. The children have to ask another question to be certain which shape it is.

Assessing 'Understanding shape'

The activity above is a very useful assessment activity as you can observe the use of the vocabulary of shape as well as getting a sense of children's understandings of the properties of shapes through the questions that they ask. Another very useful assessment task is to ask your pupils to classify shapes in a number of ways. Use a wide range of concrete shapes which the children can sort physically. These are available from many suppliers of mathematical resources. Using Carroll diagrams as sorting 'grids' is a useful technique as this requires the pupils to look at properties very carefully. You could use properties of symmetry, for example:

	No rotational symmetry	Has rotational symmetry
No lines of symmetry		
One line of symmetry		
Two lines of symmetry		
More than two lines of symmetry		

or ideas of regularity:

	Regular	Irregular
Triangle		
Quadrilateral		
Pentagon		
Hexagon		

This allows you to focus on the wide range of varieties of polygons that exist and use specialist language where appropriate. So a regular triangle is an equilateral triangle, a regular quadrilateral is a square and so on. This same activity can be adapted for three-dimensional shapes.

Cross-curricular teaching of 'Understanding shape'

The idea of this section is to draw on the key ideas within the chapter to develop a cross-curricular project which you can explore with your learners over a series of lessons. This allows you and your class to develop your subject knowledge together.

The ideas of design and packaging are ideal for developing into a cross-curricular project for your class. This sort of activity is useful for an end-of-term celebration. Perhaps the school is holding a summer fair and needs to award prizes or 'wrap' surprises for some of the games. The pupils need to work out how they can design the nets which will 'fold up' to make the packages which will hold the prizes as securely as possible. They will also need to visualise the 3D shape which will result from the 2D net so that they can decorate the net before making it up into the package.

Other possibilities are designing patchwork quilt designs. Many patchwork quilts are made up of a central pattern of squares with triangular surrounds. If the class were to make four pieces of patchwork each they will need to work out how big a quilt they could make, and how many squares and triangles will be required to make the quilt.

© Michael Boys / Corbis

A final possibility which also asks the pupils to use the idea of tessellations is to calculate how much it would cost to make and hang bunting around the classroom. Tessellation is the process of covering a two-dimensional space with repeating two-dimensional shapes.

Most individual pieces of bunting are isosceles triangles so the pupils will need to work out the most efficient way to cut these out of pieces of material. There is also much scope for measurement to differing degrees of accuracy in this activity.

Summary

This chapter has shown you how the ideas of visualisation, categorisation and position underpin 'Understanding shape'. To be able to understand shapes you need to be able to see the shapes and manipulate them in your 'mind's eye'. This is a skill that can be developed – you may need to develop it in yourself before you can work with your pupils. Or, it may be that by helping your pupils to become better at visualising you become more skilled yourself. The chapter opened with an example of a visualisation activity you can try with your pupils – it is well worth building your own bank of these activities and using them regularly.

There has been a focus on the properties of shapes – a knowledge of the range of possible properties is important in order to be able to classify shapes. So another area to concentrate on with your pupils is developing their vocabulary of shape. Use posters and displays to make sure the vocabulary is clearly displayed so it becomes a part of the language of the classroom. It is important that you model the language of shape constantly – in the same way that you will often use number facts when taking a register, you can use the language of shape whenever you notice new shapes, whatever the subject.

Finally, the language of description has been emphasised. You have seen how important the four quadrants are in placing a point in space and how shapes can be transformed into new shapes by reflection and rotation.

Reflections on this chapter

I wonder if you see 'Understanding shape' in a slightly different way than you see learning and teaching aspects of number? Sometimes my students don't regard the topic as 'important'. But it is, not only in terms of being successful in assessments which all include shape, but also as a way of viewing and describing the world. You may well have discovered a new skill – that of visualisation. I find it very difficult to visualise things, maybe as a result of not learning it at school, and this inhibits me when I am trying to solve practical problems around the home, such as deciding how I might pack the car boot, or arrange a room in the best way.

Understanding shape also seems to motivate children – they enjoy talking about the shapes, they enjoy making new shapes, they enjoy describing what they are seeing. I hope that you feel able to draw on all the practical aspects of shape in your work with your pupils. Don't forget that understanding shape is a dynamic and practical area of mathematics, and we can't learn about it without being dynamic and practical.

I also hope that you feel the language of shape has been demystified. It isn't complicated, but there is a lot of vocabulary to learn and remember. However, this is just a matter of regular use. Talk about shape with your pupils on a daily basis. Have a shape of the week and add a property a day. Play the shape-in-a-bag game whenever you have to fill five minutes at the end of a lesson and soon you will all have really well-developed vocabulary of shape.

Self-audit

Carry out this audit to explore how your learning has progressed as a result of working on the ideas in this chapter. Include the results in your portfolio.

1 Draw four sets of axes in all four quadrants with the coordinates labelled up from −5 to +5. (See page 133.)

   For each question you should draw the initial shape on the set of axes in one colour and the second shape in another colour. Then write down instructions which explain how to move from the first shape to the second shape. You should use at least two sets of instructions each time and include reflections, rotations and translations if you can.

   (a) Initial shape, right-angled triangle (−1,1), (−1,5), (−5,−1); dotted shape (1,−1), (5,−1), (1,−5).

   (b) Initial shape, rectangle (−2,3), (−2,5), (−5,5), (−5,3); dotted shape (0,−2), (0,−5), (−2,−5), (−2,−2)

   (c) Initial shape and 'L' shape (2,1), (5,1), (5,4), (4,4), (4,2), (2,2); dotted shape, rotate through 90° about (2,1) then translate 6 in the direction −x.

Now draw your own starting and finishing shape together with instructions of how to get from one shape to the other.

2 Draw four shapes. They should include at least one triangle, one quadrilateral and one pentagon. Underneath the shape write the instructions to help a friend draw the shapes. You will need to include the length of the sides and the approximate angle at each vertex.

   Underneath the shapes write down a list of each shape's properties and the shape's name.

Possible ways to classify the shapes on page 130:

   Opposite sides parallel

   Opposite sides congruent

   At least one obtuse angle

   At least one right angle

   All sides congruent

   All angles congruent

   Two consecutive sides congruent

   Parallelogram

   Quadrilateral

   Regular polygon

   Opposite angles congruent

   Pentagon

   Hexagon

   Octagon

Rhombus

Isosceles

Trapezoid

Concave polygon

Convex polygon

Going further

'Shape and space at Key Stage 2' by Jenni Back, Chris Brooksbank and Geoff Faux

This short article consists of three experienced mathematics teachers discussing how they approached a particular task involving pattern making, and the different resources they brought to the task. They all used the same task with their pupils, and they describe the learning that took place.

Back, J., Brooksbank, C. and Faux, G. (2007) 'Shape and space at Key Stage 2.' *Mathematics Teaching*, 201, 27–31. Available on the web at http://www.secondarymathsite.co.uk/Primary/Organisations/ATM/ATM5/MT201%20Back,%20Brooksbank%20&%20Faux.pdf or from the Association of Teachers of Mathmatics, Derby.

Mindstorms by Seymour Papert

This is the seminal text which brings together Papert's vision for the ways in which computers and ICT can transform the ways that children learn and how the programming language of Logo which is predominantly used to explore shape and space can be utilised to support children in developing independent thinking skills. While this is a research text there are lists of immediately applicable ideas.

Papert, S. (1993) *Mindstorms: Children, Computers and Powerful Ideas*. London: Basic Books.

CHAPTER 8
MEASURING

Introduction

All of the activities that I have introduced you to in this book are activities I have used in my own teaching. I was working with a group of 6- and 7-year-olds in a city school in Leeds using weighing scales and comparing relative mass of beans and pulses when I noticed one of the teaching assistants using her hand to measure out different amounts of pulses. I talked to her later and she explained that when she was cooking she used her hand, cupped to a greater or lesser amount, as a measure which would compare to a teaspoon, or a tablespoon, or any measure in between. I realised that this was a 'unit' of measurement that I hadn't seen used before but which many of the children I worked with would be used to. It reminded me of the importance of learning from the cultural diversity within the classrooms that I work in.

As with activities involving shape and space, activities involving measuring allow us to notice pupils excelling, who have not always succeeded immediately when working with number. I often start to see those learners who have a well-developed sense of spatial awareness coming to the fore, and that those who have experience outside the classroom of constructing, or cooking, are able to bring this prior experience to bear. Those children who sometimes struggle to remember their times-tables can easily estimate how long a shelf needs to be to fit into a space, or can quickly stack building blocks into a box. Another reminder that we should not use the term 'ability' in such an unthinking way.

Reflecting on the story with which I opened this chapter, it is worthwhile pausing for a moment to think about the measures we have a good sense of. I could probably estimate a pint and half-a-pint fairly accurately, but I still forget whether I need to order half-a-litre or a litre when I am drinking abroad, so I default to 'large' or 'small'. In my spare time I run, so I have an understanding of distances like 10 km. It is 8 miles from my house to work, a cricket pitch is 22 yards long, and so on. The starting point to this chapter reflects on which units of measurement we have a good understanding of and those which we cannot 'picture'.

Starting point

Portfolio task 8.1

Write a list of the units of measurement you have a sense of as I did above. Try to complete the list below – what do you think weighs about 1 kg, has a capacity of about a litre or measures about 1 cm?

1 mm	1 g	1 ml
1 cm	1 kg	10 ml
1 m	100 kg	500 ml
1 km		1 litre
10 km		100 litres

Which measurements did you find easy and which did you find hard? Talk to your friends about it and think about how your prior experiences have informed your knowledge of measurements.

Measuring is not just about units of measurement; other key skills are reading scales and measuring instruments, including clocks, and understanding concepts such as area and perimeter. We will explore all of these areas in detail throughout the chapter. Firstly, let us see how children's understanding of measuring is developed during their time in primary school.

Taking it further

In their book *Children Doing Mathematics* published by Blackwell in 1996, Terzinha Nunes and Peter Bryant show how children can be very successful in mathematical activities outside the classroom as they bring their intuitive understandings to bear on everyday problems. However, when they are faced with the same problems in school they often struggle as they try to apply 'school learning' to the problem rather than following their own strategies. Chapter 4 in the above book describes how children's prior experience impacts on their learning of measurement, and offers suggestions for the ways that teachers can draw on children's own understandings in the classroom. The book explores children's prior understandings of measurement in the way that Martin Hughes, whose book you have been introduced to in Chapters 5 and 6, examines young children's capacity to develop calculation skills out of the formal classroom.

The most important message from the book is that children's understanding of mathematics is not generative. That is, that children cannot generate knowledge they have not learned through engagement in teaching activities. This challenges a traditional Piagetian viewpoint. However, they also produce evidence that shows that children bring with them well-developed understandings of aspects of mathematics, and that teachers should draw on these to support children in their learning. They also suggest that children will respond to mathematical problem solving in a different way if the problem occurs outside the classroom, often employing a wide range of reasoning skills, rather than in the mathematics classroom when they may try to use rules that have previously been imposed by a teacher. This reminds us that when teaching measurement we should spend time finding out how and when our learners measure outside the classroom and use this learning as our starting point. We should also draw on as many real life, practical contexts as possible when teaching the skills of measurement.

Progression in 'Measuring'

Foundations for 'Measuring'

Initially children will begin to understand the language of measurement and comparison using vocabulary such as 'greater', 'smaller', 'heavier', 'lighter' to compare quantities. To introduce children to ideas of time you should also use vocabulary such as 'before' and 'after'. So, at this stage children should be engaging in a wide variety of practical activities which allow you to develop this vocabulary with them.

Beginning to understand 'Measuring'

At first children should carry out activities which involve measuring and weighing in order to compare objects. They will use suitable **uniform non-standard units** and then **standard units** for this comparison. (In non-standard units, uniform means that we use something that has a uniform measurement, so we can measure length using multilink cubes, or use a fixed number of wooden blocks to compare weights. Standard units are those in common usage, such as metres, litres and kilograms and all the related units.) Once children have an understanding of using non-standard units to compare they can start to use a range of measuring instruments such as metre sticks and measuring jugs. Pupils will continue to estimate, compare and measure, by now relying on standard units. They will be able to choose suitable measuring instruments to help them. At this stage you should introduce them to scales and teach them how to read the numbered divisions on a scale, such as a weighing scale or measuring jug. They will also be using a ruler, which is another scale, to draw and measure lines to the nearest centimetre.

To build children's sense of time you can introduce them to vocabulary related to time such as days of the week and months. They can also begin to to tell the time to the hour and to the half-hour. You will develop their sense of time using seconds, minutes and hours. They will then be able to tell the time to the nearest quarter of an hour and be able to identify time intervals even across an hour. So, for example, they will know that it is 15 minutes between five to six and ten past six.

Becoming confident in 'Measuring'

At this stage pupils will come to understand the relationships between the standard units – kilometres and metres, kilograms and grams, and so on. They will be able to record their measurements using appropriate units. They will develop their skills reading scales, becoming able to read them to the nearest division and half division, including reading scales that are only partially numbered. As a next step they will learn the abbreviations for standard units and will understand the meanings of 'kilo', 'centi' and 'milli'. The basic units are metre, litre and gram – these are the basic units as they do not have a prefix. The prefixes tell you what multiple of the unit you require. So 'kilo' tells you that you need 1000 of the unit; 'centi' tells you this is 1/100 of the basic unit and 'milli', 1/1000. This leads on to decimal notation, so your learners will understand that 1.5 metres is the same as 1m 50cm. They will be reading scales and recording readings to the nearest tenth of a unit.

They will be reading the time on 12-hour digital clocks and to the nearest 5 minutes on an analogue clock, as well as measuring time intervals so they can work out beginning and end times for given time intervals. For example, they will know that if a TV programme lasts 30 minutes and starts at 9.40 it will end at 10.10. Once they have an understanding of this pupils will move on to be able to read timetables and time using the 24-hour clock and use a calendar to work out time intervals.

You will also introduce measurements linked to rectangles, including measuring the **perimeter** and finding the **area** of **rectilinear shapes** by counting squares in a grid. The perimeter of a shape is the distance all the way around its outside edge – this is measured in mm, cm or km. The area of a shape is the amount of space it takes up – this is measured in square mm, square cm or square km, written mm^2, cm^2 or km^2. A rectilinear shape is one that can be split up into a series of rectangles.

Developing these ideas pupils will be able to convert larger to smaller units using one place of decimals. For example, they will be able to change 7.3 kg to 7300 g. They will be able to interpret readings that lie between two divisions on a scale and draw and measure lines to the nearest millimetre.

They will also be calculating the perimeter of regular and irregular **polygons** and using the formula for the area of a rectangle to calculate area. A polygon is any shape with straight edges – a regular polygon must have all sides the same length and all the angles between the sides the same, otherwise the polygon is irregular. The formula to find the area of a rectangle is length multiplied by width.

Extending understanding of measuring

At this stage pupils will be operating up to two places of decimals – for example, changing 4.82 m to 482 cm. They will be able to read a wide variety of scales and will understand that the measurements made on scales are only approximate to a given degree of accuracy.

They will be able to calculate perimeters and areas of rectilinear shapes and estimate areas of irregular shapes by counting squares.

Developing these skills pupils will operate up to three decimal places knowing that 2541 ml is the same as 2.541 litres. They will apply their knowledge of measuring to solve a range of problems, and will also be able to calculate using imperial units (such as pints and ounces) still in everyday use, having an understanding of their approximate metric values.

Pupils will also be able to calculate the area of a **right-angled triangle** given the length of two **perpendicular** sides and be able to calculate the volume and **surface area** of a **cube** and **cuboid**. A right-angled triangle is a triangle in which two of the sides join at a right angle. The two perpendicular sides are the two sides that join at right angles – perpendicular means 'joined at right angles'. The surface area of a 3D shape is the total area of all the faces of the shape. A cube is a 3D shape. All its faces are squares. A cuboid is a 3D shape with all its faces rectangles.

This section illustrates how, from the building blocks of the foundation stage where children are developing the language of comparison, they progress to the stage where they are accurately estimating, measuring and comparing up to two decimal places; reading any scale accurately; telling the time; and calculating area and perimeter of rectilinear shapes. The next section outlines the big ideas and key skills which underpin 'Measuring'.

Big ideas

Conservation and comparison

We measure in order to compare objects. We need to see if something is the right length to fit in a particular space, or if it will hold objects of a certain length. One of the earliest principles children come to understand is that the measurements of a particular object stay the same wherever we place it. Young children may describe something as longer than something else if they are not aligned.

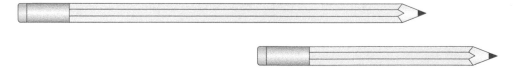

In this case they may say that the shorter pencil is 'bigger' or 'longer' than the other. Young children need to use non-standard units such as pencils, wooden rods and cubes to come to an understanding that measurement is conserved, or stays the same, before they move on to using standard units. These difficulties with ideas of conservation are discussed in more detail later.

Units of measure

Units of measurement have been agreed by mathematicians and scientists in order to make measurement consistent throughout the world. In the UK imperial and metric units are used, but metric units, first introduced in eighteenth-century France, are the system taught in schools. Metric units are in common usage as they are based on powers of 10 and so are easier to work with.

Imperial units are as follows:

- **Length**: 12 inches in 1 foot; 3 feet in 1 yard; 1760 yards in 1 mile.
- **Area**: 144 square inches in 1 square foot; 9 square feet in 1 square yard; 640 acres in 1 square mile (an acre is about 4840 square yards).
- **Volume**: 1728 cubic inches in 1 cubic foot; 27 cubic feet in 1 cubic yard.
- **Capacity**: 5 fluid ounces in 1 gill; 4 gills in 1 pint; 8 pints in 1 gallon.
- **Mass**: 16 ounces in 1 pound, 14 pounds in 1 stone; 8 stone in 1 hundredweight (cwt); 20 cwt in 1 ton.

Looking at this list you can probably see why the decision was made to focus on metric units! Metric units are sometimes referred to as SI units (Système International d'Unités). The table below shows the SI units together with the conversions to imperial units.

Attribute	SI unit	Abbreviation	Imperial units	Abbreviation	Conversion
Length	Metre	m	Inches, feet, yards, miles	in ft yd	1 in = 2.54 cm 1 ft = 0.30 m
Mass	Kilogram	kg	Ounces, pounds, stones	oz lb st	1 oz = 28.35 g 1 lb = 0.45 kg
Time	Second	s			
Area	Square metre	m^2	Square inches, acres	sq in	
Volume	Cubic metre	m^3	Cubic inches, cubic feet	cu in cu ft	
Capacity	Litre	l	Pints, gallons	pt gal	1 pt = 0.56 l

As you read in the opening section to the chapter, metric units are easy to use as the prefixes (kilo, milli, centi) tell you the conversion between the units.

Scales

All measurement is against a scale based on the unit we are using for comparison. Measurement is against a continuous scale: that is, we are always measuring approximately. If we say a line is 3.2 cm long, what we are actually saying is that it is 3.2 cm long to the nearest tenth of a centimetre. It may be 3.21 cm or 3.19 cm but we have decided that saying 3.2 cm is accurate enough. Reading scales is one of the key skills to teach children – it is also useful to teach them how to create their own scales to measure. This helps them see the importance of standardisation and also the approximate nature of measurement.

Teaching points

Teaching point 1: Conservation of mass and capacity

In the 'Big ideas' section earlier in the chapter I suggested that young children do not always remember that you need to place the ends of two objects together to compare length. Similarly, if you move an object so that it is in a different orientation, the children may need some convincing that the length of the pencil has remained the same (or has been 'conserved').

Before we explore children's understanding of conservation of mass it is worth defining **mass**. In everyday usage, mass is more commonly referred to as weight, although the precise scientific definition is the strength of the gravitational pull on the object: that is, how heavy it is. The distinction between mass and weight is important for extremely precise measurements which may be affected by slight differences in the strength of the Earth's gravitational field at different places, and for places far from the surface of the Earth, such as in space or on other planets. This means that you can convert exactly between weight and mass on the Earth's surface. This confusion between mass and weight is heightened by the fact that in much of the metric world, weight is not dealt with, and mass is used in its place almost exclusively. The main difference is that if you were to leave the Earth and go to the Moon, your weight would change but your mass would remain constant.

Conservation of mass is an even more difficult concept for young children. An activity I use which begins to get children thinking about this is to put four or five boxes of different shapes and sizes on a table and ask the group to place them in order of mass. I will have deliberately placed the heaviest object in the smallest box. Once we have ordered the boxes I will get the group to compare the masses of the boxes by lifting them up. They are often amazed that the smallest box is the heaviest as they have the misconception that the mass of an object is directly linked to its volume.

Another activity which deals directly with this misconception is to take a large spherical piece of Plasticine or Play-Doh and place it in a balance so that it exactly balances with a counterweight. Then move the Plasticine from the scale and roll it flat. Ask the group if they think it will be lighter, heavier or the same. Children will often think that it will now be lighter, as it is 'thinner'. They will be surprised that this is not the case.

Another example of this is to place three or more containers in front of the children. The container should range from very wide-based containers to long thin ones. Pour the same amount of liquid into each container. The liquid will not come very high up the wide-based container but the same volume may fill the container with the smaller base.

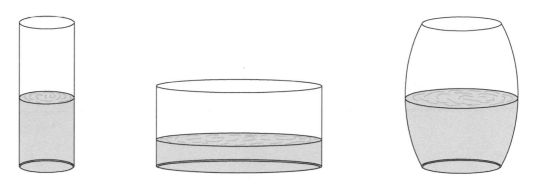

Lots of practical experience of weighing a wide range of objects, and measuring capacity, is the most effective way to deal with this misconception.

Teaching point 2: Conservation of area

I was working with a small group of children finding the areas of rectangles by counting squares. After we had agreed that the area of this shape was 18 cm²

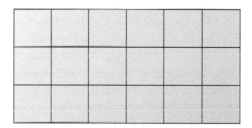

I asked the group to make new shapes by cutting across diagonals of the squares. We created three new shapes, all including triangles:

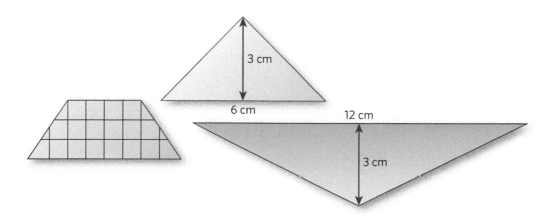

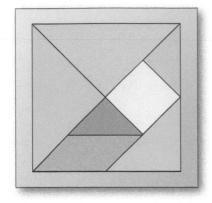

A tangram.

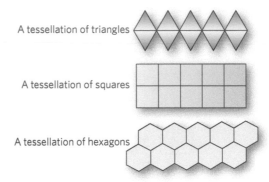

A tessellation of triangles

A tessellation of squares

A tessellation of hexagons

A tessellation is created when a shape is repeated over and over again, covering a plane without any gaps or overlaps. It is sometimes referred to as 'tiling'.

I then asked the group what they thought the areas of these shapes would be. None of them believed that the area would still be 18 cm². In fact Helen had to count each one three times to convince herself. She said, 'That can't be right. Look, this one is much more spread out and so it should have a bigger area.' In Helen's view the fact that one of the shapes was longer suggested that it should have a greater area.

A good way to develop children's understanding of conservation of area is to use tangrams or other tessellating activities to create a wide range of shapes with the same area. A tangram is a Chinese puzzle consisting of a square which is cut up into seven pieces. These pieces can be used to make many different shapes. As these are all made from the same pieces they will all have the same area.

In the activity described in the following Resource inspiration box children are asked to rearrange 4 cm squares to make different shapes. Although the shapes look very different, they all have the same area as they are all made up from the same 4 cm squares. The link is made to perimeter as a way of supporting children in coming to an understanding that shapes with the same area can have different perimeters. This also consolidates the children's understanding of perimeter. A similar activity for more experienced learners can be set as the following open-ended investigation.

> Explorers in a gold field are each given 100 m of rope and four stakes. Each explorer uses the four stakes and the rope to section off the piece of land they will dig in order to find gold. What are the dimensions of the shape they should make to enclose the largest area they can?

You may like to try this activity for yourself.

Teaching point 3: Using appropriate units

The activity that opened the chapter was designed to start you thinking about appropriate units. It can be very confusing that length can be measured in millimetres, centimetres, metres and kilometres. Then when we measure area we can use the equivalent measures,

Resource inspiration

Area and perimeter

If two centimetre squares are put together, there is only one way to link them:

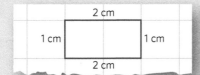

The perimeter is (2 × 2 cm) + (2 × 1 cm) = 6 cm

If you put four squares together, you can make these shapes:

A

B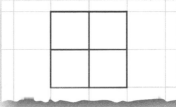

C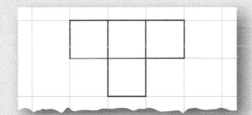

D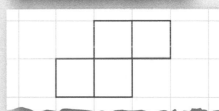

❶ Find the perimeter of each of these shapes.

❷ There is one more four-square shape you can make. Make this shape and record its perimeter.

❸ Which four-square shape has the shortest perimeter?

❹ Use six squares. How many different perimeters can you find?

❺ Repeat with eight squares, then try ten and twelve squares. Find all the possible perimeters for each number of squares.

❻ Look for rules or patterns to predict which shape gives the longest perimeter and which shape gives the shortest.

although we tend mainly to use square centimetres and square metres. The best way to support children getting used to appropriate units is to use contexts which they are familiar with and ask for appropriate units rather than asking them to carry out the measuring activity. In this way they can focus on the units, rather than the act of measuring.

Teaching point 4: Relationships between dimensions and length, area and volume

Your pupils may simply try to remember a process when you ask them to solve problems to do with perimeter and area and volume rather than think through what the problem is asking them to do. I can think of occasions when learners have asked me whether perimeter is 'that one where you add everything together', or simply multiplying any numbers that they can see on a diagram when asked to find an area, as they remember that you 'multiply to find area'.

Try this activity with the class you are teaching as a way of supporting them in coming to a deeper understanding of the relationship between perimeter, area and volume. In this way the language of area, perimeter and volume will make more sense to them as well as the relationships between these three ways of describing measures.

Portfolio task 8.2

Decide which of these statements are true and which are false:

- If you double the dimensions of a rectangle you double its perimeter.
- If you double the dimensions of a rectangle you double its area.
- If you double the lengths of the sides of a rectangle, but leave the width the same, you double the area.
- If you double the dimensions of a cuboid you double its volume.

For the false statements write down an equivalent statement which is true. Try to describe why this is true.

Teaching point 5: Misreading scales

Children can make a range of errors reading scales. Firstly you will have noticed children not always measuring accurately because they don't line up their ruler correctly. They may start from the edge of the ruler rather than the zero point (this is not always at the end of a ruler), or sometimes you may notice children starting at the 1 cm point and so they will add 1 cm to the true measurement.

An activity which can help children correct this for themselves is to have a series of lines down one side of a page and a series of measurements down the other side. Children have to measure the lines and match them to the appropriate measurement. Avoid using the answer which an error of measuring starting at the 1 cm mark would give the pupil. Any child who is habitually making this error will then have to self-correct in order to 'match' the correct answer.

Children also sometimes forget to make sure that a measuring cylinder is placed on a flat surface when they are reading the scale. They move the cylinder to their eyes rather than their eyes to the cylinder. You need to check that children are placing their eyes level with the liquid so that they read the scale accurately. You can illustrate this to the children by tipping a cylinder and showing them how 'inaccurate' the reading can be.

Teaching point 6: Misreading clocks

The best way to support children in learning to tell the time is to have both analogue and digital clocks in the classroom, and to refer to them as often as possible. Children rarely see analogue clocks – they will have a digital reading on their mobile phone, or on a TV at home, so you may need to model using an analogue clock frequently.

Taking it further

In *Mathematics Teaching* 209, July 2008, Rona Catterall describes the way she introduced 'telling time' to her class of 6-7-year-olds. This is a detailed article about the methods Rona used after she became frustrated with her children struggling with the skills of telling the time and is available online at **http://www.atm.org.uk/ mt/archive/mt209.html**.

One example she uses is how you can use a child's understanding of their age to help with telling the time. She reminds us that a child sees their age to be of great importance. So she asks one of her class how old they are. 'I'm 6,' they reply. The teacher asks if they can say they are 7? 'No,' says the pupil, 'I'm not 7 until my next birthday.' 'It's just the same with this clock,' says the teacher, with the time set at half-past six, 'we can't say it's seven o'clock until the hand has gone all the way round.'

I introduced a class of mine to an analogue clock a few years ago and they laughed almost as if I had brought in an ancient timepiece. I set the clock at half-past twelve (12:30) as this was lunchtime and asked the group what time was shown by the clock. The range of answers included:

- 6 past 12
- 6 to 12
- 12 and a half.

All of these were sensible ways of interpreting a new scale. When we are introduced to a new scale out of context we decode it the best we can. I decided the best thing I could do was to discover all the possible errors with the children and so I set them the task below.

Portfolio task 8.3

This clock is showing 3:45. Write down all the ways you could say this time.
These are some of the answers that my class gave – explain the errors the children are making:

- 45 minutes to 4
- 9 minutes to 4
- 9 minutes past 3
- 18 minutes past 9

One of the changes I have noticed over the last few years is that the number of different ways of describing the time has reduced. As people become more used to reading digital clocks and move away from analogue clocks the descriptions of time are always accurate to the nearest minute. So if I ask a pupil in my class what the time is they will tell me, 'It's eleven forty-seven' rather than 'just after quarter to twelve'. This is an interesting illustration of how technology imposes itself on our day-to-day mathematical practices.

In practice

The following lesson plan and evaluation describe a lesson taught to a group of pupils who had been working on measuring using uniform standard units. As they have developed an understanding of the relationship between centimetres and metres the particular focus was developing their understanding of the relationship between grams and kilograms. This will help them to make connections between the units of measurement of length and of mass. I particularly wanted to focus on the fact that there are 100 cm in a metre but 1000 grams in a kilogram. This will allow me to introduce the meanings of the prefixes 'kilo' and 'centi'. I am making sure that the children work practically so that they come to have an understanding of 'how much' 1 kg, 500 g and 10 g is. The program 'Scales' was used to explore the children's knowledge of properties of the shapes. This program is available on the companion website to this book.

Topic: Understanding the relationship between grams and kilograms

Age group: Lower primary

Objectives

Know the relationship between kilograms and grams

Choose and use appropriate units to estimate, measure and record measurements

Key vocabulary	Context
Gram, kilogram, weight, heaviest, lightest	This is the fourth lesson of the week and so far we have used hand spans to measure lengths and widths and then measured hand spans to the nearest 1/5 cm to calculate lengths. We have estimated lengths to the nearest centimetre and then moved on to using metre sticks. This should support the children in making connections between kilograms and grams in this lesson

Resources	Starter activity
Mini-whiteboards and pens; 1 kg, 500 g, 100 g, 50 g and 10 g weights; pan balances; collection of items to weigh; three large sheets of paper	I'll ask the children to sit in their 'talk partner' pairs. The pairs have 2 minutes to write down as many different units of measurement as they can think of. After 2 minutes I will go round the pairs getting one unit from each pair to record on the board until we have collected everyone's answers. I'll draw a table on the board – length, capacity, mass and time. Individuals then pick a unit and tell me which column to put it in

Main activity	Teacher	Pupil activity
Whole group activity	I will ask the children to move to their numeracy tables, which I have set out with the balances and a range of everyday items to weigh. Groups should estimate which item on their table is the heaviest and bring it to the scales at the front to weigh. I will ask the class if they think it will weigh more or less than 1 kg. I will also ask if they think it is heavier/lighter than the previous item and model how to write down the weight	Pupils pick up the objects to estimate the weight in terms of heaviness/lightness They will draw on their previous knowledge as more items are weighed. They will observe the way I am using the different weights to balance and then the method I am using to record the weights
Group activity Children operating above expected levels	I will ask members of the group to estimate the weight of the objects before they weigh them, encouraging them to draw on their previous measurements to come up with sensible estimates	This group will weigh all their objects and record the weights. They will then arrange them in order of weight and complete a table allowing them to record the measurements formally

Main activity	Teacher	Pupil activity
Children operating at expected levels	This group will work with the 1 kg, 500 g and 100 g weights only. They will weigh the objects and complete the following chart: Objects less than 100 g Objects between 100 and 500 g Objects between 500 g and 1 kg Objects heavier than 1 kg	I will focus my attention on this group and encourage them to estimate the answers first before measuring. If necessary I will fetch extra weights and move on to measuring more accurately
Children operating below expected levels	This group will work with the 1 kg, 500 g and 10 g weights. I will give them three large sheets of paper labelled 1 kg, 500 g, 10 g. Pairs of children from the group will find objects that weigh approximately 1 kg, 500 g and 10 g and place them on the appropriate piece of paper	The TA will work with this group and if necessary the children can leave the room to find a wider range of objects

Plenary

I will use the 'Scales' program on the IWB. I will use the 'compare' setting to place two objects on the scales – I will ask children to estimate the weights each time and then in pairs to calculate the difference in weight using the number line for support

Rationale and evaluation

The starter activity was very effective. Talk pairs are always a good way to get responses and I could see pairs noticing each other's units and 'copying' and building on each other's ideas, which I encouraged. I made the point that it is very useful to use each other's ideas to develop our own thinking and I tried to discourage pairs from hiding their boards to keep their answers 'secret'. The classification activity was also useful – I moved this on so that we looked at the units within each classification and talked about what we might measure with each unit. This did mean that I spent much longer on the starter than I meant to, but I decided that, as understanding the relationships between units was a key idea, it was a good decision.

As I had extended the starter I decided to move straight into the group activities, otherwise I felt the children would not have sufficient time using the scales, which was important. I was able to move quickly between the tables to set up the activities and quickly realised that there was sufficient expertise within my higher attaining groups to carry out the activity. This suggests that the activity wasn't challenging enough for them, although they were well motivated and engaged with the activity. I extended this activity by asking the group to record the measurements in two ways – 1 kg, 300 g or 1300 g. This did challenge them, although Megan also suggested 1.300 as a measure which impressed me. I asked them to focus on using kg and g as I think the idea of 1.300 being equivalent to 1.3 would have led to some misunderstandings.

The groups who were estimating gradually became more effective in their estimation. Initially it appeared as though they were making 'random' guesses, but with support from me and the TA they were able to draw on their prior experience and by the end of the session had a sense of more and less than 1 kg, as well as being able to compare weights.

Because of this I changed my planned plenary and used the introductory activity I had planned as a plenary. Each group used a different set of objects and this helped me both consolidate the learning of the children and assess their development during the lesson.

Portfolio task 8.4

Devise a lesson plan which is appropriate for a group of learners you are working with. The focus should be an aspect of 'Measuring' that is appropriate to the age group you are working with.

Make sure you think carefully about the context and evaluate the lesson. Incorporate either the 'Scales' program or another interactive program which models a scale for weighing within your planning.

Add this lesson plan and evaluation to your subject knowledge portfolio.

Observing teaching 'Measuring'

On the companion website you will find a video which shows a teacher introducing an activity which involves her pupils in measuring 500 millilitres of fluid. She sets an imaginary context for this by dressing up as a 'witch' who requires the potion. Watch the clip from the beginning and think through other contexts you could use to motivate the pupils. Could you enter into the role more convincingly? In this role play the teacher does not play a role – she is really just the teacher dressing up.

Observe the different ways in which the children record their five measures that will total 500 millilitres. How could you encourage them to think of as many different ways as possible?

How might you adapt this lesson for use with the pupils you are currently teaching?

Assessing understanding of 'Measuring'

The most effective way of assessing your pupils' measurement skills is to observe them engaging in activities which involve measuring. For early learners this will involve you asking questions about how many small containers your pupils might think will pour into larger ones, or how many hand spans will measure a table, or how many strides there will be across a classroom. For older learners this can take the form of using containers with a given capacity and estimating the capacity of larger containers using this knowledge. As learners become more skilled at measuring using scales you can ask them to create a measuring jug, including calibrating a scale on the jug. You might perhaps ask them to create a 1-litre measuring jug with 50-millilitre divisions, given a 100-millilitre measure.

You can assess pupils' early understanding of time by asking them to order events during a typical day and assign a time to them to the nearest hour. This can become increasingly sophisticated in terms of the accuracy of the time. If you draw on the pupils' own experience this is even better. Later you can use timetables to ask pupils to plan appropriate journeys given set criteria.

Cross-curricular project

As I suggested above, a useful way to both develop and reinforce the skills of measurement through cross-curricular projects is by asking children to make containers of appropriate sizes. The two ideas below should motivate both your younger learners and those in Key Stage 2.

Younger learners

Bring three teddy bears into the class. One should be very small, one 'medium' sized and one larger. If you want, you could link this to the 'Three Bears' story. Each group needs to make different objects for the three animals. For example, you might ask one group to make a chair, one a plate and bowl, and even an appropriate shelter. This will involve them in comparing measurements and using the language of comparison.

Older learners

Bring in a range of cereal boxes. The pupils should find ways of measuring the capacity of the box, and their task is to design a box which is a different shape but which will hold the same amount. Ask them to design the **net** for the box, including logos, as this means they have to think through how the net fits together to form the final box. An alternative to this is to ask the groups to design and create carrier bags for particular objects.

Summary

The emphasis within this chapter is on the practical nature of measuring and the importance of drawing on learners' intuitive understandings and knowledge of measurement in order to develop their skills. The progression section illustrates the importance of developing a language of 'measurement' in young children and engaging them actively in carrying out measurement as the only way to learn about 'measurement'. The key ideas which the chapter then builds on are ideas of conservation and comparison – everyday skills we will use all the time but may not have put a name to before. The teaching points emphasise the fact that we can and need to teach these skills to our learners – they aren't simply common sense. Other big ideas such as the units we use to measure and compare objects, and the scales we use to support measurement, are also described.

Reflections on this chapter

The important thing to take away from this chapter is the small number of skills we are trying to teach our pupils in order to help them become effective in measurement. The basic foci are 'units' and 'scales'. Pupils need to have a sense of what a measurement means – if your pupils leave primary school with an understanding of what a litre looks like, how far 500 m is, what 50 g feels like, and so on, they will be able to estimate measures effectively. And if you have taught them how to read and create a range of scales, they will be able to transfer this skill into many other areas of mathematics.

Self-audit

These activities focus on estimation of distance, mass and capacity. Through working on the ideas you should develop your understanding of these concepts and be better able to support those you teach.

1   Complete this table. The first column is a measurement; in the second column write down an object that is approximately that length and in the final column rewrite the measurement in either cm or m, whichever is most appropriate.

Length		
1 mm		
10 mm		
100 mm		
1000 mm		
10,000 mm		
100,000 mm		

2   Repeat this activity for weight, using g or kg.

Weight		
1 g		
10 g		
100 g		
1000 g		
10,000 g		
100,000 g		

3 And capacity, using ml or l.

Capacity		
1 ml		
10 ml		
100 ml		
1000 ml		
10,000 ml		
100,000 ml		

If you did not attempt the 'Portfolio task' activities in teaching points 4 and 5, complete them at this point. This will allow you to assess your understanding of the relationship between area and perimeter.

Going further

'Progression in measuring' by Margaret Brown and her colleagues

This article reports on a research project which explores the extent to which learners' progression in learning 'measurement' can be described. As you might expect there are idiosyncratic patterns to individuals' progression in their learning. However, the team are able to outline a general framework to describe progression in this area. It is interesting to compare this with any progression described in other curriculum documents.

Brown, M., Blondel, E., Simon, S. and Black, P. (1995) 'Progression in measuring'. *Research Papers in Education*, 10 (2), 143–170.

Primary Teachers' Perceptions of Their Knowledge and Understanding of Measurement by **Michelle O'Keefe and Janette Bobis**

This is a paper presented to the Mathematics Education Research Group of Australia. This study focused on primary teachers' perceptions of their knowledge and understandings of length, area and volume. It also explored their understanding of how children's growth of measurement concepts and processes develops. Data gained from in-depth interviews revealed that teachers' knowledge was often implicit and that they struggled to articulate their knowledge of measurement concepts and children's trajectories of learning.

O' Keefe, M. and Bobis, J. (2008) *Primary Teachers' Perceptions of Their Knowledge and Understanding of Measurement*, available at http://www.merga.net.au/documents/RP462008 .pdf, accessed 18 July 2012.

CHAPTER 9
HANDLING DATA

Introduction

Several years ago I carried out some work in a Year 5 class in Leicester. The class I was working with included children from a wide variety of backgrounds. I was interested in the group posing their own problems and using their own mathematical skills to come up with solutions. One group suggested carrying out a survey into attitudes towards racism.

They designed a questionnaire, decided who they would use this questionnaire with and then analysed the responses and reported back to the class. Their reports used bar charts, line graphs and pie charts with each group describing why they had chosen particular representations to illustrate their data. Some of their results are given below:

- How would you feel if someone made fun of your skin colour?

I would hit them	16%
I would be sad	34%
I would be angry	38%
I would think they were ignorant	12%

- What would you do if no one would let you play because you looked different to them?

I would ask them why	42%
I would let a teacher know	58%

- Two people wrote 'I would be sad and play with someone else' and another wrote 'I would wish I could change my skin colour.'

- If you were on a bus and you had a spare place next to you how would you feel if there were lots of people standing and no one would sit next to you?

  I would think they didn't like me because I am different   64%

  I would ignore it and be happy because I wasn't squashed   36%

This approach to handling data made direct links to the children's lived experience; it also allowed the teacher to bring mathematics directly into the Personal, Social and Health Education (PSHE) curriculum which focused on these issues for the next three weeks. It opened the teacher's eyes to issues they hadn't been aware of – the day-to-day impact of prejudice on their learners when they travel on public transport, and the damage to self-esteem suffered when children are made to feel that 'they want to change their skin colour'.

I would suggest that the children came to understand the mathematics of data handling more deeply from this project than they would have done from surveying shoe sizes. It was a question that they were committed to, and they had to decide how to 'tell the story' accurately with the data so that people could understand the issue.

Starting point

Portfolio task 9.1

Look at this column graph:

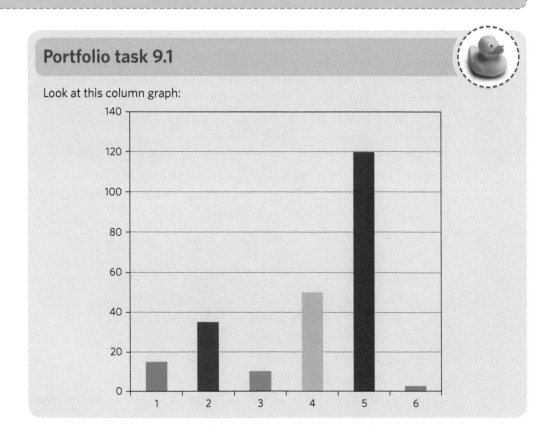

Write down three different sets of data that the graph could be illustrating. You can define for yourself what the numbers 1–6 along the *x* axis (the bottom) stand for. If you work with friends on this describe how you decided on your answers.

This may seem like starting at the end but the key reason for 'Handling data' is to be able to come to decisions about what the data represents. Often learners do not know how to interpret data; they learn how to collect and organise the data but do not realise that there may well be alternative interpretations that could be drawn from the data. It is important that our pupils see the big picture from the beginning and understand that interpretation is just as important as collection and representation of data.

The data-handling cycle is shown below:

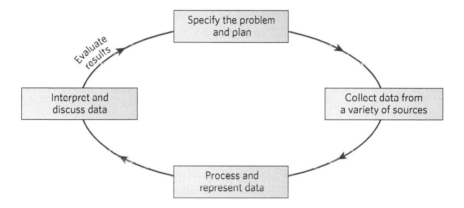

This diagram emphasises the importance of both problem posing and interpretation, and is the key 'Big idea' for this chapter. So skills in these areas are just as important as understanding how to collect data and the different ways you can represent it.

Progression in 'Handling data'

This section illustrates the progression for teaching 'Handling data'. The terms in bold are defined and explained for you in the 'Big ideas' section.

Foundations for 'Handling data'

At the early stages you will work with your learners, sorting familiar objects to identify their similarities and differences and counting how many objects share a particular property. You will support the children in presenting their results using pictures, drawings or numerals.

Beginning in 'Handling data'

At this stage children will be able to research a question by recording information in lists and tables and present outcomes to data-handling activities using practical resources, pictures, **block graphs** or **pictograms**. They will also use diagrams to sort objects into groups according to a given criterion and suggest a different criterion for grouping the same objects. Later they will start to collect and record data which they will represent as block graphs or pictograms to show the results. They will begin to use ICT to organise and present data and will use lists, tables and diagrams to sort objects. They will be able to explain the choices they are making.

Becoming confident in 'Handling data'

These children will use a wider range of diagrams to record data including **tally charts**, **frequency tables**, pictograms and **bar charts** to represent results and illustrate observations. They will use ICT to create a simple bar chart and use **Venn diagrams** or **Carroll diagrams** to sort data and objects using more than one criterion. They will be able to answer a question by identifying what data to collect and how best to organise, present, analyse and interpret the data using tables, diagrams, tally charts, pictograms and bar charts, and using ICT where appropriate. They will also be able to compare the impact of representations using different scales.

Pupils will progress to be able to interpret data through constructing frequency tables, pictograms and bar and **line graphs** to show the frequency of events and changes over time. At this stage they will also understand how we use the **mean**, **median** and mode of a set of data.

Pupils should be introduced to the language of **probability** and the occurrence of familiar events using the language of chance or likelihood. The pupils should understand and use the **probability scale** from 0 to 1 and find and justify probabilities based on equally likely outcomes in simple contexts.

Extending learning in 'Handling data'

At this stage you can teach your pupils how to describe and predict **outcomes** and to solve problems by collecting, selecting, processing, presenting and interpreting data, drawing conclusions in order to identify further questions to ask. They could construct and interpret frequency tables, bar charts with grouped **discrete data**, line graphs and pie charts. They will explore hypotheses by planning surveys or experiments to collect small sets of **discrete** or **continuous data**, selecting, processing, presenting and interpreting the data in order to identify ways to extend the survey or experiment.

My aim is that this section illustrates to you the progression in the ideas that help us collect and interpret data. In the early years children are sorting objects and talking about the decisions being made in order to sort according to particular criteria. Then, as pupils progress, they are introduced to an increasing range of charts and diagrams that can be used to represent data until they are able to write a short report detailing the results of a survey they have carried out and justifying their choices of methods and representation.

Big ideas

The data-handling cycle introduced earlier is the 'Big idea' when working with children on developing their understanding of this strand. Collecting, organising and interpreting data are at the heart of the mathematical ideas here. Another important way to understand and interpret data is through the key ideas underpinning probability and chance so these concepts are explored in this section.

Collecting data

Before we begin to collect data we need a question we are trying to answer. It is important that learners are exploring data to answer questions that they want to know the answer to – and that they are supported to explore new questions that are raised by the data they have collected.

A question that has interested groups of children I have worked with is: 'What is the ratio of your height to the circumference of your head?' We begin by estimating answers, usually guesses from '4 times' upwards. We then start measuring and plot the measurements on a scatter diagram. This means using one axis for 'height' and one axis for 'distance round head'. Each child finds the point on the chart where they would place their data, marks a cross and initials it. By plotting boys and girls in different colours, and pupils and adults in different colours, the children notice that although the ratio is about 3:1 it may be slightly different for boys and girls, and for adults and children. One group decided that they would go into a foundation class and see if the ratio was different for very young children. Even though scatter graphs may not traditionally be introduced until secondary school, the children were fascinated to see this way of illustrating data.

Organising data

One of the important skills in handling data is deciding the most appropriate way to organise the data once it has been collected. This depends on the sort of data you are collecting and the questions you want to answer.

Discrete and continuous data

Discrete data can be counted – examples would be the ways that children travel to school (five pupils travel by bus) or children's birthdays (three children have birthdays in May). Continuous data are measured – examples would be heights, weights and time. Continuous data has to be grouped in order to represent and interpret it. So, for example, if the children wanted to find out how fit their class was compared to other classes, they could devise an activity timing how long it takes individuals to run 25 m. In order to represent the data the times would have to be grouped – perhaps into two-second intervals. The children would need to decide the most appropriate interval after collecting the data. It is worth organising the data using a range of intervals – the children can then decide which is the most useful.

Pictograms, bar charts, line graphs and pie charts

Initially you will encourage young children to create pictograms through a practical activity. For example, the children could explore a shop in the role play area and draw pictures to record their favourite purchases. Using questions such as 'What can you tell about what people in your class like to buy?' would encourage more in-depth interpretation of the data. You could also introduce different roles into the role play – the children could be teachers out shopping, or people who work on a building site. They could create different pictograms for these different groups of people.

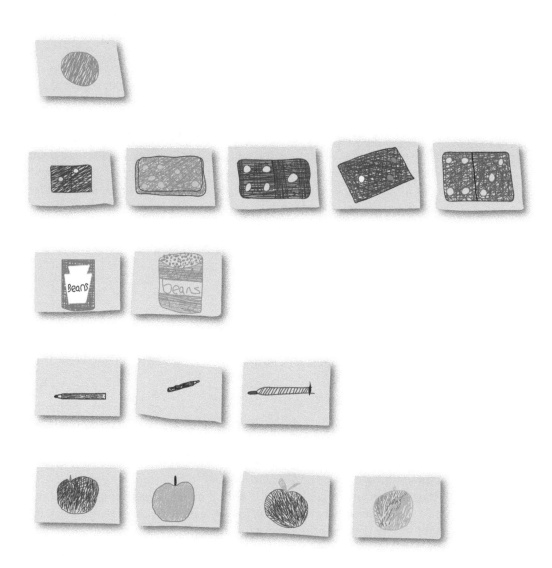

Resource inspiration

Bar and line charts

In this activity you can see in the bar chart and line chart below, two representations of data on the same page that encourage the children to explore which representation they think

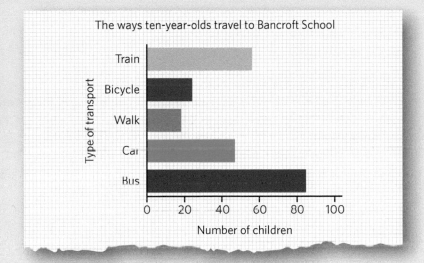

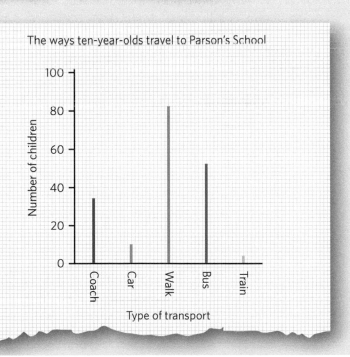

shows the data most usefully. Your role when working with data represented in this way is to use the page for discussion. Ask questions such as:

✱ Which representation is most useful?

✱ What does the data show – about the children?

✱ Where do you think this school is?

As a follow up to this activity, which focuses on interpreting data, you could collect similar data from your class, or from the school, and then compare the data for your class with the data for 'Bancroft School' and 'Parson's School'.

Line graphs are used to look at trends over time. You will often see these types of graphs on the news. You can collect and interpret data using line graphs to answer questions like, 'Is it too hot/cold in our classroom?' 'Does the classroom take a long time to warm up in the morning?' 'What happens on particularly sunny or very cold days?' This data can be graphed on the same set of axes to allow for comparisons. The figure below shows the type of axes you would use to record temperature change in the classroom.

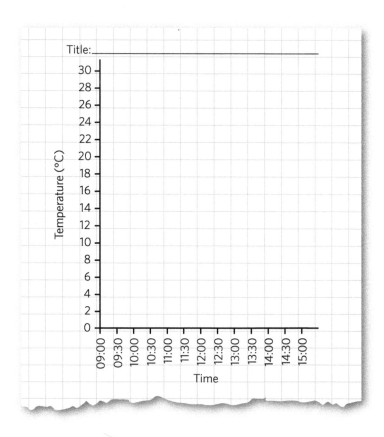

Children are also expected to be able to interpret pie charts. Pie charts show the proportions of data. Work on this in the task box below and add it to your portfolio.

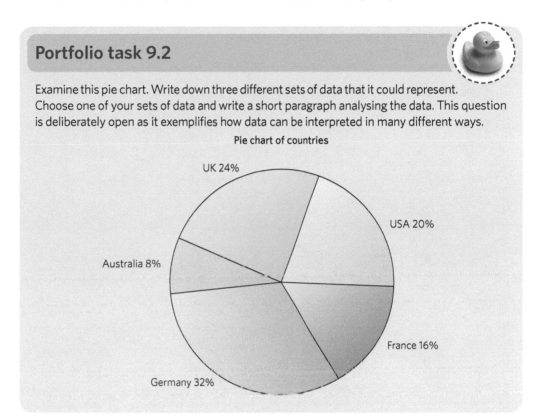

Portfolio task 9.2

Examine this pie chart. Write down three different sets of data that it could represent. Choose one of your sets of data and write a short paragraph analysing the data. This question is deliberately open as it exemplifies how data can be interpreted in many different ways.

Pie chart of countries

UK 24%
USA 20%
France 16%
Germany 32%
Australia 8%

Venn and Carroll diagrams

Venn diagrams and Carroll diagrams are used to sort objects. Carroll diagrams are actually named after the author Lewis Carroll, who wrote *Alice in Wonderland* and was fascinated by mathematics. People have explored *Alice in Wonderland* for the mathematics it contains, and Lewis Carroll also wrote academic books on geometry. Venn diagrams were introduced by a mathematician called John Venn in 1880.

The task below illustrates the different uses of Carroll and Venn diagrams. In fact you have already used Carroll diagrams for sorting in Chapter 7.

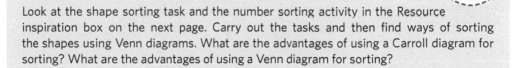

Portfolio task 9.3

Look at the shape sorting task and the number sorting activity in the Resource inspiration box on the next page. Carry out the tasks and then find ways of sorting the shapes using Venn diagrams. What are the advantages of using a Carroll diagram for sorting? What are the advantages of using a Venn diagram for sorting?

Resource inspiration

1 Carroll diagram

Sort the shapes and write the letters in a Carroll diagram like the one below.

(a)

(b)

(c)

(d)

(e)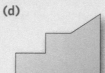

(f)

(g)

(h)

(i)

(j)

(k)

(l)

(m)

(n)

(o)

(p)

(q)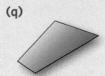

(r)

(s)

(t)

	Symmetrical	Not symmetrical
More than four sides		
Four sides or fewer		

2 Venn diagram

Write the multiples of 6 and 7 on this Venn diagram. The intersection should show the numbers which are in both the 6 and 7 times-tables.

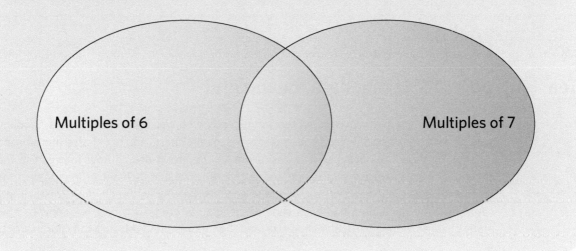

Chance and probability

Children have intuitive ideas about probability through the language that they use. Look at the phrases below and complete each sentence:

- It is very likely that …
- Once in a blue moon …
- There's a 50/50 chance that …
- It's unlikely that …
- It's certain that …
- It's impossible for …

Now organise these phrases on a line so that the least likely to happen is at the left-hand end and the most likely at the right-hand end. You have just created a probability scale. All probability is measured on a scale of 0 to 1, with 0 being impossible and 1 being certain; percentages are sometimes used, with 100% being certain. There are three ways that we can assess the probability of an event happening. Firstly we draw on prior scientific knowledge – an example of this would be predicting a 70% probability of rain given current weather patterns. Another way of assessing probability is to carry out an experiment – we could work out the likelihood of a piece of toast landing 'butter-side down' by dropping

100 pieces of toast and seeing how many actually landed 'butter-side down'. Finally we can calculate probability based theoretically on equally likely outcomes. The way we calculate the probability of throwing a 5 on a six-sided dice is by listing the six equally likely outcomes: 1, 2, 3, 4, 5 or 6. Throwing a 5 is one of these outcomes, so the probability of throwing a 5 is 1/6 (1 out of 6). More formally we write this as p(5) = 1/6.

Teaching points

Teaching point 1: Making data meaningful

I was observing a first-year student teacher recently who was introducing a data-handling session with her class. She had been asked to 'teach tally charts and bar charts' and advised to 'stick to shoe sizes because it is easy'. She let the group decide how to organise the collection of data, which was pleasing, so the children arranged themselves in groups of the same shoe size. This, however, removed the need for tallying as the children could simply count how many children had each shoe size and so wrote down the **frequency**, or how many children wore a particular shoe size, and then represented this as a tally, for example 4 = IIII.

They then drew the bar chart without noticing that the total number of children represented by the chart was more than the number in the class. The class did not engage with the data collection in any meaningful way as they weren't really interested in the outcome. This is in contrast to the activity with which I opened the chapter. Another area which children have been interested in has been linked to the environment – one class became very engaged in finding out which class in their school was the 'greenest'.

Taking it further

In their article 'Curricular opportunity and the statistics of lines' in *Mathematics Teaching* 181, December 2002, Paul Andrews and Heather Massey suggest that 'data, unless collected within a meaningful context and then analysed purposefully, is not worth collecting. No-one in the real world collects data for the sake of collecting data.' They also suggest that learners often carry out data-handling and statistical enquiries in subjects other than mathematics to a much more sophisticated level than we expect in mathematics sessions.

The lesson they describe appears very simple on the surface – they ask pupils to estimate the length of five pre-drawn straight lines. The pupils complete a table which asks for their estimate, the actual length, the error and the percentage error. However, they then ask the class to explore some complex questions:

- Are humans more accurate when estimating long or short lengths?
- Does relative error increase or decrease with length?

- How much do humans vary in their estimations of length?
- Do humans tend to overestimate or underestimate lengths?

These questions can also be asked of curved lines and angles, which allows the teacher to explore and develop skills in handling data, drawing on other areas of the mathematics curriculum.

Teaching point 2: Making sensible observations from data

This teaching point follows directly from the point made above. If learners do not see the data as meaningful, or have not been involved in formulating the questions which they are trying to respond to through collecting and analysing data, they may well see only simplistic, closed interpretations of data.

The interpretation of data should take place alongside the representation of data. In this way children are always making decisions about the most appropriate form of representation. Children should also be encouraged to come up with alternative interpretations of data so that they become used to being critical about the way that data is represented and interpreted.

Taking it further

In the paper 'Exploring the complexity of the interpretation of media graphs', published in *Research in Mathematics Education* (Volume 6, 2004), Carlos Monteiro and Janet Ainley describe the way they used graphs from the media to develop a 'critical sense' in learners' interpretation of data. They suggest that there are three main types of graph reading:

1 *Reading the data*: that is, lifting information from the data to answer specific questions.

2 *Reading between the data*: that is, finding relationships and patterns within the data.

3 *Reading beyond the data*: that is, using the data to predict future patterns or to ask new questions.

The example used earlier in the chapter exploring the relationship between a person's height and the circumference of their head showed learners carrying out all three processes.

The researchers used graphs and charts from the media to explore the ways in which student teachers interpreted data, encouraging them to read the data in the three ways described above. They found that the student teachers drew on four aspects of prior knowledge to interpret the graphs:

1 Their mathematical knowledge to describe the quantitative relationships they observed (that is, relationships based on numbers).

2 Their personal opinions to make generalisations based on the data.

3 Their personal experience to make generalisations based on the data.

4 Their feelings and emotions to describe how the data made them 'feel'.

Thinking again about the data-handling activity which opened the chapter, you can see an 'emotional' response to the data as it is related to a real-life experience.

Teaching point 3: Using mean, median, mode appropriately

For many people the word average is used interchangeably with 'mean'. There are, in fact, three different sorts of 'average': the mean, the median and the mode.

The mean is the 'average' that is most commonly used. You calculate the mean by adding up all the different items of data and dividing by the total number of items. So, if you are finding the mean height of all the children in your class, and you have 28 children, you would find the total height by adding all the individual measurements together and then dividing by 28.

The median is the middle value when all the data is arranged in order. This is a measure of 'central tendency' in the same way as the mean, but is helpful if there are extremes in the data, or 'outliers'. So if we have a list of house prices in a particular area, say:

£78,000, £150,000, £175,000, £180,000, £200,000, £210,000 and £750,000

the mean works out as £249,000, which isn't a useful measure if you are trying to decide whether you can afford a house in the area. The median is £180,000, which is more informative in this case. If there is an even number of values the median value is exactly half-way between the two central values.

The mode is the value that occurs most frequently – this time shoe sizes are a good example. You could ask the children in your class to decide how many of each shoe size they would stock if they were to set up a shoe shop for children and teenagers. This is the data for a mixed group of boys and girls:

Shoe size	Frequency
2	2
3	4
4	5
5	5
6	9
7	6
8	3
9	0
10	1

The mode is size 6, so they would stock more of this shoe size. To make it more challenging you may describe the size of the population that may visit the shop. If there are two values which are most popular, the data is said to be **bi-modal**.

A final measure which is used is the **range**. This measures the spread of the set of data. So, in the example of house prices above the range is £672,000 (78,000–750,000).

When you are exploring and interpreting data with your class it is worth asking them to find all three measures of average and the range, and then decide which is the most useful measure to answer the question you have asked of the data.

Portfolio task 9.5

Try and find:

1 Six numbers with a mean of 6.

2 Eight numbers with a median of 4.

3 Ten numbers with a mode of 7.2.

Teaching point 4: Probability – equally likely outcomes

A boy once gave me the best explanation of probability and equally likely outcomes I have ever heard. He was carrying out an experiment tossing a coin and had tossed three 'heads' in a row. His friend said, 'The next one is bound to be a "tail".' The first boy responded, 'Don't be silly, the coin hasn't got a memory.' And he was right – the probability of tossing a 'tail' is always 1/2, or 50% or 50/50, whatever you have just thrown. Similarly, lots of children seem to think that it is harder to get a 6 when throwing a dice than any other number. This isn't the case – the chance is 1/6, the same as the chance of getting a 1, or a 2, or any other number. I wonder if children just remember times when they couldn't get a 6, to start or finish a board game, and so think this is more difficult.

The outcomes of an experiment are equally likely to occur when the probability of each outcome is equal. Tossing a head or a tail on a coin, or throwing a 1, 2, 3, 4, 5 or 6 on a six-sided dice, are called **equally likely outcomes**. To find the probability of an event happening you need to decide which equally likely outcomes are acceptable and divide that by how many equally likely outcomes there are. So, for example:

Probability of throwing an even number on a six-sided dice = 3/6 or 1/2.

There are three possible outcomes that are acceptable – throwing a 2, 4 or 6 – and there are six possible outcomes altogether.

You can explore theoretical probabilities when events are not equally likely by carrying out a range of experiments. For example, tossing a match box – you can get the whole class tossing (empty) match boxes. If you were to toss it a total of 100 times and it landed on the end 22 times, the side 4 times and the faces 74 times, the probabilities would be 22%, 4%

and 74% respectively. You could also explore how the judicious placing of Blu-Tack changes the probabilities. You could set a challenge to try and reach 50% probability of landing on one end by 'weighting' the box.

In practice

The following lesson plan and evaluation describe a lesson taught to a group of 10- and 11-year-old pupils who had been working on handling data with a particular focus on using data to explore real-life questions. They had also been using the 'Data Charts' program which you can find on the companion website to this book. I wanted to work on an extended activity with the group so that they could see the data-handling cycle as a continuous process. I also wanted the group to see that often a data-handling investigation throws up new questions for us to consider.

Topic: Collecting, processing, presenting and interpreting data

Age group: Upper primary

Objectives

To solve problems by collecting, processing, presenting and interpreting data. To draw conclusions and iden-tify further questions to ask. To suggest, plan and develop lines of enquiry

Note

I will use a whole morning for this activity rather than try and fit it into a single hour, or run over several les-sons, as I feel this will lose continuity

Key vocabulary

Survey, data, frequency table, hypothesis

Resources	Starter activity
Mini-whiteboards	Write on the whiteboard 'The children in this class enjoy reading.' Ask the class to vote on this. Choose one of the group who voted for the statement – ask them to describe in detail what they mean when they say 'The children in this class enjoy reading.' Do the same with someone who disagreed. Ask the children to work in pairs for five minutes and come up with several statements about the class which may or may not be true. They should write these on mini-whiteboards. Take feedback from the groups and agree which are the six most interesting questions to ask about the class. Phrase these as hypotheses and tell the class they are going either to prove or disprove these hypotheses. The children will choose which group to work in, depending on the question they are most interested in

Main activity

Each group should spend 10 minutes deciding how they will test their hypothesis. For example, the group exploring 'We think this class enjoy reading' might decide that someone who reads 10 books a month and likes at least three different genres enjoys reading. The whole class should comment on each group's criteria. Once each group has amended their criteria based on the feedback they have been given, they should develop a questionnaire – this time ask them to get feedback from you.
Finally the group collect the data. They complete frequency tables and use the program 'Data Charts' to display their data. Each group will prepare a short PowerPoint presentation to present their findings

Plenary

Each group present their findings – I will ask for feedback from all the other children, using the two stars and a wish system. (That is, each group assesses each other's presentation giving them two positive features – 'stars' – and one way of improving it – a 'wish')

Rationale and evaluation

I was pleased that I planned to run this over a morning rather than trying to work in blocks of an hour. I needed the flexibility to manage the time differently, and the session didn't fit naturally into my normal structure for the numeracy sessions. In the end the groups didn't get to present their ideas at the end of the morning – in fact I had to build in some flexible time during the week for groups to finish their presentations as they took very different time scales. I should have expected this, but it was important that the groups could take the time they needed over preparing their presentations as it allowed them to draft and redraft. I asked each group to show me their data as pie charts, bar charts and line graphs if they could. I then asked them to make the decision about which was the most useful representation. I think this is the first time that they have thought carefully about how pie charts are better at representing 'proportion' than bar charts. Jan said, 'I'm going to use a bar chart for the information that has lots of numbers that are important but the pie chart when I just need to show where the "most" is.' I thought this showed a good understanding of the alternative representations.

All the groups found the hardest part was deciding on the initial criteria – I needed to support them carefully initially, as all the groups wanted to use just one criterion. So, for example, they asked, 'Do you like to read?' rather than 'Do you read action stories, or poetry books, or science books?' In the end I had to structure the learning by asking for three criteria they could explore. However, when we revisited the criteria at the end and started thinking of new questions to ask, they could see how they might devise criteria. There has been some impact I think, as yesterday I said, 'Well done Class 6, you've worked very hard today'. Graeme chirped up, 'What do you mean exactly by we've worked hard?'

The all attainment groups allowed people like Shauna who are normally very quiet to take a lead. She became very animated as she worked on the hypothesis 'Children in this class are good at looking after animals' as that is her passion. Similarly Lauren and Westley became the IT experts for their groups and showed them all sorts of techniques for using PowerPoint.

The groups' skills in peer assessment were also developed – they are becoming much more sophisticated in using the two stars and a wish feedback system. Earlier in the year the responses would have been along the lines of 'it was very colourful' or 'it could have been neater'. This time there were comments such as 'I think a pie chart would have been a better way of showing the data because you could very quickly see the different fractions.'

Observing 'Handling data'

There are two examples of how to explore the data-handling cycle holistically on the companion website: http://www.playbackschools.org.uk/programme/2016/data-handling (just use the first two clips).

In the video the teacher takes a holistic view of the data-handling cycle, collecting, recording and analysing data about school meals. He sets this as a genuine question suggesting that the new school cook wants some feedback. He chooses to use human charts as one way of representing the data. Watch the clip and then think about the following questions:

- What are the advantages of using the pupils to create human bar charts?
- Can you think of other ways of involving learners so directly in representing data?

Watch the second lesson in the clip, which links the data-handling cycle to athletic achievements. Here the children actively engage in 'athletic' type activities and record the results. After watching the clip think about these questions:

- How would you safeguard children's self-esteem if using this activity?
- How would you make sure that pupils who are less confident in their athletic ability were involved in the activities?

Focus on the use of cameras and video to help in assessing these activities and the range of activities which require the use of different units in measurement. This activity shows how data handling can be used as a part of a cross-curricular project.

Assessing 'Handling data'

It is important that the activities you use to assess data handling treat the data-handling cycle holistically while allowing you to assess the component parts. Many of the activities that you have been introduced to in this chapter can be used as assessment activities. For example, the activity presented on page 181 can be used to assess children's abilities in classifying data and explaining the different choices available to them when sorting data. Most importantly it allows you to assess your pupils' ability to explain the choices they are making.

Similarly the activity presented in the bar and line charts Resource inspiration box, if extended into an activity which compares this data with data collected about your class, allows you to assess learners' abilities across the data-handling cycle.

Cross-curricular approaches to 'Handling data'

One of the most effective mathematics projects I have worked on was setting up a healthy tuck shop for the school. In order to get the project off the ground we had to carry out a large-scale data-handling activity. I asked the class to decide what information they would need to find out if we were setting up a healthy tuck shop. This included:

- What do we mean by a 'healthy' food?
- What healthy foods would you buy?
- How much would the children in school spend at a healthy tuck shop?
- Where would the best site for the healthy tuck shop be?
- When would be the best time to run the tuck shop?
- How much would it cost to buy the stock?

The children opted to join a group they were interested in and then carried out the research necessary to answer the question. They then had to present their findings to the school council as it had the final decision about funding the tuck shop. The research was a success – the tuck shop was funded and ran successfully for several years.

Summary

The main focus of this chapter has been the data-handling cycle reproduced here:

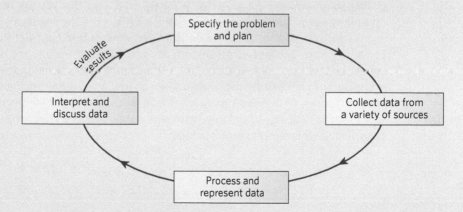

You should have a clearer understanding of each part of the cycle and how important it is to see the cycle as a whole, and that working with children to see the cycle as a whole is central to learning how to handle and interpret data.

You have seen the range of ways in which data can be represented, and have been reminded of the ways in which the spread of data can be measured, such as mean, median, mode and range.

Reflections on this chapter

Data handling can be an exciting and motivating area to explore with the children you teach. It is also, arguably, one of the most important areas of mathematics in which to develop skills in order to be able to make sense of and understand the world around us as presented through the media. I would hope that by gaining confidence in seeing data handling as a process of posing questions, gathering data which is then interpreted to answer those questions, and finally using this process to ask new questions, you will have become excited at the prospect of working through this cycle with your learners.

It is possibly the only area of mathematics that can be taught through a totally cross-curricular approach; indeed it can possibly only be taught in this way. Similarly it is an area of mathematics that can be taught by drawing on the children's interests as a starting point. Several years ago I was having a drink with a cousin of mine whom I don't see very often. Out of the blue she asked me if she should stop taking the contraceptive pill. I was taken aback and asked why she wanted to know. She told me that she had read in the paper that being on the pill doubled her chance of getting thrombosis in her legs. I asked her to show me the article and was able to explain to her that even doubling the risk still meant that the risk of thrombosis was very small. I realised she had asked me because I was 'good at maths', in her words. She didn't feel confident in making important decisions based on her data-handling skills. So, I would argue that teaching data handling is very important – enjoy it!

Self-audit

Gather some achievement data that you have on a class that you are teaching. This may be previous achievement on optional SATs, it may be results on reading ages – it can be any quantitative data. Decide what you want to find out from the data, such as comparing boys' and girls' achievements, or a particular subject area you have been focusing on, and write a list of questions. Use the data-handling techniques you have met in this chapter to analyse the data. Make sure you use range, mean, median and mode, and comment on which of these measures is the most useful. Also use a range of ways of representing the data. Use your analysis to write a short report on the achievements of your class. Include this report in your portfolio.

Going further

If the World Were A Village **by David Smith and Shelagh Armstrong**
This book is an invaluable resource that allows you to work with your pupils on issues of global importance while introducing the pupils to ways of representing and interpreting data. The book uses the construct of imagining the world was a village of 100 people to present data around issues such as access to electricity, the number of languages spoken globally, and poverty.

Smith, D. and Armstrong, S. (2004) *If The World Were A Village: Imagine 100 People Live in a Village.* London: A & C Black.

Bad Science by Ben Goldacre
This is a great book to share with your older learners as it exposes how statistics can be used to make mistaken observations about science. It is based on Goldacre's *Guardian* column and is written in an entertaining and witty style.

Goldacre, B. (2009) Bad Science. London: Harper Perennial.

'Data handling' by J. Michael Shaughnessy, Joan Garfield and Brian Greer
Michael Shaughnessy and his colleagues contributed this chapter on data handling in the first *International Handbook of Mathematics Education*. It explores the historical role of data handling in mathematics curricula around the world, and pays particular attention to the way in which ICT can support the learning and teaching of data handling.

Shaughnessy, J. M., Garfield, J. and Greer, B. (1996) 'Data handling'. In Bishop, A., Clements, M.A., Keitel-Kreidt, C., Kilpatrick, J. and Laborde, C. (eds), *International Handbook of Mathematics Education*, pp. 205–237. Dordrecht: Kluwer Academic.

CHAPTER 10
TEACHING AND LEARNING MATHEMATICS IN THE EARLY YEARS

Introduction

Millie came home from school the other night and sat at the kitchen table while I made a cup of tea. She fetched a pencil and a piece of paper and said to me, 'I'm just going to do my work.' After a couple of minutes I asked her what she was doing. 'I've got to finish off my sums,' she said. I looked at the paper and saw she was writing numbers and the equals, plus and minus signs randomly across the paper.

I was interested that at age five, Millie was describing this as 'doing work' rather than learning, and described anything to do with numbers as 'sums'. This chapter offers a broader view of mathematics in the early years and aims to illustrate how, by planning a wide range of mathematical experiences for your young learners, they will come to see how mathematics is embedded in many aspects of their day-to-day experience.

Portfolio task 10.1

Activity

Try to work on this with a group of friends. One of you should read out this list of numbers and ask the others to draw the images they see when each number is read out:

8; 25; 6; 13; 100; 1,000,000

Starting point

There will be a range of images drawn – discuss the reasons behind the images that people have chosen. These are often influenced by life experiences. So, for example, people may see boxes of eggs for 6:

This is a useful image. It means that as well as seeing 6 we see 6 as 2×3 or 3×2; we may also see 5 as an egg box with one missing, so we know that $6 - 1 = 5$. As the numbers get bigger we may have more abstract images, or images that don't help us relate to the size of a number. I often hear children referring to any big numbers as 'millions and trillions and millions' – this just really means 'big'.

So children's early mathematical experiences are very important in providing them with images that they will carry with them as they grow.

When Harry was three we were sharing a book called *Window* by Jeannie Baker (Walker Books). This is a beautiful book consisting of drawings of the view through a window on each birthday of a child from age 1 to 20. In each picture the birthday card is displayed so that the numeral can be seen. As we flicked through the book Harry made no comment until we reached the child's 15th birthday. Harry looked at the card and said, 'I know that one – that's 15. Sam is 15.' Sam, my eldest, and at that time a hero of Harry's, had just had his 15th birthday. I remembered that he had asked me to show him 'how to write 15' when I told him that Sam was 15 years old. So even though Harry was not writing numbers in order he was recognising numbers that were important to him – and beginning to order and describe his world using numbers.

Similarly my two sons were out with their grandad when they were very small, and walking down our road. One of them started chanting 2, 4, 6, 8, 10, 12 until he reached our door and said, 'We live at 14'. We had, of course, at an early age made sure the boys knew their address in case they got lost. The other one picked up the chant using the houses on the other side of the road, counting 1, 3, 5, 7, 9, 11. Here we can use evidence of young children noticing patterns in number and using these patterns to describe and navigate their world.

Children know bus numbers, know how many brothers and sisters they have, know about sharing, may have a sense of money, a sense of size from very young. We cannot and should not assume that we are working with blank slates when we start exploring number or shape, or handling data with our young learners. They have been using mathematics since they were born – an exciting task is to discover how they are using their mathematics to understand and describe their world.

This chapter will explore how every child brings with them their own mathematical understanding and is capable of developing this understanding, with a 'teacher', who may be an early years practitioner, another adult, a parent or a friend.

Taking it further

In her article 'Handing control to 5 year olds' published in the ATM journal *Mathematics Teaching* 184 in September 2003, Cynthia Collins describes how she allowed her group of young learners to create their own rules for playing together when engaged in mathematical activities. The activity she describes allowed her to explore children's personal, social and emotional development, as they negotiate their ways of playing and learning together, and at the same time support them in developing their mathematical understanding. She gave her group a box of felt-tip pens and a pile of square pieces of card. She told the group she needed a new set of number cards for the number washing line in the classroom. One of the group decided to take charge and gave each of the group some cards – they then had to decide who would write which number. At first everyone started writing 1, 2 before realising this would mean they ran out of cards. Immediately one boy changed his cards to 11 and 12. The group then decided they had finished and laid the cards out in order. When they looked at the number line they had left a long gap between 7 and 11 and they realised there were numerals missing. They completed the task and called the teacher back over, satisfied that they had solved the problem. By leaving the children to the task they had drawn on their understandings and had engaged in the activity over an extended period. They had also very carefully and thoughtfully negotiated their roles within the group.

Problem solving, reasoning and numeracy

Early years practitioners and teachers of young children will develop young learners' mathematics through playful activities in a broad range of contexts to allow learners to explore, enjoy, learn, practise and talk about their developing understanding of mathematics. Young children's mathematical development occurs as they seek patterns, make connections and recognise relationships through finding out about and working with numbers and counting, with sorting and matching, and with shape, space and measures.

Another important role that a teacher plays is to support children in talking about the activities they are engaged in, allowing them to describe how they are solving problems and encouraging them to ask new questions about the areas they are exploring. A word that I often hear being used when teachers are talking about effective lessons is 'pace'. They will tell me that they were pleased with the pace of the lesson – they felt as though they covered a lot of ground. Early years practitioners may hold a different view of effective mathematics teaching. They should aim to allow children sufficient time, space and encouragement to discover and use new words and mathematical ideas, concepts and language during child-initiated activities in their own play. So, don't be afraid to let children explore mathematics over extended periods of time – and try not to interrupt too early.

The sense of allowing children to explore and develop also applies to their jottings and notes. It is important to allow children to explore their own ways of recording their thinking. The opening of the chapter outlined the importance of the environment in supporting children's mathematical activity. Through carefully planning the environment, both indoor and outdoor, you can encourage the children to see and explore mathematics that is all around them. Using stories, games, songs and role play to develop young children's mathematical understanding is vital. So keep a lookout for as many books as you can which can support mathematical understanding.

Portfolio task 10.2

Choose one of the books that you enjoy sharing with young learners. Jot down some notes for your portfolio about the way you can use this book to develop children's mathematical skills and understanding.

Numbers as labels for counting

When we use the term 'numbers as labels for counting' we mean the cardinal numbers 1, 2, 3, 4, 5 and so on, rather than 'labels' such as bus numbers or house numbers.

Early skills in number that we would aim to teach at this stage are:

- Saying and using number names in order in familiar contexts.
- Counting reliably up to 20 everyday objects.
- Recognising numbers 1 to 20.

Effective practice which would contribute towards children achieving these objectives would include encouraging children to create their own displays to record choices that the group make – for example, preferences for school lunch, ways of travelling to school, birthdays. As mentioned earlier, you will bring counting into everyday practice through the books you are sharing, and use a wide range of nursery rhymes and songs every day. These will include songs that involve counting back – for example,

Five green and speckled frogs,
Sat on a speckled log.
Eating the most delicious worms
YUM, YUM.
One jumped into the pool,
Where it was nice and cool.
Then there were four green speckled frogs
GLUG, GLUG.
Four green and speckled frogs, . . .

Or

Ten fat sausages, sizzling in the pan,
Ten fat sausages, sizzling in the pan,
And if one went POP!
and the other went BANG!
There'll be eight fat sausages,
sizzling in the pan,
Eight fat sausages, sizzling in the pan.
And if one went POP!
and the other went BANG!

If you are lucky enough to be working in a multicultural classroom make sure you ask the parents for counting songs and rhymes from their cultures to enrich your collection. It is worth spending more time on counting back than on counting on in planned activities. I would aim for a ratio of 2:1, i.e., twice as many counting-back activities as counting-on activities.

You will also make sure that you have number lines, number washing lines and 100 squares on display and number games available for children to play when they are able to choose their own activities. Chapter 4 expands these ideas in much more detail and should be read in conjunction with this section.

Calculating

The foundations for calculating will be laid if your young learners can:

- Begin to use the language of addition and subtraction in practical activities and discussion.

- Use language such as 'more' and 'less' to compare numbers.

- Find one more or one less than a number between 1 and 10.

- Begin to relate addition to combining groups and subtraction to 'taking away'.

Effective practice in developing calculating skills would involve posing questions as you read stories – 'How many friends will be left when one gets off the bus?' – as well as using everyday events in the setting to pose questions: 'How many girls are here today?' Encourage children to record what they are telling you, allowing them to record in their own way and talking about the choices they are making. Use number lines and make use of number lines physically, allowing children actually to jump forwards and backwards on a number line.

Chapter 6 details the progression in 'counting' as children move through the early years into the primary. If you work through this chapter it will help you understand how counting skills develop as children move through the primary years.

Taking it further

Ian Thompson, currently a visiting professor at Edge Hill University, has edited one of the most useful books about teaching early number. Published by the Open University Press and now in its 3rd edition, *Teaching and Learning Early Number* is an accessible guide to recent research exploring how young children begin to make sense of counting and the number system. The book explores developing mathematics through play, assessment of early mathematical knowledge through interviewing children, and children's early recording of number activities, as well as detailing recent research on the complex process of learning how to count. For example, the different ways in which children make errors in counting out loud are examined. These include continuing with a count in order but omitting numbers, or repeating numbers and then recounting from that number. The authors show how using puppets to count with the children can encourage them to recognise and correct their mistakes.

Shape, space and measures

In the early years you will develop children's understanding of shape, space and measure if your learners are able to:

- Use language such as 'greater', 'smaller', 'heavier' or 'lighter' to compare quantities.
- Talk about, recognise and re-create simple number patterns.
- Use language such as 'circle' or 'bigger' to describe the shape and size of solids and flat shapes.
- Use everyday words to describe position such as 'in front of' and 'behind' or 'above' and 'below'.

Again these objectives should be achieved through practical activity. You will provide a range of 2D and 3D shapes, including large boxes and cartons for children to play with. While they are engaged in building and making you can introduce names and model the language of comparison by asking which is the biggest square or the smallest triangle. You will bring a range of shapes and solids into the role play areas that you construct, talking with the children about the shapes as you construct the role play areas and as you join in the children's role play. Observe the use of the role play areas carefully to see how children use the resources you have provided; this will help you decide which role play settings are richest for mathematical activity. When you go out for walks, or are playing outside, use positional language: Who is at the end of the line? Who is behind Tony? Who is in front of Emma? Who is next to Tom?

Taking it further

The book *Mathematics with Reason* edited by Sue Atkinson and published by Hodder and Stoughton in 1992 is subtitled *The Emergent Approach to Primary Maths*. This is a book which, although research based, is structured around teachers and early years practitioners describing the ways that young children learn in their classrooms and settings. You'll read about children planning a picnic, making maps and designing natural wildlife areas. The PROBLEMS acronym, first introduced by the Open University, is widely used to analyse the process through which these young learners are encouraged to solve problems:

Pose the problem.

Refine the problem into areas for investigation.

Outline the questions we need to ask.

Bring the data home.

Look for solutions.

Establish recommendations.

Make it happen – put the solution into action and test it out.

So what next? Start the process again.

Sue Atkinson also describes the importance of supporting young learners in developing their own, intuitive methods for solving problems. The following extract shows the joy that working to support children in developing their own understandings can bring:

[Unlocking children's own intuitive methods] is one of the most thrilling things in teaching. It's like that magic moment when a small child rushes up to you, her face glowing with pleasure and tells you she can read. When those special moments come you can stand back and watch the child race off, powered with her own understanding.

I hope this section has offered a clear view of the sorts of mathematical activity which may be seen in an early years setting. The most important point to emphasise is that this should all be taking place through talk and activity. The subject knowledge that you need here is the ability to find the mathematics in the everyday – and the confidence to draw out the mathematics all day, every day.

Assessment in the early years

Effective assessment in the early years is an analysis and review of children's learning in order to make informed decisions about what you will plan to meet their next learning needs. This is the basis of assessment for learning: you are not assessing simply to find out what a young learner can do, you are observing their skills and understandings so that you can decide what **you** do next. There are a range of things you might look out for. Some practitioners choose to keep notes in a journalists' notebook during the day; you will see some practitioners using Post-it notes and occasionally photographs so that they can reflect at the end of the day on children's individual progress and the next steps in learning they should provide. The following sections provide you with areas to focus on when you are assessing your learners' current understandings in order to plan for their next stage of development.

Numbers as labels for counting

As you sing number songs and rhymes with actions with the children, make a note of their responses. Observe how confident the children are with with their actions. Do they initiate the actions or are they following their friends without understanding what the meanings of the actions are?

When you count with children using displays, observe whether the children point at the numbers on the display and name them accurately, and see what range of numbers they refer to.

You will be estimating small numbers of objects and can note down how accurate their estimates of numbers of things are. Similarly when you use the language of comparison on a day-to-day basis you can note when children begin to use the language of first, second, third. You could also make a note of how the children refer to numbers they use in everyday life – house number, number of brothers, and so on.

When carrying out counting activities with the children you can take note of their developing skills in this area. At what stage do they understand the one-to-one principle, the stable order principle – when do they realise that the last number in a count always gives the total? (See Chapter 4.)

Calculating

As you observe and engage the children in activities involving calculating you can look for how accurately children share things out between them. See if the children share accurately and make a note of how they go about sharing. Observe the children to see if they know whether or not the sharing has been fair by noticing that groups of objects have the same number or different numbers of objects in them.

You can pose questions whenever you have planned a 'sorting' activity. See if the children work out how many more or less there are in some groups and notice how the children respond if you combine two groups and ask them how many all together. Alternatively, if you remove objects from a group, what forms of records are they developing to record your actions?

Shape, space and measures

At an early stage you will be noticing how the children respond to shape sorting games and the language they use to describe shapes. Listen to their vocabulary when describing the properties of shapes. You will want to listen out for language such as 'bigger' and 'smaller' or 'heavier' and 'lighter', or 'in front' and 'behind', as well as simple shape properties and names.

Make a note when children start noticing shapes in the environment or responding to you, pointing out shapes around the classroom. You can also observe the children working on practical activities such as modelling or wrapping presents to see if they are estimating sensible amounts of materials. You can talk about where the children live in order to see if they can describe routes they have taken to school and start to draw very simple maps.

Don't see any of the questions above as 'testing' the children – you can pose these questions, engage the children in the activities I have described and observe how they respond. As children become more familiar with the activities and as they hear their teachers and friends model more complex mathematical vocabulary you will notice the children develop their understandings.

Below there are examples of activities which are rich in assessment opportunities – the first will help you to explore children's understanding of counting.

Create a set of 'lily pads', numbered 1 to 20, that the children can stand on. The first activity is asking a group of children to put them in order so that you can 'play a game'. It is very often mathematically worthwhile for the children to help you prepare for an activity. You can notice how the children order the lily pads: Who takes control? Who decides on the correct order? Then ask the children to start on 1 and hop on the lily pads until they reach 15 or start on 12 and hop back to 2. For some children you could ask them to hop in 2s and others could count out loud the numbers they land on. You can also create number frogs – frogs with numbers on them that children have to match to the correct lily pad. Alternatively children can make their own number frogs.

This activity allows you to assess children's developing understanding of shape, space and measures. Provide the children with a large collection of newspapers, Sellotape, paper, modelling straws, pipe cleaners – the wider the range of resources, the better. Initially talk about all the different sorts of 'houses' the children can think of. Ask the children which houses are 'big', 'small' and 'medium sized'. Try to get children to explain how they are making the decisions about which category to place a 'house' in. Give the group three different animals. Their task is to make a house for each of the animals. This assessment task relies on the teacher observing the process very carefully. It may be appropriate to use a digital camera to record the activities the children are involved in. Make sure you ask probing questions like:

- How do you know that will be big enough?
- How could you check the animal will fit?
- How big is that house?
- Which house is the biggest?

Observing teaching in the early years

The video clip available on the companion website to this book describes how a school in Birmingham introduced personalised learning programmes for its learners in the early years in order to transform the view of mathematics for all learners in the primary school. As well as offering lots of starting points for teaching this extended clip gives you a clear sense of what effective mathematics teaching in the early years might look like. The reflective discussions between the practitioners will help you understand the reasons for the developments they are making.

Watch the clip and then make notes in your portfolio about the following questions.

- What are the implications for your teaching in the later years?
- What are the key things that primary classrooms should learn from early years practice?

The clip is available at http://www.tes.co.uk/teaching-resource/Teaching-and-Learning-EYFS-Maths-6084067/.

Summary

This chapter has outlined how problem solving and reasoning underpin numeracy learning in the early years. It has also emphasised how your teaching should engage the young learners in games, songs and active learning through which their understandings of number and shape and space will emerge. The importance of playful activity for mathematics learning is revisited on several occasions.

There are suggestions for the early and developing skills that you will focus on at this stage and a range of foci for assessment are offered. There is a clear emphasis on assessment for learning. That is, your assessment is made to inform your plans for the next stages in learning for individual learners.

Reflections on this chapter

I hope that the chapter has shown how mathematics in an early years setting can appear as natural and everyday as all the other activities across the other areas of learning for the children. The curriculum and activities that you can plan and provide should engage and challenge the children – and hopefully you will enjoy engaging with the children. Children are developing their sense of identity as they work with you – if part of that identity can be that they see themselves as successful in mathematics and able to tackle mathematical problems, you will have succeeded as their first mathematics teacher.

Going further

Mathematics through Play in the Early Years by Kate Tucker
This book offers lots of advice and practical activities for those of you working in early years settings. It is a really helpful book for all teachers as the activities are easily adapted for learners at all stages, and learning through play is important across the primary school. There are chapters which explore creative ways of recording children's learning, suggestions of how to involve parents, and case studies which will support you in developing your own individualised approach to mathematics teaching.

Tucker, K. (2010) *Mathematics through Play in the Early Years.* London: Sage.

Thinking and Learning about Mathematics in the Early Years by Linda Pound
This book draws on the research about young children's mathematics development to support teachers in finding ways to plan for playful and engaging mathematics. There is particularly useful advice on ways to link mathematics to everyday situations and ways to plan for cross-curricular activity.

Pound, L. (2008) *Thinking and Learning about Mathematics in the Early Years.* London: Routledge.

The Little Book of Maths Outdoors by Terry Gould
This is a very practical book which supports all early years practitioners in developing their ideas for mathematics outdoors. It is vital that children see mathematics all around them and that they are not limited to learning mathematics on a mathematics table, or in a numeracy corner. This book has been well received by early years practitioners and will be helpful for all of you wanting to plan activities for your learners in outdoor spaces.

Gould, T. (2011) *The Little Book of Maths Outdoors: Little Books with Big Ideas.* London: Featherstone Education.

CHAPTER 11
ISSUES OF INCLUSION

Introduction

Understanding and becoming successful in mathematics can have a huge influence on individual life chances. None of you would have been able to gain places on teacher education courses without achieving a 'C' in GCSE mathematics. In 2008 in answer to a parliamentary question the schools minister announced that 42% of pupils in English schools achieved five GCSEs at grades A–C including English and mathematics. This percentage falls to 13% in schools where over half the children are entitled to free school meals. This statistic shows how success in mathematics, and access to the improved life chances that offers, is not equally distributed. This chapter explores issues of inclusion – it aims to offer you support in helping *all* your learners to achieve their potential in mathematics.

Starting point

In 1997 Mike Askew, Margaret Brown, Dylan Wiliam and colleagues from King's College in London explored the links between teachers' practices, beliefs and knowledge and pupil learning outcomes in mathematics. They interviewed and observed 90 teachers and 2000 pupils. The full results are available in the book *Effective Teachers of Numeracy: Report of a study carried out for the Teacher Training Agency* (King's College). In this book the authors identified three sets of beliefs which they suggested were important when understanding the impact of teacher beliefs on effective teaching of numeracy. These were:

- **Connectionist** – a connectionist teacher values pupils' methods and teaching strategies with an emphasis on establishing connections within mathematics. This means that learners are able to see the links between the different areas of mathematics they are engaged with and can see the 'big picture' rather than view mathematics as a set of separate skills to be learnt in isolation from each other.

- **Transmission** – a teacher with these beliefs sees mathematics as a collection of separate routines and procedures to be taught to pupils.

- **Discovery** – these teachers see themselves as facilitators of learning and see mathematics as an area to be discovered by pupils.

You will recognise these terms from the audit questionnaire you completed in Chapter 2. The research showed that teachers with a strong connectionist view were most effective in terms of pupils making progress in their learning of mathematics. A key belief for connectionist teachers is that 'most pupils are able to become numerate'. This means that they believe that all pupils are able to move forward in their mathematics learning. The challenge for teachers is to find the most effective ways for pupils to learn mathematics.

This chapter explores the ways in which you can adapt and develop your practice to include all children in your class, whatever their learning needs are.

Chapter 3 opened with this number square:

1	3	5	7	...
2	6	10	14	...
4	12	20	28	...
8	24	40	56	...
...	...	...	...	...

I posed the questions 'What patterns can you see?' and 'Will 1000 appear?' I have used this activity with learners aged 10–70, with primary school pupils, secondary school pupils and degree-level mathematicians. Some groups of pupils focus on exploring patterns; the simplest patterns here are odd and even numbers, series of numbers that increase by 2, by 4, by 8, and so on. Another group noticed that the numbers in the first column are powers of 2 ($2^2 = 4$, $2^3 = 8$, and so on). Older learners used algebra to explore the patterns in the square, and academic mathematicians came up with a proof that showed all numbers would appear once and only once.

As a teacher exploring ways of teaching for inclusion through mathematics, a key skill you will need to develop is the ability to plan activities that are accessible to the range of learners in your class. However, as well as offering accessibility, these activities need to offer challenge too.

Another activity I have introduced you to previously in Chapter 9 has engaged a wide range of pupils. If you remember I ask the children to try to think about the relationship between the distance around their head and their height and come up with some conjectures.

I always ask learners to work in all attainment groups for this activity, and I will explore the outcomes in a little more detail here. The children measure each other's height and the circumference of their heads to create a scatter graph using initials rather than dots so that each child can see themselves in the data. A scatter graph is a graph of plotted points which shows the relationship between two sets of data. For this activity, distance round head was measured on one axis and height on the other.

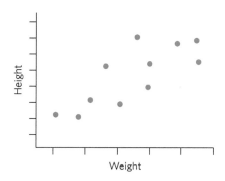

Different groups will interpret the graph in different ways. Some find the 'line of best fit'. The line of best fit is the line that can be drawn on a scatter graph which is the best approximation to all the points on the graph. If you have drawn it accurately the total distance of all the points from the line should be the same for points on each side of the line.

Some children used calculators and individual measurements to see if there was a pattern; some looked at boys and girls in the data to see if there were generalisations that could be made. But the whole class were engaged in exploring the data. At the end of the activity the teacher turned to me and said, 'That was interesting, the weaker mathematicians were the most successful.' In this class the teacher usually grouped her children by prior achievement in mathematics tests. These tests were usually number based. The teacher had noticed that for this activity prior achievement in a 'number' test did not predict how well an individual would engage with ideas if data handling and problem solving.

In an inclusive classroom all learners would be achieving to the best of their ability; and different learners may well excel in different areas of mathematics rather than individuals attaching labels of 'good at mathematics' to themselves. A key lesson for me here was how important it is to vary the groupings we operate within schools. When I visit my students in schools many still operate with fixed groups for mathematics sessions. They may start a session by asking children to get into their 'numeracy groups'. If we never vary the groups that our children learn mathematics in, we limit the range of their peers that they can learn from; we also limit the possibility for children to excel in different areas of mathematics as they quickly come to understand they are in the 'bottom group' for mathematics and put limits on their own understanding.

This became clear one day when I was sitting with a group in a Year 2 classroom. One boy in the group said to me, 'Can you do all of your times-tables?' I told him I could, so he said, 'You need to go and sit with the blue group – they're the cleverest and we won't know our tables until next year.'

Taking it further

Professor Jo Boaler, currently working at Stanford University in the United States, has researched into the impact of setting by ability in English schools for many years. She suggests that this practice means that many learners spend much of their time in school being given low-level and uninteresting activities. Many of these children are capable of achieving more if they are given appropriate learning activities.

In interviews she carried out she was moved by the pleas of learners in low groups who said that they just wanted to learn but were constantly given activities that they did not feel stretched them. She notes that some people believe the practice is right because it keeps the high achievers away from low achievers. However, her research shows that high achievers do not do any better in high sets than in mixed-ability groups, and for some students, being in a high set is a source of considerable anxiety. She also shows us that comparisons of test performance in different countries always show that countries that set students the least and at the latest date have the highest performance. The reasons for this are obvious: once students are told that they are low achieving and given low-level work, their learning diminishes.

Her conclusion is that a mixed-ability, multi-dimensional approach means that success is an option for all learners.

If you are interested in reading more about these ideas, there is a wide range of research studies available on Professor Boaler's home page: **http://www.sussex.ac. uk/education/profile205572.html**.

The rest of this chapter focuses on ways in which teachers can meet the specific needs of particular groups of learners who may currently be underachieving in mathematics.

Children with special educational needs

It is important to remember that there will not necessarily be a correlation between children you teach who are identified as having a special educational need and their ability at mathematics. For example, a child in your class who is dyslexic may be a high achiever in mathematics or may achieve less well. There is often no direct correlation between a special educational need and attainment in mathematics. However, there are steps you can take that ensure you are giving all children the best possible chance to achieve their potential. It is vital that you become aware of the impact of an individual child's specific need, and use this to support your planning.

The main implications for your planning are ensuring that activities are accessible for all learners so they can find a way to get into the activity, while ensuring the activities offer sufficient challenge for all pupils.

This might mean that you have to adapt resources that have previously been used to teach a particular idea. For example, I have seen a group of children who are learning about 'adding money to 10p' set the following set of questions.

Copy and complete these number sentences:

$2p + — = 10p$ $\quad$ $9p + — = 10p$
$4p + — = 10p$ $\quad$ $5p + — = 10p$
$7p + — = 10p$ $\quad$ $1p + — = 10p$

This very closed activity was accessible to children who already had the necessary skills, but several of the children in the class found it hard to make a start on the activity. Similarly those children who understood the task found it very easy and completed the activity without being challenged.

An alternative to this is for the teacher to ask, 'How many different ways can you make 10p?', providing learners with 1p, 2p, 5p and 10p coins. Try this activity for yourself and you will see that it offers accessibility and flexibility.

If you plan the structure of your lessons carefully you can maximise the possibility of all your learners progressing in their learning. For example, in the sections of the lesson which focus on discussion led by the teacher it will help to plan questions specifically for pupils achieving below expected levels. By careful targeting of questions rather than asking for 'hands up' you can draw all pupils into the activity. This also allows you to focus on and develop key vocabulary. You may choose to sit these children close to you, or to use teaching assistants to work with them in oral sessions. Another good way to involve all pupils in oral sessions is through 'talk partners'. You can set up 'talk partners' and place those children who are achieving below expected levels with peers who are achieving well. Using paired discussions will support both sets of learners.

Careful thought about the resources you can use will also support your learners with specific learning needs. Flash cards and illustrated wall displays will support all learners in developing appropriate vocabulary. The use of number lines, 100 squares and other number apparatus will also support children in developing mental images of the ways in which the number system works.

There will be children you will meet in your career who have been identified as having specific learning needs. There are suggestions below as to how you may support these particular groups of learners. Don't forget, however, that most of these ideas will improve the learning experience for all your learners.

Children with emotional and behavioural difficulties

'EBD' stands for Emotional Behavioural Disorder (often referred to as 'Emotional and Behavioural Difficulties') and refers to a condition in which the behaviour or the emotional response of children is so different from the rest of your class that they impact on the child's learning. This may take the form of disruptive, antisocial or aggressive behaviour; poor peer relationships; or hyperactivity, attention and concentration problems.

You may find that unstructured, open-ended tasks can exacerbate behavioural difficulties. If children are uncertain how to start an activity, or are unclear what your expectations of success are, they may avoid starting the activity in case they 'go wrong'. Similarly, if they are unclear what you are looking for as success in the activity they may not take a risk in case they 'get it wrong'. It may help to provide a clear structure and set time-specific targets. Try to be consistent in your routines; in particular, the cycle of demonstration, modelling and summarising is very important for this group of learners. Giving children responsibility and involving them in demonstrations by bringing them to the front can support them in developing positive behaviour patterns. Also aim to avoid interrogational questioning, as this may lead the learners to feel humiliated, and this is a common cause of inappropriate behaviour; this is where using talk partners can help. Make sure you offer this group of learners challenge – they will soon realise if you are offering them low-level tasks, and this can lead to inappropriate behaviour too.

Children with autism

The National Autistic Society, on its website http://www.nas.org.uk/autism, describes autism as follows:

> Autism is a lifelong developmental disability. It is part of the autism spectrum and is sometimes referred to as an autism spectrum disorder, or an ASD. The word 'spectrum' is used because, while all people with autism share three main areas of difficulty, their condition will affect them in very different ways. Some are able to live relatively 'everyday' lives; others will require a lifetime of specialist support.
>
> The three main areas of difficulty which all people with autism share are sometimes known as the 'triad of impairments'. They are:
>
> difficulty with social communication
>
> difficulty with social interaction
>
> difficulty with social imagination.

These are described in more detail below.

> It can be hard to create awareness of autism as people with the condition do not 'look' disabled: parents of children with autism often say that other people simply think their child is naughty; while adults find that they are misunderstood.
>
> All people with autism can benefit from a timely diagnosis and access to appropriate services and support. (Visit www.autism.org.uk for further information.)

You need to be careful when setting up group or pair work as this can be problematic for children on the autistic spectrum. It is important not to avoid group and pair work but you need to make sure that routines are followed consistently, in particular routines for moving into groups or pairs. For example, always sitting in the same pair on the carpet will help. Classroom transitions are another point of the lesson that can cause difficulties for children with autism. Plan for these transitions carefully, be very clear about how the transition will be managed and keep them calm and orderly – if you just send groups back to their tables without instructions this will prove difficult for children with autism. If they become overwhelmed by noise and movement they should be allowed to go to a quiet, calm place for a while. (So, it is important to have such a space in your classroom.)

Using familiar equipment also supports these children in their learning, as novelty has little appeal. Extensive use of metaphor can also cause difficulty as children with autism are likely to interpret what you say literally. Making time to observe the children to check their understanding is important. Using picture sequences to break down activities into manageable tasks can also support progression.

Recent films and stories in the media seem to suggest that many people on the autistic spectrum can calculate huge numbers in their heads and have photographic memories. Unfortunately such stories give the false impression that all children with autism have these special skills. Most people on the spectrum do not have any special talents for mathematics. However, it can be true that children on the autistic spectrum will exhibit keen interests in particular subjects, and so may know a great deal about very specific areas.

Finally, allowing a child to 'fiddle' with their fingers or small objects can help with concentration and focus.

The following suggestions for children with dyspraxia will also prove helpful for children on the autistic spectrum.

Children with dyspraxia

Dyspraxia is thought to affect up to 10% of the population. It is an impairment in a child's development in terms of the way the brain processes information to help us organise our movements. It affects the way that we plan what we are going to do and how we do it. Dyspraxia can lead to difficulties in terms of perception, language and thought.

Avoid giving a series of instructions for a task as this may well confuse a child with dyspraxia. This will mean that you may have to differentiate, giving some groups more complex instructions while breaking the instructions down for others. Giving 'thinking time' is useful for children with dyspraxia – saying, 'In 30 seconds I will ask you to tell me three number pairs that sum to 100' for example. Using individual whiteboards to rehearse answers will also support these children.

Children with dyslexia

Dyslexia is a specific learning difficulty that mainly affects reading and spelling. Dyslexia is characterised by difficulties in processing word sounds and by weaknesses in short-term verbal memory, and its effects may be seen in spoken language as well as written language. The current evidence suggests that these difficulties arise from inefficiencies in language processing areas in the left hemisphere of the brain which, in turn, appear to be linked to genetic differences.

You should avoid asking a child with dyslexia to read questions aloud unless you are sure they will be comfortable doing this. By checking individual needs you will know what specific support your dyslexic learners may need. It may be that coloured filters will support them in reading text, or printing on a particular colour of paper. The use of highlighters to pick out key words is an important skill for all pupils and will support dyslexic learners across all subjects.

Providing visualisation activities will help dyslexic learners – indeed they may excel in this area and be able to support other children in becoming more skilled at visualisation.

Children with dyscalculia

Dyscalculia describes children who have specific difficulties in carrying out calculations as a result of damage to specific regions of the brain. Recent research suggests that dyscalculia can also occur developmentally, as a genetically linked learning disability which affects a person's ability to understand, remember or manipulate numbers or number facts. The term is often used to refer specifically to the inability to perform arithmetic operations, but it is also seen as leading to a specific difficulty in conceptualising numbers as abstract concepts. This may be described as having 'number sense'.

Ways that you can support learners with dyscalculia include providing a wide range of concrete manipulatives to help understanding to develop before moving into the abstract concepts. This will also assist in providing learners with strategies to visualise. When working on problem solving or word problems, try to provide opportunities to use real-life situations or items to assist with visualisation.

It can also help to provide opportunities to use 'pictures, words or graphs' to help with understanding. Make sure you promote a 'can do' attitude as much as possible; praise and a positive outlook can start to overcome the fear of mathematics that learners with dyscalculia may have developed.

Children who are gifted and talented

The Department for Children, Schools and Families (now Department for Education) suggested that providing an appropriate learning experience in mathematics for gifted and talented learners in our schools is a matter of equity. As with all other pupils they have a right to a mathematics education that will allow them to fulfil their potential. It is appropriate then that a section exploring the particular issues for learners who have been identified as gifted and talented should feature in a chapter exploring inclusion.

Identifying a learner who is gifted and talented in terms of mathematics does not mean identifying those learners who are achieving very highly in tests. Gifted and talented learners may often be those children who take on leadership roles in group work, who show high-level practical skills or can see creative solutions to complex problems.

The following are characteristics that gifted and talented children *may* exhibit. They will:

- Be very articulate.
- Offer quick verbal responses.
- Communicate well with adults.
- Show unusual responses to problem-solving activities.
- Be able to work things out in their head quickly.
- Have a good memory.
- Be easily bored.
- Show a strong sense of leadership.

So it is important in planning your lessons that you work to the strengths of these learners. Create opportunities for them to articulate their thoughts; this may be best in small-group work so they don't dominate whole-class sessions. You may occasionally want to work in 'achievement' groups so that these learners can challenge each other, but it is also important that these learners articulate their thoughts with a wide range of pupils. Through describing their own thinking to their peers they will come to understand their thinking processes better.

Similarly, plan activities which demand quick verbal responses and offer leadership roles to this group of learners. Most importantly, watch out for signs of boredom and always have open, extension activities ready.

One website which will help you add stretch and challenge to your classroom is the NRICH site http://nrich.maths.org. This site is coordinated by Cambridge University and offers a wide range of activities and free resources for teachers. For example, in October 2012 the theme for the month was 'Playing with Numbers' and the site offered activities such as this one.

Zios and Zepts

On the planet Vuv there are two sorts of creatures. The Zios have three legs and the Zepts have seven legs. The great planetary explorer Nico counted 52 legs. How many Zios and how many Zepts were there?

These activities can be carried out interactively on-screen too.

Taking it further

In 1999, Keith Jones and Hannah Simons from Southampton University carried out an independent evaluation of the use of the online NRICH materials. They discovered that over two-thirds of the users of the site were boys and that a large number used the site at home. This suggests that teachers were not using the site regularly as a part of their own teaching and were not making sure that girls had access to the materials. The main impact on pupils of using the site was that they gained a wider appreciation of mathematics and began to view mathematics as an interesting subject which they might enjoy studying outside the classroom. The interactive nature of the site was seen as a particular advantage. This research is available from the University of Southampton in a booklet entitled *Online mathematics enrichment: an evaluation of the NRICH project*.

Portfolio task 11.1

Here is another NRICH problem to have a go at.
I am decorating 20 biscuits for my daughter's party. I line them up and put:

- icing on every second biscuit
- a cherry on every third biscuit
- chocolate on every fourth biscuit.

How many biscuits have no decoration on them? How many have icing, a cherry and chocolate?

If I ice 50 biscuits how many will have all three decorations on them?

Make notes in your portfolio about your thinking while you solved this problem. How do you think it would 'stretch' your high-attaining learners?

Multicultural and anti-racist approaches

The mathematics that we teach in schools is not value or culture free. Multicultural and anti-racist practice does not assume that any other practice is overtly racist, rather it acknowledges that the historical and social context in which our current system of schooling has developed may advantage some groups over others. It also takes the view that these systems can be challenged in order to ensure access to mathematics learning for all learners.

Values and cultural beliefs are embedded in:

- The content of the curriculum that we offer to pupils.
- The ways in which we teach that content.
- The environment in which children learn mathematics.
- The view of mathematics we bring to the classroom as teachers.
- The ways that we measure success in our mathematics classrooms.

So a multicultural and anti-racist approach to mathematics teaching would:

- Include content that develops pupils' understanding of cultures other than their own through reflecting on cultural and linguistic diversity.
- Use resources that draw on pupils' cultural heritage, counter or challenge bias in materials such as textbooks, or draw on pupils' own experience.
- Present positive images of learners as mathematicians and use familiar contexts as starting points, as well as illustrating the diverse cultural heritage of the discipline of mathematics. This may include photographs of your current learners being successful in mathematics, or people from the communities you draw your pupils from who are successful in mathematics.
- Use teaching strategies that both develop pupil confidence with mathematical language and develop positive attitudes towards linguistic diversity. Children here will see linguistic diversity as a benefit to the classroom and would expect to hear a range of languages in the classroom.
- Encourage collaborative teaching and learning which offers challenge to the pupils, encourage learners to express and examine their own views, encourage learners to become involved in their own learning, encourage learners to pose their own problems.
- Develop anti-racist attitudes through mathematics by using data that critiques stereotyped views of particular groups of people. So, for example, looking at images in newspapers and carrying out a data-handling activity may well show the images that newspapers present of minority ethnic groups in a small number of roles, as sportspeople,

or as underprivileged. It is interesting to contrast these images with those found in newspapers such as *The Voice* or *The Asian Times*.

- Monitor achievement and grouping by ethnicity to ensure equal access to the curriculum.

This set of bullet points can be seen as a series of prompts for planning. It accepts the need for the numeracy strategy to form the basis for planning but offers a way in which key questions can inform the planning so that values of multiculturalism and anti-racism pervade the planning.

An activity which would support this view of teaching and learning uses a 100 square in a range of scripts or languages to develop children's understanding of place value and the Hindu–Arabic number system. (The Hindu–Arabic number system is the system widely used in European schools; it is also called the decimal number system or sometimes the European system. This system has developed from combining the Hindu and Arabic representations of number.)

In this activity give groups of children 100 squares in a range of scripts which you have previously cut up to form a jigsaw. They have to reconstruct the 100 square – this will draw on

১	২	৩	৪	৫	৬	৭	৮	৯	১০
১১	১২	১৩	১৪	১৫	১৬	১৭	১৮	১৯	২০
২১	২২	২৩	২৪	২৫	২৬	২৭	২৮	২৯	৩০
৩১	৩২	৩৩	৩৪	৩৫	৩৬	৩৭	৩৮	৩৯	৪০
৪১	৪২	৪৩	৪৪	৪৫	৪৬	৪৭	৪৮	৪৯	৫০
৫১	৫২	৫৩	৫৪	৫৫	৫৬	৫৭	৫৮	৫৯	৬০
৬১	৬২	৬৩	৬৪	৬৫	৬৬	৬৭	৬৮	৬৯	৭০
৭১	৭২	৭৩	৭৪	৭৫	৭৬	৭৭	৭৮	৭৯	৮০
৮১	৮২	৮৩	৮৪	৮৫	৮৬	৮৭	৮৮	৮৯	৯০
৯১	৯২	৯৩	৯৪	৯৫	৯৬	৯৭	৯৮	৯৯	১০০

The Bengali 100 square.

and develop their understanding of the 100 square they are used to working with as they explore it with a new set of eyes. A wide range of resources is available from the 'Learning Live' website: http://www.learninglive.co.uk/teachers/primary/numeracy/teaching/index.asp.

Children with English as an additional language (EAL)

In January 2004, 21 local authorities piloted a programme designed by the Department for Education (then the Department for Education and Skills) and aimed at raising the achievement of bilingual learners in primary schools as this group of learners were not achieving as well as the rest of the population. The project involved each authority receiving the funding to appoint an EAL consultant to work in participating primary schools to support them in developing the curriculum better to support bilingual learners. While this project resulted in improving the achievement in English there were no significant gains in mathematics or science. In an evaluation reported by Tom Benton and Kerensa White published by the National Foundation for Educational Research in 2006, *Raising the Achievement of Bilingual Learners in Primary Schools*, it was suggested that this may have been because initial interventions were not as consistent in mathematics lessons as in English lessons. This means that teachers may not support EAL learners in developing their linguistic skills in mathematics sessions as much as they would in English sessions.

Schools which are effective in supporting bilingual learners realise that these learners enhance our classrooms. The pupils bring a wealth of experience to the classroom which offers a wide range of starting points for exploring mathematics. As I have mentioned previously, the advice on how best to support bilingual learners will also benefit all the learners in your class.

Try to encourage learners in your class to use mathematical language in a wide range of different contexts: some familiar, such as counting up the school dinners, talking about how many children are away; and some new, so whenever you introduce new ideas in any subject try to explore these ideas mathematically. Bilingual learners may need to listen to mathematical language to allow both mathematical and language development. This means that discussion becomes very important. This allows learners to both hear and use mathematical language. To support this discussion use visual resources and engage in practical activities too. Bilingual learners should also be encouraged to develop fluency in their home language through mathematics by engaging in discussions with teaching assistants or peers who share their language.

Observing inclusive mathematics teaching

The video clip available at http://www.teachfind.com/teachers-tv/special-needs-inclusion and on the companion website to this book shows how a piece of IT called a Visualiser is used to support deaf children in a mathematics lesson. This allows a teacher to 'film' their demonstration and record, or add text to the piece of video. This particular clip shows the equipment being used in a secondary school to demonstrate the construction of bisectors of angles. Watch the clip and then reflect on the following question in your portfolio.

What could you use the Visualiser for in your classroom? Can you think of a lesson you have taught recently which would have been enhanced by the use of a Visualiser?

Summary

This chapter took as its starting point the importance of supporting all learners in becoming as good at mathematics as possible. This is vital in order to maximise their life choices. Through drawing on a range of research studies and advice from organisations with the interests of children with specific learning needs at heart, you have learnt about a wide range of strategies you can use to support the learners in your class. The key areas I have focused on have been children with specific learning needs, children who have particular gifts in mathematics, and children from minority ethnic groups, all of whom may not reach their potential if we do not adapt the way that we plan and teach.

Reflections on this chapter

As you read this chapter you may well have realised that most of the suggestions for changes and adaptations to mathematics teaching would benefit all learners in your classroom. By focusing on the needs of specific groups of children that you teach, you begin to plan for individual needs. And by doing this all learners will become more engaged in the mathematics you are teaching.

Going further

Mathematics for Dyslexics (including Dyscalculia) **by Steve Chinn**
This book is now in its third edition. As well as outlining the difficulties that learners with dyslexia or dyscalculia may have in the classroom it offers suggestions for you to support these pupils in overcoming these difficulties. The mixture of theory in the first part of the book together with practical examples in the second half of the book should help you in developing your practice to be more inclusive.

Chinn, S. and Ashcroft, R. (ed) (2006) *Mathematics for Dyslexics (including Dyscalculia)*. London: Wiley-Blackwell.

Overcoming Difficulties with Number: Supporting Dyscalculia and Students who Struggle with Maths **by Ronit Bird**

This is a more practical book which offers teaching plans for pupils aged 9–16 who have dyscalculia. The focus is on practical activities, visualisation and building self-esteem. A resource bank including games and other activities is provided on an accompanying CD.

Bird, R. (2009) *Overcoming Difficulties with Number: Supporting Dyscalculia and Students who Struggle with Maths.* London: Sage Publishing.

CHAPTER 12
ICT AND TEACHING AND LEARNING MATHEMATICS

Introduction

As a teacher in the twenty-first century it is vital that you can use your skills in ICT to support your teaching and that you are able to design opportunities for learners to develop their own ICT skills. It is an area that I have seen many students excel in. It is also an area in which you will notice your own learning progress, from the first time you try to write on an interactive whiteboard and can't make anything legible, to confidence in working with a range of technologies.

This chapter takes an overview of ICT, describing how we can best select from the wealth of software available to make sure we are genuinely designing opportunities for learners to develop their skills rather than just filling time working at a computer. The chapter also discusses how you can use calculators to support children's learning, drawing on the research around the use of calculators in primary schools. The view that I take towards calculator use is described in more detail below.

Starting point

Ten years ago I was asked to write a 'comment' piece for *Micromath*, the journal of the Association of Teachers of Mathematics, which focuses on the use of technology to support the teaching and learning of mathematics. As I was writing the article David Blunkett, the then minister for education, had made a statement that suggested children should not be 'encouraged' to use calculators until they were 8 years old. More recently it was seen as important that children in foundation stage had calculators available to support their role play areas, especially if these are shops or cafés and such like.

However, the worry that calculators somehow 'inhibit' the learning of mathematics persists to the extent that government policy in 2012 suggests reverting to a limited use of calculators in the primary classroom.

Whatever government policy suggests, I would argue that teachers in primary schools and early years settings should have calculators available all the time for the children they teach, whatever their age. A teacher's role is to teach their learners how to use calculators effectively, and to notice when they are useful. For example, if you are teaching multiplication by 10 you can give children a range of numbers and ask them to multiply these by 10 using a calculator and write down what they notice. Try it for yourself with these numbers:

14
157
13.8
2051
18.7
483.1
15.85
72.876
95231

By exploring multiplication by 10 in this way the learners themselves will realise that you don't 'add a nought' when multiplying by 10. This is a commonly held misconception.

Suggesting that calculators should not be available is a bit like suggesting that children shouldn't be able to use a ruler as it might stop them estimating lengths. Calculators are just one of the tools of the trade for mathematicians – our job is to teach children how to use them well.

Fortunately the use of computers to support learning has not been seen in the same way. Teachers I speak to, although some may lack confidence in their own technical abilities, usually speak positively about the impact that interactive computer software can have on supporting children's learning. In fact, on occasions, I think that computers are overused in the classroom. This chapter explores the use of calculators and computers to support the teaching and learning of mathematics. In both cases the focus is on the effective, efficient and appropriate use of these powerful tools.

Progression in using calculators

The fact that calculator use is seen as an important area is illustrated by the fact that there have been several guidance papers exploring the use of calculators in the teaching and learning of mathematics.

The National Numeracy Strategy, which was statutory in English schools until 2011, offered the following suggestions as to how teachers can use calculators to support teaching and learning throughout the early and primary years. These recommendations are still helpful for primary teachers. Key purposes for calculator use can include:

- Teaching children how to use the calculator effectively so they can decide when it is appropriate to use a calculator and when mental methods would be quicker and more efficient.
- Supporting the teaching of mathematics when the focus is on solving a problem rather than the process of calculation.
- Using the calculator as a tool to support children in exploring number patterns.
- Consolidating children's learning of number facts and calculation strategies.

This can be developed into the following progression map for developing children's calculator use.

Foundations in using calculators

Initially children may well see calculators at home or in out-of-school contexts. It is important that these are replicated in school. Provide a calculator in any role play environment where it is sensible or realistic to have one. This allows young learners to use calculators to support their creative play and to begin to explore how the keys on a calculator operate. Young children also enjoy using calculators to display numbers that are familiar to them, such as their age, or their house number.

Beginning to use calculators

When children are learning to read and write numbers up to 20 they can use calculators to illustrate two-digit numbers – and keying in these numbers can support them in their early understanding of place value. A 6-year-old child wanted to use a calculator to show me 17 (their brother's age) and asked me how to 'spell seventeen'. We looked at the possibilities – 17 or 71 – and then by looking at a number line agreed it should be 17. I have also worked with 6- and 7-year-old children to explore adding and subtracting 10 using a calculator. So, for example, I would write:

19
13
18
11
16

and ask the children to use a calculator to subtract 10 from each number and ask them to tell me what they notice.

As children are asked to learn the 2, 5 and 10 times-tables, it is useful to show them how to use the constant function on a calculator to notice the patterns that are formed in the times-tables. (If you don't know how the constant function on your calculator works, read the handbook – if you haven't got a calculator, buy one!)

An activity that uses a calculator to support the development of mental skills is shown below:

5	9	3	8	2	12	9	19	15	5

Draw the number track on your whiteboard and ask your pupils to work in pairs with one calculator between them. The aim is to move from one box to the next using a calculator so that the calculator display shows the appropriate number after an operation and a number have been keyed in. The pupils take it in turns and in this way will keep a check on each other.

Developing the use of calculators

As pupils come to understand partitioning, a calculator game that can support them is to ask one pupil to write a three- or four-digit number on a piece of scrap paper, say 3582. Their partner then has to remove the digits from the display one at a time using the calculator. So one way to do this would be:

$$3582 - 3000 = 582$$
$$582 - 500 = 82$$
$$82 - 80 = 2$$
$$2 - 2 = 0$$

You can add challenges to this game. Change the order in which the digits must be eliminated, ban the use of particular keys, try to eliminate two numbers at once. I promise you that the children in your class will very quickly come up with interesting and challenging rules for the game.

At this stage children can be introduced to the following calculator skills and learn how to:

- Clear the display before starting a calculation.
- Correct mistakes using the clear entry (CE) key.
- Carry out one- and two-step calculations involving all four operations.
- Interpret the display correctly, particularly in the context of money.
- Recognise negative numbers on the display.

The most appropriate way to focus on these skills is to provide problem-solving situations which will require children to develop these skills. Some teachers use self-assessment such as 'I can' statements so that their learners can notice for themselves when they develop these core skills.

As learners become more confident in their mathematics I would be expecting them to use the calculator for the following:

- Estimating the likely size of answers and checking calculations. I often stop children pressing the $=$ button on the calculator and ask them to estimate the answer – they are then very excited if they are proved correct by the calculator.

- Carrying out measurement calculations and interpreting the answer. For example, if I add 1 m 35 cm to 2 m 15 cm I will get 2 m 50 cm, but the calculator will show 2.5 rather than 2.50.

- Solving problems involving fractions – to do this pupils will need to recognise decimal equivalents of fractions. This in itself is a useful exercise to carry out using a calculator.

Portfolio task 12.1

Write the following fractions as decimals by using a calculator. For example, if you want to find 3/5 as a decimal you key in 3 ÷ 5 = . You should see 0.6.

3/4
1/2
4/5
1/4
1/5
2/10
7/10

Convert 1/5, 2/5, 3/5, 4/5, 5/5 to decimals.
   Do the same with 1/10, 2/10, 3/10, 4/10, 5/10, 6/10, 7/10, 8/10, 9/10, 10 /10.
   What do you notice about your answers to 'fifths' and tenths'? Now explore all the other fractions from 1/3s to 1/12s. Describe the patterns you are seeing.
   Can you see how this activity helped develop a sense of the value of fractions, and would have been impossible without the use of calculators?

Extending the use of calculators

Your most confident pupils pupils should be able to use a calculator to:

- Solve multi-step problems.

- Recognise recurring decimals. If you try to change 1/3 into a decimal using a calculator you will get 0.33333333; similarly, sevenths and ninths give recurring decimals.

Taking it further

A calculator-aware curriculum

Between 1986 and 1989 a research project called the Calculator Aware Number (CAN) project took place. Initially the project was based in 15 schools but by the end of the process hundreds of schools had become enrolled. Perhaps more importantly, all the schools which started the project, led by Hilary Shuard from Homerton College, Cambridge University, remained with it to the end.

The philosophy of CAN was that 'Children should be allowed to use calculators in the same way that adults use them: at their own choice, whenever they wish to do so.' The key principles that underpinned this philosophy were:

- Children should always have a calculator available, and the choice to use it should be the child's not the teacher's.
- Traditional paper and pencil methods for the four operations will not be taught.
- There should be a teacher emphasis on practical investigational and cross-curricular mathematics.
- Children should engage in mathematical activities which involve a range of apparatus.
- Teachers should support learners in developing confidence in talking about numbers using precise mathematical language.
- Mental methods should be emphasised and sharing children's mental methods encouraged.
- Teaching and learning 'number' should occupy less than 50% of the time spent teaching and learning mathematics.

Research carried out into the long-term impact of the CAN project was reported by Kenneth Ruthven in *Research Papers in Education*, 12 (3), 1997, in the paper 'The long-term influence of a calculator aware number curriculum on pupils' attitudes and attainments in the primary phase'. This study compared the attitude and attainment of pupils in post-project schools matched with non-project schools. This used national tests at ages 7 and 11 to compare attainments. The study found that more pupils attained at high levels in post-project schools than in non-project schools at age 7, but this was also the case for low attainment. This suggests that there had been a greater differentiation of attainment in post-project schools than non-project schools. Teachers in post-project schools thought that this may be the result of their not offering enough support and structure to lower attaining pupils carrying out open, unstructured activities.

Interestingly by age 11 there were no differences in post-project and non-project schools in terms of either attainment or enjoyment. That's to say, both groups of pupils did equally well in tests and when asked if they enjoyed mathematics the responses were the same whichever group the pupils belonged to.

The appropriate use of computers

When I visit schools I am excited by the number of schools which have facilities for using interactive software to support the teaching and learning of mathematics. However, I am also concerned sometimes when I see how the technology is used and find myself asking the question: 'Is this software enhancing the learning of mathematics or is it simply replacing practices that might be more appropriately carried out by teachers?'

I had been observing an engaging lesson exploring a group of Year 2 children's understanding of time. They had been discussing times that they knew – the time they got up, the time they left for school, the time they went to bed, the time their mum got in from work, and so on. They had recorded these times on clocks, both analogue and digital, and this had led to some complex discussions about how to record times and why the big hand tends not to be where you would expect it to be. The lesson continued as we moved into the IT suite: the children all showed considerable skill in quickly logging on and finding the appropriate program. This asked multiple choice questions requiring them to attach the correct written time to the time on the clock. The room fell silent as the children took it in turns to answer the questions. I noticed two strategies to get the correct answer: try each answer in turn until you get affirmation from the machine; or ask your friend. All discussion had stopped and as I asked children how they were applying their prior knowledge they suggested that wasn't the point. The idea was to get as many answers correct as they could in as short a time as possible. For me, what had been a lesson which drew the children into exploring and developing their own understandings of telling the time had become a very traditional mathematics lesson focused around routine and practice and for which the main motivation was not learning mathematics but finishing the exercise.

So, how can we measure the effectiveness of a piece of software? There are some key criteria I use with my teacher education students to analyse the effectiveness of a range of resources from number lines to coat hangers. You may find it useful to apply these criteria to any ICT you use as a learning and teaching resource.

The first question I ask is: 'To what extent does the resource provide an image or a representation of the mathematical idea you wish to teach?' In other words, does it model the mathematics that you are asking the children to engage with?

An example of this that is seen in classrooms around the country would be the number line. This models the 'big idea' of place value as well as supporting children in developing mental strategies for carrying out calculations. One example would be the zoom number line, which is one of the programs available on the companion website, introduced to you in Chapter 4. Here the traditional number line has been developed to create a zoom number line. This number line allows the teacher to define the central number of the line and to alter the scale.

This capability of zooming in and out of a number line offers a view of the number system that is only available using ICT. It also meets the criteria of representing the number system and modelling the mathematics of place value. More than this, it allows us to begin discussions about such ideas as rational and irrational numbers. A rational number is one that can be placed exactly on a number line; an irrational number, such as pi, is a recurring decimal and we do not know exactly where it is on the number line. We can also see that no matter how far we zoom in on the number line, there will always be another 'zoom' to be made. We can talk about infinity with primary mathematicians – and they love it.

The second question is: 'To what extent does the resource encourage learners to describe what they are doing?'

An example of this in everyday classroom practice is the teacher asking children 'How have you worked that out?' as a normal part of their teaching. Of course, a resource cannot force learners to describe what they are thinking, only good teaching can do this – however, a program which can be used to support learners thinking 'out loud' is a good place to start. The 'Number Boards' program which was used in Chapter 5 is an example of a piece of software that can be used to support the teacher in developing their learners' ability to articulate their thinking. The number boards are randomly generated and the criteria for the range of numbers can be set by the teacher.

Once the class have explored one 'number board' the software can then immediately create another grid which allows children to repeat processes in a way which is not available without using ICT. Learners can be encouraged by the teacher to describe why they are making decisions at each step, or other learners can be asked to give instructions to the learner at the interactive whiteboard – of course, justifying why they are asking them to make a particular move.

The third question is: 'To what extent is the resource able to offer a range of representations of the same mathematical idea?'

In Chapter 9 the software used in the 'In practice' section allows you to illustrate data using a range of representation. Here the software can enhance the learning by allowing teacher and learner to move between the 'big picture' and the specifics of the mathematical context. It also allows pupils to compare quickly the representations and decide which they think most effectively represent the data. They have not had to invest time and effort on drawing the different representations and so will be happy to decide that a bar chart is more useful than a pie chart. If they had spent time drawing a pie chart it would have been difficult to motivate the same children to draw a bar chart in order to decide which was the most appropriate representation.

The final question I ask is: 'Does the resource offer a context for applying or practising skills?'

The program 'Scales' which is used in the 'In practice' section in Chapter 8 allows children to draw on their previous knowledge to explore balancing and reading scales. Children can apply contextual knowledge about how heavy specific articles are. The software allows learners to apply this prior knowledge and question it while engaging in a balancing activity and practising the skills of reading scales.

It is always exciting to see young learners motivated and excited by their developing understandings of mathematics. ICT has a vital role to play in supporting their learning and showing them that mathematics is something they can do and something that has an internal logic which they can explore and ask questions of. My aim here is to suggest that an important role for the teacher is to ensure that the software we use when working with our learners genuinely enhances their learning. Who knows? You may even find yourself waking up in the middle of the night with some mathematical questions!

Summary

This chapter has illustrated how calculators and computers can be effective tools for teaching and learning mathematics. I have aimed to give you the confidence to encourage children to use calculators at all stages of their learning. Using the guidance from the National Strategy I have illustrated how calculators can be used progressively to develop mathematical skills appropriate to the age of learners so that they can develop both appropriate mathematical skills and appropriate calculator skills. In this way you have seen how the calculator is both a tool for learning mathematics and a tool for carrying out mathematics. Finally, by drawing on a radical piece of curriculum development, I hope I have convinced you that using calculators in the classroom is not harmful to children's mathematical development.

To support you in using appropriate software to support your teaching and to enhance your pupils' learning I raised questions which aim to help you in deciding which particular pieces of software will be useful.

Reflections on this chapter

Mark kept coming up to my desk and swapping a ruler that he was using for a new one. After he had repeated this four or five times – I was an over-patient teacher sometimes – I asked him what he was doing. He told me that he was trying to find a ruler that worked. I was confused so I asked him what he meant. He said that he was measuring a line and he knew the answer was 8 cm but all of these rulers kept giving him '8 and a bit'. When I went over to see what he was doing, he was using the end of the ruler as his starting point rather than the '0'. Once I had shown him this he didn't see the need to keep changing rulers!

It strikes me that those who suggest that calculators might inhibit children's learning of mental methods or slow down their learning of written calculation are trying to solve Mark's problem by taking away the ruler rather than showing him how to use it. A calculator cannot inhibit children's learning – the way that we teach children how to use it can, but then that is within our control. I hope that this chapter has offered you a way to view calculators and computers as powerful mathematical tools that we are in control of and maybe even encouraged you to get your old calculator out of your bag and explore how you can best use it both to teach your learners and to carry out mathematics yourself.

Going further

ICT and Primary Mathematics **by Jenni Way and Toni Beardon**
In this book the arguments made in this chapter about the value of using calculators in the primary classroom are expanded. The chapters are written as case studies which describe how teachers have developed powerful learning experiences for their learners through the imaginative use of a range of digital technologies. There are lots of practical ideas for you to try out in your classrooms.

Way, J. and Beardon, T. (2003) *ICT and Primary Mathematics*. Open University Press.

ICT and Primary Mathematics (A Teachers Guide) **by Nick Easingwood and John Williams**
This book covers similar ground. This is more practically focused with sections covering the use of databases and spreadsheets. Teaching using log and the floor turtle and advice on using an interactive whiteboard.

Easingwood, N. and Williams, J. (2004) *ICT and Primary Mathematics (A Teachers Guide)*. London: Routledge Press.

GLOSSARY

2D: Two-dimensional. Describes a shape that has length and width, but not depth. 2D shapes move so that we can see them in any orientation.

3D: Three-dimensional. Describes a shape that has length, width and depth. 3D shapes can roll, slide, build and balance.

acute angle: An angle less than 90°.

algorithm: Finite sequence of instructions. An explicit, step-by-step procedure for solving a problem, often used for calculation.

area: The amount of space a shape takes up. Measured in units such as square millimetres, square centimetres or square kilometres, written mm², cm² or km².

array: A set of numbers or objects arranged in order, often in rows and columns.

axes: Reference lines that cross at right angles; used to locate points by their coordinates.

bar chart: Diagram that uses bars or rectangles to represent discrete data.

bi-modal: Data that contains two values that are equally common.

block graph: Diagram similar to a bar chart, in which each block represents one item of data.

cardinal number: Whole number that tells us how many there are in a set of objects. Cardinal numbers can be written as words (one, two, three …) or using numerical symbols (1, 2, 3 …).

Carroll diagram: Diagram used to represent data in a tabular, yes/no format.

centre of rotation: Point about which an object rotates.

closed shape: Shape whose sides all join together.

common multiple: Multiple that is shared by two or more numbers. So a common multiple of 3 and 6 is 12, as 3 and 6 are both factors of 12.

concave shape: Shape that has at least one interior angle greater than 180°.

congruent shapes: Two shapes that will fit perfectly on top of each other.

continuous data: Data that has an infinite number of possible values, such as heights, weights and time.

convex shape: Shape whose interior angles are all less than 180°.

coordinates: Pair of numbers such as (2, 3) or (21, 4), used to define or locate a point by reference to a pair of axes.

counting on: Technique for performing simple calculations (addition, subtraction) by reference to a number line.

cube: A 3D shape with all its faces squares.

cuboid: A 3D shape with all its faces rectangles.

decimal notation: System used to express numbers and parts of numbers as multiples and sub-multiples of 10.

degree of rotational symmetry: The amount by which a shape with rotational symmetry must be turned for it to look the same as before.

denominator: The lower part of a fraction, representing the number of parts into which the whole has been divided. For example, the denominator of 5/7 is 7.

directed number: Number with a plus or minus sign attached, to show whether it is a positive or negative number. So ⁺7 means 'positive' 7 and ⁻3 means 'negative' 3.

discrete data: Data that can be counted.

edge: The boundary line of a 2D shape, or the straight line where two faces of a 3D shape meet.

equivalent fractions: Fractions with the same value, such as 6/8 and 3/4, or 70/100 and 7/10.

faces: The flat regions of a 3D shape.

factors: The various numbers that divide exactly into a given number. For example, the factors of 12 are 1, 2, 3, 4, 6 and 12.

frequency table: Used to record observations of frequencies.

frequency: The number of times a particular value occurs.

generalise: To make a statement that is true about a wide range of cases.

improper fraction: Fraction with its numerator larger than or equal to its denominator, such as 7/4 or 4/3.

inequality: Statement showing which number is greater or less than another.

integer: Number that has no decimal or fractional part; sometimes called a whole number. Can be either positive or negative. Integers should not be confused with natural numbers.

inverse operations: Arithmetical operations that are the opposite of each other, such as multiplication and division.

irregular shape: Shape with sides and angles that are different lengths and sizes.

line graph: Diagram used to represent continuous data.

line of symmetry: Line about which a shape with reflective symmetry can be folded so that the two halves fit exactly on top of each other.

mass: The amount of substance in an object. Not to be confused with its weight, which is the strength of the gravitational pull on the object – that is, how heavy it is.

mean: Average value, calculated by adding up all the different items of data and dividing by the total number of items.

median: The middle value of a set of data when all the data is arranged in order.

mixed number: A number that contains both a whole number and a fraction, such as 3¾.

mode: The value that occurs most frequently in a set of data.

natural number: A positive integer, such as 1, 2, 3, 4.

net: Two-dimensional shape that can be folded to make a three-dimensional shape.

numerator: The upper part of a fraction, representing the number of parts of the whole that have been taken.

oblong: A rectangle that isn't a square.

obtuse angle: An angle between 90° and 180°.

open shape: Shape that has a gap between two corners.

operation: The four operations are addition, subtraction, multiplication and division.

order of rotational symmetry: The number of times a shape with rotational symmetry is repeated before it makes a complete 360° turn.

ordinal number: Number used to indicate position, such as 1st, 2nd, 3rd.

origin: Point at which coordinate axes cross.

parallel lines: Two lines that are always the same distance apart and will never meet, no matter how far you extend them.

parallelogram: Quadrilateral with opposite sides parallel.

partitioning: Splitting a number to enable you to carry out a calculation mentally: so, for example, 24 = 2 tens and 4 units = 20 + 4.

perfect square: The square of a whole number. For example, 36 is a perfect square as it is 6×6 or 6^2.

perimeter: The distance all the way round the outside edge of a shape; measured in mm, cm or km, for example.

perpendicular lines: Two lines at 90° to each other.

perpendicular: Describes the relationship between two objects – such as lines or surface – that meet at right angles (90°) to each other.

pictogram: Diagram that uses pictures of objects to represent discrete data.

polygon: Any shape with straight edges.

prime factor: Factor of a number that is also a prime number

prime number: Number with only two factors: itself and 1.

prism: Solid object with two identical ends and all flat sides.

probability scale: Numerical scale from 0 to 1, or from 0% to 100%, used to measure probability.

probability: The likelihood of an event occurring.

pyramid: Solid object with a base that is a polygon, and with sides that meet at the top.

quadrant: Any one of the four equal areas created by dividing a 2D area up using two perpendicular axes.

range: A measure of the spread of a set of data.

ratio notation: Used to express the proportional relationship of one value to another as two numbers: for example, 30:100.

rectangle: Any quadrilateral with four sides.

rectilinear shape: Shape that can be split up into a series of rectangles.

reflection: Transformation of a shape about a mirror line.

reflective symmetry: The property of a shape that can be folded in half so that the two halves fit exactly on top of each other.

reflex angle: Angle greater than 180°.

regular polygon: Polygon with all sides the same length and all angles between the sides the same; any other sort of polygon is irregular.

regular shape: Shape with all sides the same length and all interior angles the same size.

rhombus: Quadrilateral with four equal sides.

right-angled triangle: Triangle in which two of the sides join at a right angle.

rotation: Transformation a shape about a centre of rotation.

rotational symmetry: Property of a shape that looks the same after it has been rotated through less than 360°.

rounding: Reducing the number of digits in a number but keeping its value roughly the same.

similar shapes: Shapes that are not congruent, but whose sides are all in the same ratio.

specialising: Looking at specific examples in order to get started on a problem.

square number: The result of multiplying (squaring) a number by itself.

square root: Number that produces a required number when multiplied by itself (squared).

square: Quadrilateral with four equal sides and four right angles.

standard units: Units that are in common usage, such as metres, litres or kilograms, and all the derived (related) units.

surface area: Total area of all faces of a 3D shape.

symmetry: The property of a shape that is made up of identical parts facing each other or when rotated round an axis.

tally chart: Diagram that uses sets of ticks of hash marks to represent discrete data.

transformation: Process of moving a shape on a grid, by translation, reflection or rotation.

translation: Transformation of a shape that alters its position, but leaves its dimensions and orientation unchanged.

uniform non-standard units: Quantities that are uniform in size (e.g. multilink cubes or wooden blocks), and are used to measure something, but are not part of a standard system such as the metric system of units.

Venn diagram: Diagram that uses overlapping shapes (usually circles or ellipses) to show the relationships between groups of things that share something in common.

vertex: Point at which two or more edges meet.

vertically opposite angles: Angles made where two lines cross. They have the same value.

INDEX

Note: Glossary page numbers appear in **bold**.